Dial A Guru Series

Get Out of Your Own Way!

How to overcome self- sabotaging beliefs and habits at home and in the workplace

Edited by
Dawn Campbell

Co-Authored by
Barbara J. Cormack
Cathy Radcliffe
Danielle Lindsay
Dawn Ann Campbell
Jennifer Rahman
Susan Hay
Tina Sibley
Tomasz Nędzi

Published by PenCraft Books, LLC

Get Out of Your Own Way!

© 2016 Dawn Campbell, Barbara J. Cormack, Cathy Radcliffe, Danielle Lindsay, Dawn Ann Campbell, Jennifer Rahman, Susan Hay, Tina Sibley, Tomasz Nędzi. All Rights Reserved

Dawn Campbell and co-authors asserts their moral rights to be identified as the editor and co-author of this work.

For more information: www.dialaguru.eu

ISBN: 978-1-939556-14-1(Kindle)
ISBN: 978-1-939556-16-5 (Print)
ISBN: 978-1-939556-17-2 (PDF)

First published: August, 2016 USA

Published by: PenCraft Books LLC,
7348 Maple Terrace, Traverse City, MI 49686, USA

No part of this publication may be reproduced, stored in a retrieval system or transmitted in any form or by any means, electronic, mechanical, photocopied, recorded, scanned, or otherwise: except as permitted under Section 107 through 118 of the 1976 United States Copyright Act; without prior written permission of the Publisher.

Limit of Liability / Disclaimer of Warranty: While the author has used their best efforts in preparing this book, they make no representations or warranties with respect to the accuracy or completeness of the contents and specifically disclaim any implied warranties. The advice and strategies contained herein may not be suitable for your own situation, and where appropriate you should still consult with the author or another professional. The author shall not be

Get Out of Your Own Way!

liable for any loss of profit or any other commercial or personal damages, including but not limited to special, incidental, consequential, or other damages.

Disclaimer: In the hands of anyone seeking to improve their personal, and or professional life, the Dial A Guru series of personal and business self-help books represents a constructive and valuable resource for anyone's *success tool kit*. This book has been collectively written by a group of qualified, highly experienced and talented professionals. Inspired to write, these professionals have come together to share their valuable expertise to help us learn functional skills, which when implemented will bring beneficial results. Access to such information means we are increasing our knowledge base. Knowledge means power and power helps us make more informed choices. The first proactive step on this journey is to accept we are each of us all responsible for our own choices. The views expressed in this series are solely those of each author based on their personal and professional experience.

Contents

Dedication	1
Foreword	3
Introduction	7
How to Use This Series	11
Section One Creating Complete Confidence	13
What is confidence?	18
How can we develop more confidence?	35
Strategies for maintaining confidence	44
Cathy Radcliffe - Biography	52
Section Two Releasing Your Future	55
How does your current thinking affect your future?	61
Universal Thought Process	67
This is achieved by learning how to releasing your future	73
Barbara J Cormack - Biography	80
Section Three Powerful Public Speaking	83
What Public Speaking Will Do for You and Your Business	84
The Art of Public Speaking	93
The 3 C's: Confidence, Content, and Charisma	98
Tina Sibley - Biography	132
Section Four Be Healthy, Fit and in Flow	133
Nutritional Health	134
Physical Fitness	161
Mental Flow	162
References	166

Susan Hay - Biography 167
Section Five Escaping from Toxic Relationships 169
Surviving Toxic Romantic Relationships 185
Strategies for dealing with toxic parents.................. 192
Tomasz Nedzi - Biography 204
Section Six Reflexology for Health 207
The Healing Power of Reflexology............................ 208
History of Reflexology and its development 217
Case Studies and Coping Strategies for a wide range of illnesses 233
Danielle Lindsay - Biography.................................... 246
Section Seven Breaking the Change Barrier 249
Creating positive change to reshape your destiny 250
The positive power of negative thinking 263
Changing your past story to create a better future................ 277
Jennifer Rahman - Biography.................................... 287
Section Eight 7 Keys to Vitality 289
Self-care is not selfish 290
7 keys to vitality 296
Strategies for becoming a Centerian 302
Dawn Ann Campbell - Biography 332
Dial A Guru Series 335
Feedback... 337
Calling all authors-in-waiting 338
About PenCraft Books, LLC 340
Editor and co-author of the Dial A Guru initiative................ 342

Dedication

This series is dedicated to the many hundreds of trainee coaches I've mentored and coached, from around the globe, over the past decade. It has been my privilege to help you overcome your saboteurs while you retrain. Also to support you in setting up your own coaching practice in what is a truly rewarding and results orientated profession.

Way too many of you to name in person, though many of you know who you are. Not least because you stayed in touch, shared your successes, become friends, or have become joint venture partners; like these sought after, famed and compassionate professionals who have helped me create this wonderful series.

It is said "We each have two lives, the one we live, and the one we dream of living". *Dial A Guru* authors are passionate about helping us be brave and authentic enough to live the life we dream of living.

So huge thanks go to our co-authors who have shared their inspirational stories about how they overcame their own adversities, and how their strategies now help others overcome theirs.

Thank you also for challenging and reminding me that *there's always a better way*, and ultimately, for encouraging me to put you all together to create this series for the benefit of the widest possible audience.

Get Out of Your Own Way!

Foreword

Stop for a moment and imagine yourself in ten years' time; imagine that nothing much has changed in your personal, professional or business life.

How does that make you feel?

When we do this exercise in my workshops, people usually feel depressed at the idea. I can actually see the horror registering on their faces as they consider the implications of not making any progress at home, or in the workplace.

Yet that's the reality for most of us as we trundle through life day in day out without making the proactive changes needed to actually create the future we want. That's why so few talented people actually fulfil their full potential. Of course we've usually fabricated a good reason for our short comings, mostly though we blame the world for not giving us our lucky break. In reality we know the true reason lies deep within us.

We hold ourselves back for a myriad of reasons. Maybe we need a boost of confidence; perhaps we are tired and simply do not have the energy to make changes. Possibly we are lacking the knowledge or skills to progress. Or we may simply not know what is holding us back; we just know intuitively that life could be so much better than it currently is.

That's why we need useful books like this that are co-authored by a team of writers who have the expertise to offer a wide range of assistance to a wide range of issues. Writers whose guidance is backed up with tried and tested exercises and insightful questions. All of which have been designed to help us identify *what* is holding us back, and *how* we can overcome our issues. After that, it's up to each and every one of us to choose *when* we're ready to break free of self-sabotaging thoughts and behaviours.

Sounds simple doesn't it, but the reality is we know it's not. That's why step by step you will be taken on a journey of self-discovery: from confidence building to becoming fitter and healthier; from dealing with toxic relationships to breaking through the barriers of creating positive change and ultimately, learning how to release your ideal future.

As you read through each of the eight sections in this series you will find some topics will ring truer for you than others. They are the ones you'll want to pay more attention to; they are the areas that are holding you back from being all you are capable of being.

I suggest you do not just skim through this book, but instead carefully focus and work your way through it. If any of what you read makes you angry or upset that could be another sign to stop right there and have a good think about why that is. Be honest with yourself as you do this, always making sure you deal with the issues that come up *as* they arise.

This is where the accompanying workbook proves invaluable. It encourages you to record where you are now with where you'd ideally like to be in ten years' time. Additionally what has to change to ensure you achieve the future you desire.

By the time you've worked your way through this series you

Get Out of Your Own Way!

will have cleared the way to making real progress in your life, by which time you'll deserve a well-earned pat on the back.

Good luck and here's to enjoying the road ahead one step at a time.

Anne Jirsch

Author of four books including international best seller *The Future is Yours.* To find out more visit www.annejirsch.com. Email Anne at annejirsch@hotmail.co.uk for your free copy of her e-book *Universal Signposts.*

Anne Jirsch is a London born professional psychic and a leading world pioneer of Future Life Progression (FLP). She has a large worldwide following which includes: heads of industry, politicians and celebrities from the world of film, music and sport. She is the author of four books: *Instant Intuition, The Future is Yours, Cosmic Energy and her latest Create Your Perfect Future* which is an international best seller available here

http://www.amazon.co.uk/s/ref=nb_sb_noss?url=search-alias%3Daps&field-keywords=anne+jirsch

She has appeared on numerous radio shows including regular slots on BBC Radio. Anne has also appeared on Kuwait morning television, Estonian television and BBC morning news, and more recently, ITV *This Morning*

Get Out of Your Own Way!

where she hypnotised celebrity Natalie Cassidy and took her into her future lifetime. She is currently in talks with a major television production company.

She is the Chairman of *The Past & Future Life Society* and her FLP Training School is now in 14 countries. She also has representatives in Japan, Kuwait, Dubai and Estonia and travels extensively with her sell-out workshops and seminars.

http://www.annejirsch.com/products/signposts

Introduction

Having coached thousands of clients, and mentored many hundreds of coaches over the past decade, I've come to realise that it doesn't much matter what the topic of conversation is. The root-cause of the majority of issues we suffer with actually boils down to one main cause: **self-esteem, or rather, the lack of it.**

Whether we are experiencing issues, concerns, difficulties, or challenges (call them what you will), we all want the same things in life. We want friendlier, happier, more loving, sexier, romantic relationships. We also wish to communicate with more ease; that means listening, as well as influencing, so both parties are understood. We certainly aspire to attaining financial freedom, and we'd like to choose work, careers, or a business that fulfils our sense of purpose. Plus we definitely want to enjoy vital health, a zest for life and increase our chances of longevity.

So what stops us from achieving our hearts desires? Often it's because we've convinced ourselves people won't accept, like, or love us. Maybe it's because when we were younger, we didn't receive the unconditional love, or acceptance we all need to build a healthy self-esteem? Consequently, we carry around feelings of low self-worth through to our adult relationships. Possibly it's because no matter how loud we tried to be heard, we were ignored, marginalised, or worse, physically trampled on.

All these reasons and more create profoundly negative thoughts, feelings, and behaviours which we continue to act out, *until* such times as we change our perception of our self-worth. In the meantime, we don't *believe* we are worthy of being in loving relationships. We don't *value* ourselves enough to aspire to being satisfied in our dream job. Our low self-worth doesn't merit fame and fortune. We don't even feel we have the right to a fit and healthy body.

So we abuse and neglect our body, we sabotage our prospects and we engage in toxic relationships. We habitually replay all the negative comments we've ever heard growing up about *never amounting to much,* or we tell ourselves *I mustn't get above myself.*

So when someone surprises themselves by surpassing their expectations, they suffer a huge amount of stress because they feel like a fraud and are anxious about being found out. Same thing with lottery winners; they often go completely off the rails doing anything and everything they can to get back to where they were before simply because they feel undeserving and uncomfortable. They don't know how, or what to think because the paradigm of themselves and their situation has been so altered they literally can't cope.

The good news is that whatever the reason for experiencing low self-esteem in the past, it does not need to continue, or define the future, unless you let it.

Everything we think, do and believe are simply learnt behaviours, we copied them from someone else. Meaning, with motivation, commitment and a little help, we can learn new empowering, more positive and healthier ways to think and behave instead.

All we need to do to get started is to find the courage to say "enough"! Then recognise *what* it is that we want to be different in our future. Next, we need to make a concerted effort to finally become authentic; live the life we want to live rather than the life someone else thought we should live.

We achieve this by finding fresh evidence to support we are worthy of a better future. That often means making new friends who are happy to encourage us to achieve our goals, rather than hanging around with family and friends who hold us back because they don't want us to change. Gradually, our beliefs, values, attitude, behaviours and habits become more nurturing, and our self-esteem flourishes.

Books like ours become an enormously supportive tool in helping you make those changes. Consequently, we kick off with Cathy's chapters on **creating complete confidence** that will help you improve your communication skills at home and work alike. Next Barbara shares her strategies for successfully working with your mind so it's aligned to your dreams and **releases your ideal future**.

Tina steps things up a pace by explaining the **benefits of being able to speak and present in public** and shows us exactly how to go about acquiring these invaluable skills. She is followed by Susan who introduces us to her **strategy for becoming *healthy, fit and in flow*** so we learn to eat to thrive rather than to survive.

Then Tomasz bravely takes us on a revealing journey of what it's like to grow up with toxic parents, then repeat the patterns in romantic relationships, until he learns to breaks the cycle and creates a worthier self-esteem. **Reading his chapters will help you break free of toxic relationships too.**

Get Out of Your Own Way!

He is followed by the healing hands of Danni, the Reflexologist who has experienced amazing results with her client's physical and mental issues. She encourages us to **explore reflexology as a means of improving our own well-being.**

Of course we know *a change imposed is a change opposed* so change *has* to come from within. Jennifer explains this in more detail by helping us **break down our barriers to change so we can overcome this resistance**, because even when we say we want to change, we still sabotage our best efforts. Finally, I wrap things up by introducing you to the **7 keys to vitality and *how* and *why* practicing them will not only *add years to your life, but will add life to your years*.** I also explain why it's *not* selfish to practice self-care because how you look after yourself, determines how you perform in every area of your life.

So, there you have it: eight lovingly compassionate authors, writing eight insightful, potentially life-changing chapters. However, we know reading isn't enough to make a change stick. Change has to be accompanied by doing; putting things into practice, one thing at a time. So please combine reading this book with the exercises in the accompanying workbook to achieve maximum benefit, so you too can start living the life you dream of.

Wishing you the best of everything you wish for yourself.
Dawn Campbell (Editor)

Get Out of Your Own Way!

How to Use This Series

There is no right or wrong way to read this series. Some of you will feel inspired to read it cover to cover; others will prefer to dip in and out as the need arises while plotting their progress in the accompanying workbook before moving onto a new subject. Either way, I'm sure the many practical activities provided will keep you engaged and coming back for more as your confidence and skills develop.

> Sam Thorpe, International Speaker, Trainer and Author of METAMessages from Your Body said about this series "You will get the most out of this book if you approach it with curiosity. Curiosity for the journeys of the authors and a curiosity to reflect on what resonates with you, and equally what you choose to discard. This book is packed with so many opportunities for personal discovery that I suggest you keep a notepad and pen nearby, not just for the exercises that have been skilfully designed to move you closer towards that light that you seek, but to make a note of your own *light-bulb* moments when your world shifts and your light inside shines just a little bit brighter".

At the back of our books you will also find a range of valuable free resources to help you continue your journey to success at home and in the workplace. Additionally, when you visit http://www.dialaguru.eu you will find many more authors generously offering more resources for your benefit.

You'll find space to answer these insightful questions in the accompanying workbook also available on Amazon.

Get Out of Your Own Way!

Get Out of Your Own Way!

Section One
Creating Complete Confidence

by
Cathy Radcliffe

"*Self-confidence and a belief in yourself is a must. To instil confidence in others, you first must have confidence in yourself*". - Byron & Catherine Pulsifer

Confidence is a funny old subject and I don't mean of the "ha-ha" variety; rather that people often have a peculiar and confused attitude towards it. Let me clarify; I feel incredibly privileged to work as a coach and a trainer with people from all over the world. Consequently, I experience a myriad of backgrounds and cultures. Irrespective of these surface differences, something that unites us is an overwhelming struggle to develop and maintain a healthy level of self-confidence. Indeed, the latest research by Dr Joe Rubino suggests that nearly 85% of people suffer from some kind of issue related to confidence. So if you're reading this and you're thinking "she's talking about me", please know that you're in good company and there is plenty you can do.

Now as I said, confidence is a particularly funny subject. Whilst most people realise they need more, they'll often caveat any assertion to this end with a word of caution about the amount of confidence they actually want. In my coaching sessions, seminars and workshops I often hear things like;
- "I don't want to be too confident or I'll come across cocky", or
- "you can't be confident all the time", and
- "confident people are generally the loudest".

No double you'll also have heard a number of times people saying "she / he is *very* confident". The way they say it suggests there is something not quite right about being confident, or perhaps it's an undesirable quality to have. I've certainly heard it applied to me a few times in my life!

This type of assertion is simply down to confusion around *what* confidence is and *how* it's created. I strongly believe if there was a universal understanding of what confidence is, and the importance of investing time and energy into developing it, people would enjoy healthier levels of confidence. More importantly, they would be better equipped to embrace and enhance their lives to the fullest *without* the fears, worries and stresses that accompany low self-confidence. I am convinced if everyone spent time developing this valuable skill, we'd all benefit from more productive relationships, at home and in the workplace.

The Benefits of Confidence

- Higher likelihood of setting and achieving compelling goals.
- Increased feelings of well-being and happiness.
- Increased creativity and ability to think differently.
- Greater acceptance and tolerance of others.
- Optimised performance in the workplace.
- Greater collaboration and sharing of ideas.
- Increased feelings of social ease.
- Increased physical and mental health.

It's not something to be taken lightly; a clear understanding of confidence will create all of the above.

A great number of the challenges we face on a daily basis in our interactions with others stem from a lack of self-confidence. Through my studies, learning and first-hand experience I have come to believe that it actually isn't possible to be too confident as some people might assert; and that if you have what we describe as *healthy confidence* then you aren't likely to go far wrong.

It's important at this point to take a quick look at the difference between confidence and self-esteem because whilst they are intrinsically linked, there are some subtle differences. We are focusing on confidence throughout our time together, but our subject wouldn't be complete without taking into consideration the importance of self-esteem too.

In essence, self-esteem is the value you place on yourself in terms of being a worthwhile human being. It is related to a broad sense of personal value, or self-worth. If you have high self-esteem at work, you probably have it in other areas of your life too, because this is a reflection of how you see yourself.

Confidence on the other hand tends to be related to action. It's a belief that you have the capability to succeed at something. So, you can be confident about one area of your life, but totally unconfident about another e.g. "I am confident that I am a good person, but I'm not at all confident about speaking in public.

In many ways it is easier to develop your confidence than your self-esteem. Confidence builds by taking action and working on yourself, working on your inner dialogue, trying things you find hard, by going outside your *comfort zone*. Confidence is about facing obstacles and realising you're still alive even when you fail and celebrating your successes.

We're now going to take a thorough look at the subject of confidence; what it's made up of, how we can develop more of it, and how to maintain it. If you like any of my coaching clients have ever felt that confidence will always elude you, then keep reading and start looking forward to creating the compelling confidence that you deserve:

"When I first started working with Cathy my confidence was at rock bottom; whilst I have been relatively successful in my career, and have a happy personal life, something was always holding me back. I suffered from anxiety and fear of social situations. Working with Cathy has shown me that I can create my own confidence and in the time we've worked together, I've achieved more than I ever thought was possible and done things that I never would've done before. I'm happier and enjoying my life more than ever".
Simon Buckley

What is confidence?

Now, before we get started on the content, I want to make one vital point upfront that I need you to accept and never to forget. It's a universal truth that is fundamental in starting the process of creating confidence, yet one that so many of us seem to have difficulty retaining.

There is and only ever will be one of you. Whether you accept it or not, you are a totally unique individual. No one else on the planet right now, or before, has ever had, or ever will have the same unique upbringing, experiences, thoughts, feelings or learnings as you do. There is only one you. In the same way that we all recognise that our fingerprints are unique and our eyeballs are for that matter the very essence of you is a one off. You are an original.

"So what"? I hear some of you mutter "Heard that before, but what does it actually mean"? In a nutshell it means that you are, whether you like it or not, individual and by proxy, special and as such, who you are, and what you have to bring to the party that we call life, matters. A lot! Why? Because no one else has had the same experiences as you, no one else has the same genetic makeup as you, no one else thinks in the same way you do, or feels the same way you do. Remembering this is a key building block in the process of creating compelling confidence. You do matter; others have much to learn from you *if* you learn how to get comfortable sharing YOU with the world.

However you feel about yourself right now, on some level I am certain you knew that already, I am certain this universal truth resonates. Therefore, throughout the course of these chapters, I will remind you of your uniqueness and your inherent value with exercises, tools and tips that will help you create the confidence to go forth and conquer whatever it is that you want to do with your short time on our magnificent planet.

You are going to have to do the work of course. No one can do that for you, but the great thing is that you only really have to do the *digging deep* part once, and then you are good to go. Take time to work through the chapters and complete the exercises, think about the ideas shared and what they mean to you, apply them to your life from this day forward and before long, you will enjoy having created compelling confidence.

Going back to what confidence is. It's important that you are crystal clear about this up front; self-confidence isn't a *nice to have*, it's a fundamental and key part of your experience of life that will bring you all of the benefits listed above. We'll get into that in more detail a little later on, but for now, let's get back to exploring what it means to be confident. Spend a moment now using the space below to jot down key words that describe what *you* think it means to be confident. Don't read ahead just yet; it's important that you do the work of thinking about your current perception of what it means to be confident.

Get Out of Your Own Way!

How difficult was that exercise? A lot of people struggle with defining exactly what it means to be confidence and that's precisely my point; we talk a lot about confidence, about needing more of it, or having low confidence, or lacking in self-esteem, but how many of us actually know what we are talking about? Do we really know what it means to be confident? What we do know is that a lack of confidence is commonly blamed for not achieving our goals!

According to the Oxford English dictionary, the definition of confidence is: "The feeling or belief that one can have faith in or rely on someone or something."

OK, let's break that down a little bit. So it's a feeling or a belief first off, so that's an internal thing. We all agree that we generate feelings and beliefs ourselves right? External factors play a role in how we generally feel and what we believe about ourselves, and the world, but fundamentally, that's down to us. Think about it this way if you need further convincing; most of us have at one point or another needlessly upset ourselves by imagining distressing future scenarios. I know I have. I can reduce myself to tears by creating a wildly improbable future reality that scares or upsets me. On that basis, if we can create feelings and emotions so vividly, we can start to get the picture that both these things are under our control.

Now of course, it doesn't always feel like that; it often feels like external circumstances are playing havoc with our emotions and thoughts. However, it's important to recognise, and realise that you are in control of the things you think, and the things you feel.

As for the second part of the Oxford English dictionary definition, confidence is about having faith or relying on someone or something. In this instance, confidence is about believing in you. Simple as that! When you know who you are and you **believe in yourself** you have the foundations of confidence.

Two other definitions that help expand on the Oxford English definition are;
1. "Confidence is our ability to think, confidence is our ability to cope with the basic challenges of life and confidence is our right to be successful and happy, the feeling of being worthy, deserving, entitled to assert our needs and wants, achieve our values, and enjoy the fruits of our efforts". Nathaniel Brandon
2. "Confidence is the evaluation the individual makes and customarily maintains with regards to himself... and indicates the extent to which the individual believes himself capable, significant, successful and worthy". Stanley Coopersmith

It is also intrinsically linked to how you relate to other people and the extent to which you are willing to assert and stand up for yourself. As confidence is essentially an assessment of your own worth, it dictates how others perceive you as well as influencing the way they are likely to treat you. It's worth knowing that it's not possible for people to treat you worse than you treat yourself; you'll always find a way to self-sabotage! What counts most in life is improving the way you feel about yourself, not the way others feel about you. That's their bag; you are your bag.

Get Out of Your Own Way!

In a nutshell then, the essence of confidence is about knowing who you really are, accepting who you are and believing in yourself. The type of confidence we are striving for here is internal, it's about how you view yourself and it manifests itself quietly; it's about being self-assured, about knowing that you are good enough, about understanding that you have value and worth and that you can do whatever you set your mind to. When you think about confidence in these terms, you will develop a quiet, assured, inner sense of self, a belief in yourself.

Getting to Know Yourself

If we accept the confidence is about the extent to which we know and believe in ourselves, why is it such hard work? Surely we all know who we are right? Well, no actually, that doesn't tend to be the case in my experience. In fact, people often struggle so much with really knowing, admitting, or realising who they are that they'll create all sorts of external storylines for themselves that don't align with their reality. Suppressing our feelings are where and when problems around confidence start to develop.

I'll often do an exercise with my client's where I simply ask them to write down 20 statements about themselves as fast as they can. Irrespective of their situations and circumstances, 95% of people find it extremely difficult to achieve. We're going to do a similar exercise so get ready!

Give yourself a good 15 minutes to dedicate to the next exercise and don't read on until you have completed it. You will find below a number of statements that I want you to go ahead and complete with whatever occurs to you. For this exercise to work to its full potential you need to be as honest and authentic as possible. Also, go with whatever pops into your mind naturally. Don't overthink the process; go with your first thoughts.

| I know I am |
| I know I am |
| I know I am |
| I know I am |
| I know I am |
| I think I am |
| I think I am |
| I think I am |
| I think I am |
| I think I am |
| I can |
| I can |
| I can |
| I can |
| I can |

Get Out of Your Own Way!

I want
I want
I want
I want
I want

How did you get on? Well done if you managed to complete all 20 statements. Don't worry if you didn't; this type of exercise can be extremely difficult when we begin to explore ourselves authentically and honestly. Consider what you did write down; how many of the statements that you know about yourself or think about yourself are positive and empowering versus how many are negative in tone in any shape or form? If you completed this exercise as honestly as possible, you'll now have in front of you a good basic understanding of the way in which you view yourself. It is likely that the things you wrote down form a significant part of your internal dialogue and it's a critical part of confidence to ensure that your internal dialogue is as kind and compassionate with yourself as any external dialogue you have with anyone else. We're going to return to this exercise later and start the process of tweaking our self-talk to create the compelling confidence we all desire.

So why is this self-reflective exercise so difficult? Because for many of us, taking a long hard look inside and becoming what we call "self-aware" seems like an insurmountable task. Even people who consider they are already self-aware, still find it worth considering how honest they are actually being? Any residual internal feeling of unease or dissatisfaction this exercise raises tends to indicate that perhaps we haven't reached the optimum level of confidence meaning, there is still work to be done.

Confidence and Childhood

Consider this; toddlers are full of confidence; they are open, curious, honest, non-judgmental, and most of all keen to try new things. They are keen to apply themselves when they enjoy something; they're pure in their emotional reactions and generally a joy to be around for these reasons. They are not sabotaged by a lack of confidence; if they were, they'd give up learning to walk after just a few attempts.

We started off where we are meant to be; confident and happy. So what goes wrong? Typically it's the way we process and react to the things that happen to us in life that eats away at that natural state, and causes us confusion, and self-doubt to grow. In reality, it's not surprising that many of us suffer from a lack of confidence since the notion of how important it is, as well as how to develop or maintain it isn't taught in most schools and it doesn't even tend to be at the top of most parents' lists either!

As a result what tends to happen is that we spend our formative years without any strategies in this area. Consequently, when we encounter negative life experiences we take them personally, we don't learn that *failure* and *rejection* are simply labels. We don't learn how to handle feedback or criticism. We compare ourselves negatively to our peers; we compare our appearance, our family situations, how well we do in exams; the list is endless. We take to heart the careless things that people say.

Get Out of Your Own Way!

We learn to internalise instead of communicating openly and honestly. Consequently we stumble into adulthood with a whole load of uncomfortable feelings and beliefs about our self-worth based on the plethora of challenging experiences that we have had to deal with growing up. Added to which, the things we've been told about; how we are meant to behave, think and feel often don't quite resonate, hence we have the perfect recipe for low confidence!

When we aren't taught *how* to process our experiences in a healthy and productive manner, we start to question our self-worth. We start to think that we aren't good enough, we start to think that we aren't attractive enough, smart enough, or that the careless words people use to describe us are true, or that our teachers were right and we won't amount to much. Our thinking patterns change which influences our behaviour, we may retreat into our shell, or cling to someone else to give us the confidence we so badly crave. Now of course we have to deal with challenging experiences throughout our whole of life so as we get older, we develop coping strategies to detach from emotional experiences.

An inability to process experiences and feelings in a useful and constructive way manifests as an identifiable lack of confidence that most of us would easily recognise; shyness, unwillingness to set and achieve goals and so on. For others, the process is more complicated; our self-protection mechanisms will often kick in and we'll weave ourselves stories to help make ourselves feel better about our perceived failures. We won't be honest with ourselves or the people around us so we don't have to admit that we aren't entirely pleased with ourselves, or a situation that no longer serves us just to *save face*. We think that it will make us look weak, or people won't like us if we show that we are vulnerable and in need of assistance. We won't admit that we think other people are doing better than us, or have more than us because it makes us feel inferior.

We'll get stuck in a holding pattern of negativity where we feel frustrated and feel unfulfilled and this will often manifest itself in jealously towards others that we perceive have more. We'll stay in relationships that don't make us happy because we can't admit that we got it wrong and we aren't sufficiently confident that we, or the other party, will survive and thrive through any change. Or we stay in relationships because we have defined ourselves so thoroughly by that connection that the idea that they might find someone else *better* is abhorrent to us; the idea that they might thrive without us threatens our sense of self-worth.

We also stay in jobs that no longer satisfy or interest us because we don't have enough confidence in our ability to find another one. We don't assert ourselves if we feel marginalised or bullied in the workplace. We won't ask for a pay rise or a promotion because we're concerned the answer might be no. Or worse, we won't follow our dreams and passions and find a role that satisfies us because we are worried about failure.

We do things to impress other people, or try and make other people like us more; we behave submissively, accept treatment that belittles and undermines us and we find creative ways to explain this away. We wouldn't allow others to treat us the way we often treat ourselves. Recognise any of them? Of course you do, all these scenarios indicate a thorough lack of confidence!

These are all the complicated off-shoots of a deep rooted lack of confidence. As I mentioned right at the beginning, confidence isn't a *nice to have*, you aren't *lucky* if you are confident; it's an essential part of living the best possible life you can. The life that you deserve to live!

Confidence versus Arrogance

If we return to the idea that some people are suspicious of confidence, or believe that confident people are those who are the loudest, very often they are simply getting confused between the idea of confidence and arrogance. As you may, or may not already know, arrogance, self-promotion, or excessive bragging tends to indicate a lack of self-esteem. This is because the qualities that we associate with people who have the healthy type of confidence that we are striving for do not allow for arrogance or excessive self-promotion.

Confident people do not bulldoze others, or shout the loudest, or need external validation to allow them to feel confident. They don't talk over other people and they don't tell other people their opinions are worthless or wrong. They don't make their point by simply stamping all over the feelings and thoughts of others. In fact, when you accept the definition of confidence that we looked at earlier which was a quiet, inner sense of self-worth, it's clear that any requirement for external validation clearly indicates that you don't have the level of confidence you thought you had. It's certainly nice to have external validation and there's nothing wrong with communicating your success or celebrating yourself; but it shouldn't be something you need, or feel badly about if you don't get it. You aren't defined by the opinions of those around you. It's more important that you are honest about your thoughts and feelings and are comfortable to communicate them. This in itself is quite a rare commodity which is sometimes frowned upon by those who aren't able to do the same, but it's an essential part of confidence. There's nothing wrong with being direct. The most successful connections are based on authenticity and honesty.

Actually, people who have mastered the subject of confidence are often considered to be kind and compassionate, especially when others are doing their best to be direct and communicate too. Because when you really understand the natural struggle many of us go through to achieve higher levels of confidence, you'd never think to be unkind, or make careless comments about another person who is still on their journey towards optimum confidence. We're all in this together; we all have our own personal demons and our own personal difficulties so take the steps towards true confidence and all that accompanies it together.

Confidence and Comparisons

"Confidence isn't walking into a room and thinking you are better than everyone else, it's walking into a room and not having to compare yourself in the first place".

True confidence equally means that you don't feel the need to compare yourself to other people in any way that damages your own sense of self-worth. Start to reflect upon the things you think and question why you do compare. The next time you hear yourself say something along the lines of "why's X always posting all these photos, such a show off..." take a step back and ask yourself "why do I care"? In reality, what does it matter to you what anyone else is doing; it would only really matter if you aren't content with what you are doing so work on that part instead.

We waste far too much mental energy worrying about what other people are possibly thinking, doing or saying about us. We need to stop taking things personally or too seriously. Imagine what would happen if you applied that same mental energy to improving your own circumstances and working on your own confidence, imagine how you much more you could achieve, probably more than you ever believed possible. Taking these initial small steps will start the process of opening yourself up, laying yourself bare and getting real and honest with yourself.

Developing confidence in this way opens us up to being more tolerant to other people's opinions and digesting their feedback without feeling criticised. Most of the time when we take a stance around someone being *right* or *wrong* it's because we feel threatened in some way. When we are lacking in confidence we will often feel under attack if someone questions our views, or beliefs which tends to manifest in aggressive reactions. Here's a heads up for you; not everyone will agree with you, nor do you need them to! We're going to explore beliefs later, and we'll see how inherently personal they are so it's not surprising that many of our, and indeed the world's biggest issues stem from a lack of tolerance of others. Adopt a more positive approach to disagreement; get curious like a child and learn to debate a subject rather than seeing it as an argument, children are brilliant at debating. Also, consider the other person's perspective to understand both sides of any issue. You never know, you may learn something! Remember the old parable "before you criticise a man, walk a mile in his shoes."

I'm all for admiring and modelling other people's excellence so I encourage you to do the same. If you perceive that someone is better at you at something, your mind-set approach needs to be *how are they doing that, how can I do that too?* When you perceive that somebody else around you is having more success in an area that you would also like to experience, adopt an attitude of curiosity, find out what they are doing and how they are doing it and then you do the same. Know that you are capable of doing anything you want to. You are blessed with an amazing piece of kit inside your head that will allow you to achieve the most extraordinary things when you learn how to use it and focus it accordingly.

The characteristics of confidence

Let's summarise what we've just covered. The lists below are by no means exhaustive, but give a great indicator as to the main characteristics of confident people versus low confident people. How far do you identify with either list?

Characteristics of High Confidence	Characteristics of Low Confidence
• Know they are good enough • Hunger to learn and develop • Set and achieve goals willingly	• Feelings of low self-worth • Often stagnant/demotivated • Unwilling to set goals or follow through • Critical of self and others

Get Out of Your Own Way!

Characteristics of High Confidence	Characteristics of Low Confidence
• Compassionate to others • Not afraid to ask for help • Not afraid to own their mistakes • Comfortable asserting themselves • Help others shine • Optimistic and positive • Celebrate others successes • Enjoy feedback and criticism	• Reluctant to admit weakness • Make excuses/blame others • Often aggressive/arrogant • Jealous of others • Pessimistic and negative • Prone to negative gossip • Worried about others opinions

My final point related to defining confidence is as follows: not everyone is going to love you, or even like you, and that's perfectly OK. Don't worry if that feels like too big a stretch for you to get on board with at the moment. You'll get there, I promise. If someone doesn't like you, or doesn't understand you, it actually doesn't matter, or have any impact provided you don't let it. Not everybody will like everybody else it's human nature, there are too many preferences and choices available to us in the world today; the way you choose to live your life may be completely different from what others view as acceptable or reasonable and that's OK too. You can remain confident in the face of this as long as you know that you are a good, kind, inclusive person and that your intentions for yourself and for everyone you meet are positive.

Once you've done the work around becoming more honest

and open with yourself, you can let go of the need to control others perceptions of you which is a profoundly liberating experience. You'll realise that you don't ever have enough insight into someone else's world and thought processes to understand that their perception of you is coloured by their own world, their own challenges, their own struggle over knowing and accepting themselves. That's OK extend them some compassion and move on.

Seek out those people on a similar journey to you, seek out people who want to be honest with themselves and with you and want to help your confidence grow and thrive. You focus on working on yourself and supporting the people you love; let others do the same.

By now we are starting to get a clearer idea of what it means to be confident and exactly the type of mental attitude and state that we are aiming for to build and improve our confidence.

Let's do a little exercise now to assess how well we are doing. Score yourself on the checklist below on a scale of 1 – 10 where 10 would be that you fully agree with the statement and 1 would be that you don't agree at all.

Confidence Checklist

- I believe in myself and my abilities -
- I am happy with myself and my abilities -
- I work on the areas of myself that I want to improve -
- I rarely compare myself to other people -
- I am kind and compassionate to all -
- I am kind and compassionate to myself -
- I am respectful of different views and opinions -

Get Out of Your Own Way!

- I rarely experience feelings of jealously towards others -
- I feel satisfied with my life -
- I know I am doing the best I can -

How did you do? As a general rule of thumb, if you scored yourself less than an 8 on any of those statements, there's work to be done. The next section will help equip you with the strategies you need to create compelling confidence.

How can we develop more confidence?

"Whether you think you can or think you can't, you are right". Henry Ford

By now we know that confidence is essentially made up of what we believe about ourselves, our perception of our own worth and our own capacities. We've also considered the fact that for many of us, we're not entirely sure what we believe to be true about ourselves. Now we're going to get into the nitty gritty of what beliefs are, why they are so important, and how we can develop more confident and empowering beliefs for ourselves.

First up then, what is a belief? Well, in a nutshell, our beliefs make up the cornerstones of who we are; they are essentially what we understand and know about the world to be true. They are inherently personal and act as our own hard-wired code of conduct and internal guidelines impacting on our behaviour, our perception of the world and our role within it. Almost everything we do in life is affected and impacted in some way, by our own belief system.

The process of forming our beliefs starts early in childhood; a baby is born as an empty vessel believing anything is possible and with only two fears;
1. the fear of falling and
2. loud noises.

Both are hard-wired to ensure their survival. From the age of around two onwards, once we become more conscious of our surroundings, we start to adopt and acquire beliefs from the people and situations we are surrounded with. Our senses are bombarded by information from all sides on a second to second basis; we see, hear, smell, touch and taste and each individual experience of these encounters goes some way to forming the cornerstones of our beliefs.

We are affected by our environment and by perhaps random occurrences; for example a child nipped by a dog at an early age can easily grow up to be afraid of all dogs and even reluctant to keep pets. Growing up we are affected by the people that surround us; parents, teachers, friends, peers who are all unconsciously sharing their own beliefs and view of the world with us. Often they present these beliefs as absolute truths. A good example of this is religion; a child being raised in a specific religious environment will be instructed about the foundations of the chosen religion in a manner that suggests that the information is indisputable for example: "God created the world and everything in it". As a child, we are, in the main, incapable of deep analysis and lack the knowledge with which to make our own judgments. As a result, we're quick to adopt whatever we are presented with without any real questioning of the veracity or validity of it.

Another example would be that if a child is consistently told from an early age that they are "not academic" by their primary sources of information and care, they will likely accept this to be true. This will affect their view of self and is likely to influence their behaviour growing up. This scenario represents a negative *limiting belief;* one which is toxic and could be extremely detrimental to the future of that child. A deeply held limiting belief like this, formed in early childhood, will inevitably negatively impact on behaviour, habits and attitude. Due to the way our brains function, we are rarely consciously aware that they are indeed *only* beliefs, and beliefs *can* be changed. Until we become aware that we are capable of learning techniques for changing beliefs that no longer serve us, we tend to accept our beliefs as real. Consequently, we act accordingly which creates more evidence to make us believe a belief is true.

As we get older, we continue to be inundated with information from ever more sources that reinforce our belief systems. Our friends, parents, peers, colleagues remain influential, but we also have a plethora of choices available to us in the form of the media; books, newspapers, articles, advertisements, the Internet, radio, television, films, celebrity and so on. As an adult we are perhaps more likely to question, or take a view on the information that we receive, but nevertheless, deep rooted beliefs formed at an early age remain present and continue to influence our views and perceptions without us really being aware of them.

So how do beliefs impact on us? As we have already considered; our beliefs are essentially who we are, or who we believe ourselves to be. As a result they affect everything; how we act, think, speak and view our own selves and others. Beliefs shape an individual's reality and they are the foundation upon which our sense of confidence rests.

It is useful to have a basic appreciation of the way in which the brain processes beliefs in order to better understand the profound impact they can have on our attitude, behaviour and overall experience of life. Also how critical it is that we choose confident and empowering beliefs.

Get Out of Your Own Way!

So here we go; some basic neuroscience. Simply put, beliefs are stored in the brain at a sub conscious level; a level where the brain acts as a filing cabinet that simply accepts and stores information received to later recall it as and when necessary.

As we move through life, the sub conscious will bring information to the forefront when an experience or situation requires it. This information will be presented as the absolute truth generally resulting in the conscious mind behaving in a manner which is consistent with it. For example, the brain will tell us that if we have experienced a similar situation, or circumstance previously, and the outcome was X, the overwhelming likelihood is that the outcome will be repeated. As a result, if our perception is that the previous outcome was a negative one, we are likely to avoid producing the same result again and behave accordingly. This thinking fundamentally limits our potential and fear creates self-sabotage and reduces our ability to more forward or explore all options.

On top of this, the conscious mind, in an effort to make sense of the masses of information it receives on a daily basis, filters the information that we receive in direct accordance with our sub-conscious belief system. Essentially it will consistently look for evidence to support whatever it is that we believe to be true. The brain has no internal quality control for weeding out harmful or detrimental beliefs. It accepts what it is given, positive or negative.

Our conscious mind wants us to be right at all times. This means that, even in the face of contradictory evidence, we will be biased to what we believe. In the case we mentioned above about the child who honed their belief that they were not academic at an early age, will consistently look for evidence to support that this is indeed the case throughout their working career. As such, it is easy to understand how our future attitudes and behaviours are affected by our beliefs.

A person, who believes they can succeed, will succeed because their perception of the world will allow them to view any set-back not as failure, but as an opportunity, a learning experience. A person who has a deep rooted belief that they will fail, is likely to view the same set-back as supporting evidence of their eventual failure and give up their endeavours far more quickly.

For the individual who has been conditioned to believe that they are not academic, they are unlikely to set related goals that they believe they cannot fulfil. Their deep rooted belief may not let them aim for the highest grade when preparing for an exam, indeed they might not even prepare properly because their sub-conscious is telling them that they will fail anyway. As such, the importance and power of holding positive, empowering beliefs about ourselves is our best shot at living the most fulfilling life we can.

So, here are a number of things for us to consider when we relate this directly to confidence.

a) If you think you're lacking in confidence, you will be.
b) If you continue to hold negative beliefs about yourself that you don't address, they will continue to undermine your confidence.

Get Out of Your Own Way!

Let's explore a couple of diagrams that will help illustrate this point more clearly; take a look below at what would be considered to be a:

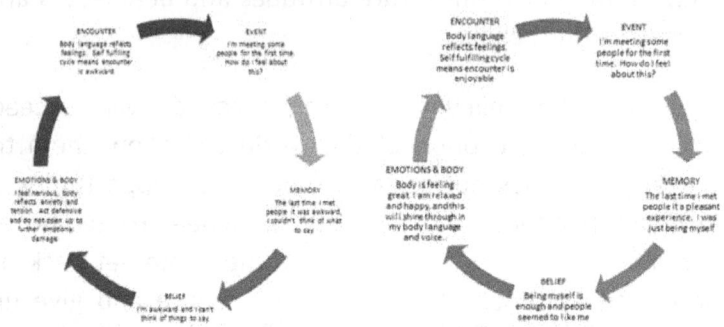

Fig 1: Negative confidence cycle   Fig 2: Positive confidence cycle

Now you can see how a self-fulfilling prophesy is achieved. One type of thought process is going to rapidly lead to consistently negative outcomes, whereas the other will yield the opposite. It's all down to what you believe about yourself to be true.

Many of us spend a lot of time beating ourselves up about the things that we do or say or the way in which we behave; consequently we forget how important it is that the voices in your head are supposed to be on your side. You have to learn to make friends with any previous versions of you and understand that from this moment on, you will, if you do the work, create the confidence that you need to live a happy, fulfilled and inspiring life, irrespective of what happened in your past.

Now you have information about how to review what your belief system is based on, we're going to review the earlier exercise and see what beliefs you want to keep because they continue to serve you, and which ones need further examination, even discarding.

Knowing what we do about the impact of beliefs on our potential and the importance of selecting healthy beliefs as the cornerstone of confidence, we need to unpick the beliefs that no longer serve us. For example, if you've written anything akin to; *I know I am difficult* or *I know I am shy* or anything similar, we want to further consider the extent to which this is likely to be damaging your own sense of self and sabotaging you from moving forward with confidence.

You can follow a relatively simple process to reframe the things that you currently think about yourself to make them a more constructive part of your inner dialogue that takes place 24/7. Follow the process below and see how you get on:

<u>1. What evidence do I have that proves this limiting belief is still true for me?</u>

You're likely to have plenty of evidence to support the disempowering things that you believe about yourself on account of the fact that you will likely have been behaving in a way which is congruent with that. Be brave and dive into the thoughts and memories that support your current way of thinking. Think deeply and visualise yourself as a third party onlooker who is dispassionately assessing the ways you have been behaving and why.

<u>2. What evidence do I have that proves just the exact opposite of this limiting belief?</u>

This is where the process gets interesting; many of us will

behave in different ways in different circumstances. So if you believe you are difficult or shy or whatever your limiting belief may be, think about the times when you *don't* behave in a way that supports that belief. At the very least, this process will open your mind up to the possibility that this particular quality or thought process isn't an embedded, intrinsic part of you in that you don't have to respond that way every time. Now think about what could be different about the circumstances where you do feel more comfortable. Then consider how you can replicate those circumstances across the board to consistently build your confidence.

3. What will happen if I continue to hold this belief?

An important part of the process, and generally one that helps us realise the full importance of *choosing* our beliefs is, being aware of what you will miss out on *if* you continue to hold a particular belief. How will you limit your potential? How will this limitation affect your overall quality of life?

4. How do other people who hold opposite beliefs to me think and feel?

Here you get to use your imagination skills to the fullest, think of people you admire and aspire to emulate that evidently hold the opposite belief system of you; so people who are brimming with confidence and are assertive. You'll know who they are because they'll likely to behave differently to you. Think about how it might be to feel and think this way yourself. Repeat this exercise until you fully desire a different belief system for yourself and are willing to fully buy into the idea that you can achieve it.

5. What would be a more empowering belief to hold onto?

This is when we start to get creative and rewrite our beliefs and take control of the quality of our internal dialogue. Now, we have to be realistic; it would be a struggle for many of us to go from thinking one thing to thinking the exact opposite in a short space of time, so we need to take baby steps to allow our thinking patterns to catch up. For example; if you've always thought of yourself as shy, it's going to be a challenge to simply think of yourself as outgoing and as a result behave in this way. It's not always a question of dramatically changing the belief, but sometimes just reframing the language you use to describe yourself. Think about it this way; what is a better way of thinking about an old belief so that you feel more comfortable with it? Let's use shy as the example; better ways of thinking about this belief could be use words like: thoughtful, reflective, considered and introverted.

Make it part of your life to automatically question the things that you believe about yourself, about others and about the world in general to assess whether they represent your beliefs, or those that you have acquired from elsewhere. Endeavour to become more curious and open in your thought processes and start by ensuring that your internal dialogue is as healthy and positive as it would be when you communicate with your loved ones and friends.

Strategies for maintaining confidence

So by now, we know what confidence is. We know how to identify internal beliefs about our self, and we know how to tweak the things that we believe about ourselves. All of which ensure we have a positive and empowering personal internal dialogue. Let's now add in the final piece of the puzzle and think about how we can maintain confidence over the long haul, especially when life, as it does, throws us a curveball.

The essence of maintaining confidence is essentially linked to the idea of competency and how competent you feel you are. People will often say to me "I'll feel more confident once I've been doing this for longer" and for many of us that's indeed the case; the feeling of confidence and competence are intrinsically linked. When we feel competent and capable, the world is ours, we boldly set out into the unknown, and we adapt and learn readily, we conquer our fears and meet our challenges. We experience heightened levels of confidence, success and mastery. In coaching, we often refer to this as the "competence, confidence loop". The more competence you have; the more confident you feel about taking on new and bigger challenges. Conversely, the more you do that, the more mastery you develop and the more competent you feel, it becomes a self-fulling prophesy.

However, as soon as our internal competence scale tips from self-assured to self-doubting, we start to erode our carefully crafted sense of confidence. When we feel that we are lacking in some way we are likely to encounter uncomfortable feelings such as: anxiety, anger, disappointment, hopelessness and the fear of failure. This will often lead us to take this out on other people and the feeling self-perpetuates, or else we'll simply withdraw.

Paying attention and investing in your competence level at any given moment is a critical part of maintaining the healthy self confidence that you need to be successful. Let's look in a little more depth at *why* it's such an important part of confidence:

- Your competence level determines what you will give your attention to. When you don't feel competent you tend not to pay attention to problems, conflicts, or bigger challenges, and opportunities that present themselves because you don't feel you can handle them. As a result, a lack of competence can often lead to procrastination.
- Your competence level will impact upon the things that you choose to do. When you feel capable and confident that you can understand, perform in and master your world, you are willing to take on harder tasks and embark upon more stretching challenges. You're likely to create goals for yourself that are appropriate and motivating. This of course generally leads to more learning and more success.
- Your competence level determines your effort level. Hard workers believe they can create positive outcomes with their effort so they work harder. It seems all too simple, but expert high performance studies have shown over and over that if you believe you are competent, you will work harder.
- Your competence level determines your overall sense of flexibility and resilience. Those people who trust their abilities to understand, learn, deliver and eventually master whatever they are doing are more

willing to adjust their action when something isn't working. They tend not to take it personally when things don't work out; they take a more dispassionate view of their own successes and failures, plus they are open to learning from their mistakes to ensure that they do even better next time.

In order to develop a sense of competency and make it a consistent part of your life, the best approach is to get more specific about the things that you are good at, the areas in which you want to develop, and the overall sense of achievement moving forward. Whether we realise it or not, human beings are hard-wired to thrive when they feel like they are making progress, learning, developing and moving towards a goal.

However, for most of us life starts to feel more difficult when we feel like we've stagnated, or are simply running the same patterns and behaviours through our heads on a daily basis. Often it's simply this realisation that can help us unlock our potential, regain our sense of confidence and move forward with renewed vigour.

Happily, we can capitalise on this knowledge by reprogramming our brain to celebrate our achievements. This ensures that we benefit from the boost of motivation and confidence that this will automatically bring. Let's do a quick exercise on this now. Write down your top twenty achievements over the past two years; achievements are personal so focus on the things that count for you; what have you learnt, overcome, what are you proud of, new things you've done/tried. For example, the first time I did this exercise, the number one thing on my list was that I'd started driving again after a good ten years of barely getting in the driver's seat. Dig deep, if you find it a struggle; you will have done far more than you realised.

My top 20 Achievements over the past two years:
1
2
3
4
5
6
7
8
9
10
11
12
13
14
15
16
17
18
19
20

Get Out of Your Own Way!

How did you get on? Typically when people start this type of exercise they find it quite challenging to bring to mind things that they have achieved. When the brain moves into recall mode though, they easily find things to celebrate that they've successfully achieved or overcome, and before long, they've generated quite a list! Don't worry if that hasn't happened to you yet. It will come.

We're going to look at another specific exercise that will help with this process. This type of exercise is really important to build into your confidence building toolkit. Not least because we are often so busy in our daily lives that we forget to take time to give ourselves credit for the things that we do and the things that we achieve. This is also a great technique to use with children; I systematically ask my seven year old daughter what the best thing was that happened to her that day irrespective of what she was doing. She now anticipates the question and can't wait to tell me about the fabulous things that go on in her life. This is a simple technique that helps develop a sense of progress and trains the brain to be proud of itself whilst maintaining a sense of moving forward.

To embed this way of thinking as a part of your everyday life, think about the following:

How did you get on? Typically when people start this type of exercise they find it quite challenging to bring to mind things that they have achieved. When the brain moves into recall mode though, they easily find things to celebrate that they've successfully achieved or overcome, and before long, they've generated quite a list! Don't worry if that hasn't happened to you yet. It will come.

Get Out of Your Own Way!

We're going to look at another specific exercise that will help with this process. This type of exercise is really important to build into your confidence building toolkit. Not least because we are often so busy in our daily lives that we forget to take time to give ourselves credit for the things that we do and the things that we achieve. This is also a great technique to use with children; I systematically ask my seven year old daughter what the best thing was that happened to her that day irrespective of what she was doing. She now anticipates the question and can't wait to tell me about the fabulous things that go on in her life. This is a simple technique that helps develop a sense of progress and trains the brain to be proud of itself whilst maintaining a sense of moving forward.

To embed this way of thinking as a part of your everyday life, think about the following:

1. <u>Set yourself challenges</u>. Make them realistic and achievable and something inspiring for example read a new book this month, learn to cook a new dish, learn a new system or tool in work. Set yourself a timeframe and PUSH YOURSELF to achieve that deadline. Don't be tempted to overstretch yourself when you start this type of technique; there's nothing more disheartening than setting yourself a huge challenge and then being unable to complete it simply because you haven't broken it down into manageable chunks from the start.
2. <u>Keep a journal.</u> Every day write down a couple of things you have achieved or worked towards that day. Get into the habit of doing this in the same way I ask my daughter to highlight the best part of her day. Persevere and avoid giving yourself a hard time if you

miss a day, or even a week. Simply return to it and start again; you'll soon find that it becomes an automatic two minute habit a day that has a profound impact on your overall sense of wellbeing and confidence.

3. <u>Practice gratitude</u>. So many studies have been conducted relating to the profound importance of making gratitude a part of your life and the significant benefits that adopting this type of mentality will bring. Remind yourself of your fortunate situation, however difficult, or disappointing your day might have been there is categorically always something to be thankful for.

4. <u>Visualisation Exercise</u>. I once encountered a wonderful visualisation exercise in developing gratitude which I use all the time which I'll share with you now. Find a nice quiet place and close your eyes. Think for a minute about all the things in your life that you are grateful for. Aid this process by setting yourself a little mental game. The premise is this; everything that you don't give thanks for will be gone once the game is completed; so you give thanks for the roof over your head, the clothes on your back, the money in the bank (however little that might be), the fridge that contains food and extends your life for longer, your family wherever they maybe, your friends, the Internet, your car, your bike, your health and so on and so forth. You get the picture. It's a humbling exercise and it's wonderful to experience. We're so much luckier than we'll ever realise. Training our brains to remember this helps to build an overall sense of well-being and develops a healthy sense of confidence and competency in our own lives.

We're reaching the end of our work together so I trust you are now feeling more confident already and more equipped to deal with the rigours of your life. Let's remind ourselves once again; confidence is essential to your overall experience of life and will allow you to feel happier, healthier, more fulfilled and more motivated to achieve the things that you want to experience in your future.

Remember it's also something that you are capable of creating yourself; whilst other people and experiences will help boost your confidence in specific circumstances, they cannot generate it for you, and they can't be responsible for your retention of confidence either. Only you can do it, you just need to know and believe that you are capable of making your desired changes. Decide what you want to change and then, as with all good things in life, put a plan in place to make it work. Start today; keep it up and most of all, start working towards a more confident future, one that offers you all the benefits that having compelling confidence brings. Good luck and let me know how I can help you further.

Get Out of Your Own Way!

Cathy Radcliffe - Biography

Cathy Radcliffe is an Accredited Executive Coach, Master Practitioner of Neuro-Linguistic Programming (NLP) accredited with the ANLP. An experienced Trainer and Facilitator specialising in the key areas of workplace communication and confidence, she has over 17 years of professional experience in general management and operations management in start-ups and SME's.

Her warm, open and direct style enables her to research, design and deliver innovative and inspirational training programs that get the most out of people and businesses by increasing motivation, effectiveness, and focus which expands self-awareness and develops a flexible effective, and influential styles of communicating.

Often described as a natural coach/trainer, Cathy has extensive expertise in helping teams and individuals achieve excellence in the workplace. She is committed to ensuring that the training she delivers responds to individual needs and knows how to embed them into the training to increase the meaningfulness of the learning programme.

Prior to focusing on her coaching and training practice, Cathy benefitted from over 17 years' professional experience engaging with people at a variety of functional levels and across a wide range of business sectors. Eight years' of which she was the Founder & Managing Director of a successful London based marketing agency. By combining her own practical knowledge and experience of the workplace with cutting edge coaching and training techniques, Cathy is able to work with individuals and businesses to facilitate lasting change in a short space of time. Consequently, she has a well-respected client portfolio.

Specialties

- Developing Communication Skills
- Confidence and Assertive Skills
- Networking Skills
- Neuro-Linguistic Programming
- Team-work & Team-building Techniques
- Management & Leadership
- Strategic Business Coaching

Cathy is currently the International Institute of Coaches and Mentors (IIC&M) Editor of their award winning monthly e-zine.

Get Out of Your Own Way!

Section Two
Releasing Your Future

by
Barbara J. Cormack

"If you think you can do a thing, or think you can't do a thing, you are right." – Henry Ford (1863 – 1947)

Get Out of Your Own Way!

Fact: you are entitled to live a life full of happiness, health, wealth, love, friendship, true expression, and peace of mind; doing what you love doing. But do you really believe that?

The simple answer could be to say a resounding *"Yes!"* Sadly, for the majority of people the opposite is true. Without realising it, *you* are the only one who has the power to sabotage you. The way you perceive yourself and your world is *programmed* from the moment of your birth. Without realising it, every time you think a thought, or feel an emotion and with every belief and value, you hold to be true; you are constantly reinforcing that programme in your own mind.

Fact. Therefore, as long as you are feeling, thinking or taking negative action you will continue sabotaging yourself *until* you give yourself permission to STOP. Stopping has the power to release your future.

As a coach and mentor, I often work with clients who have fabulous dreams, but have not allowed themselves to achieve them due to self-sabotage. Although there are many self-development courses, tools, techniques, and products available; all of them promising to help you move from where you are today, to where you want to be; *including this book*, self-sabotage will only stop *when* you take the necessary action to change. Reading about *how* to do something does not make it happen. If you want to stop self-sabotaging your dreams, then you also need to take action.

Releasing your future is essentially about how effectively you use your mind. Continue reading and you will experience a *wonderful journey of learning, self-discovery and achievement*.

Your Mind!

Although there are a number of definitions of what your mind is, it's simply the 'totality of conscious and unconscious mental processes and activities'. In other words, it's the part of you that reasons, thinks, feels, wills, perceives, judges, etc.

Now is the time to reveal the wonderful world of power within you; of your possibilities and promise.

Let's explore!

Your Conscious Mind! is the part of you that thinks and reasons. It selects or rejects thoughts. It selects or rejects ideas. It chooses what you are thinking about. It chooses what you make decisions about. It also makes your decisions. Another way of looking at this is that your conscious mind will determine the path that your life will take.

Your successes, your pains, your pleasure, your failures, and your limitations comes from what you select to think about in your conscious mind.

Your five senses (touch, see, smell, taste, hear) are experiences that you have and recognise with your conscious mind. These experiences are turned into thoughts

Get Out of Your Own Way!

in your conscious mind.

There is the well-known and fabulous quote from Earl Nightingale (1921-1989) – *'You become what you think about.'* We'll explore more about how you think and by understanding how you think, how you can change your thinking to become what you want to be.

Thoughts! are where everything begins. Without sometimes being aware your thoughts are coming from a range of places. They sometimes come from a conversation with someone else. They sometimes come from something that you've seen. They sometimes come from research that you've done. They sometimes come from a book you are reading or have read. They sometimes come from a film or movie that you are watching. They sometimes come from a website that you've seen or been reading. Sometimes they just seem to appear!

However they come, as we explore more you will also begin to understand how your conscious mind and the thoughts that you consciously think influences the path that your life has taken and will take.

Your Unconscious Mind, also referred to as your sub-conscious mind, is your power centre! Your unconscious mind, without you realising functions at every level of your being and within every cell of your body.

Your unconscious mind works in exactly the same way that your computer works when it stores your files! It has no ability to reject your conscious thoughts. It accepts them! It stores exactly what your conscious mind is thinking, using the exact words, tones, and feelings that your conscious mind is using.

If you think 'no', then you store 'no'. If you think 'yes', then you store 'yes'. If you think 'maybe', then you store 'maybe'. Your unconscious mind has no way of detection whether the information you are storing is right or wrong. It just stores it.

The thoughts that you have stored are also used by your conscious mind when you are making decisions. So if you store 'no' then often when you are faced with the same or a similar decision you will think 'no'.

An example I use is one where you go into a restaurant and look at a menu. Automatically you are drawn to those items on the menu that are familiar to you. More often than not you will not really look at those items that are not familiar and you will always say 'no' to those items where you unconscious mind tells you that you won't like it.

What happens though when you suddenly stop and truly look at what is on your menu? What happens when you question the ingredients in one of the meals? What happens when you say that you will try something that you

Get Out of Your Own Way!

haven't tried before? What happens when you try something with an ingredient that you didn't think you liked?

Henry Ford (1863-1947) said *'if you always do what you've always done, you'll always get what you've always got.'* He simply means that if you do not challenge your own thinking you will always follow the path that you've always followed.

Releasing Your Future is about challenging your way of thinking!

How does your current thinking affect your future?

Every thought that you have is expressed through everything you do (in your actions), in everything you express (in your words), and in everything that you feel (in your emotions and your feelings).

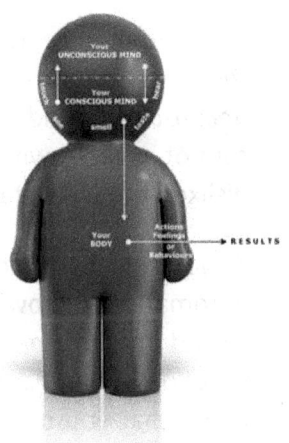

In other words, every thought you have you express in your results.

Your Body is the part of you that, although you are more consciously aware of, is really just an instrument of your mind.

Your body is moved into action through the conscious thoughts that you are thinking, or through the habits that you've created, or those thoughts you've stored in your unconscious mind. Your body is moved into action either physically, verbally, or emotionally.

Remember, and this is the key to your success in releasing your future, the actions you *select* to take determine your results.

Think of the five senses that I've included in this diagram – touch, see, smell, taste, and hearing. When you think of the way in which you experience things through one or more of these senses, those experiences are stored in your unconscious mind. You store the tastes that you like as well as the tastes you don't like. You store the textures that you like to touch, as well as those textures that you don't like to touch. You store the aromas that you like to smell, as well as those aromas that you don't like to smell.

Each experience is converted to a thought which is first thought in your *conscious* mind and then stored in your *unconscious* mind. Remember that your unconscious mind cannot on its own determine which whether you liked or disliked the smell, taste, or touch.

If you go back to my restaurant experience you will automatically know through the information that you have stored in your unconscious mind those items on the menu that you like and are drawn to, as well as those items on the menu that you don't like and won't select. Frequently you won't even think about this decision, it will happen automatically from the information you have previously stored in your unconscious mind. What happens is that your unconscious mind provides you with your answer without giving you (through your conscious mind) the opportunity to think about your response. It is this automatically generated information that will influence you to select one menu item over another.

Mind, Body, Spirit is a well-known phase that relates to how you release your future to yourself. Using the information and examples that I'm discussing, your mind relates to your *conscious mind*, your spirit relates to your *unconscious mind*, and your body relates to *your body*.

One of the secrets to living a life full of happiness, health, wealth, love, friendship, true expression, and peace of mind, doing what you love doing is that these three elements of you must be working together, and they must be working in harmony.

Get Out of Your Own Way!

'If you think you can do a thing or you think you can't do a thing, you're right.' Henry Ford (1863-1947) said this and he is right! What you *consciously* choose to think gets stored in your *unconscious* mind EXACTLY as you thought it. If you think 'I cannot do this', then this thought gets fixed in your *unconscious* mind exactly as you thought it – you cannot do it.

Over time these thoughts that you have stored in your unconscious mind become habits. These habits you will automatically continue to express in your results – in your words, in your actions, and in your emotions; without any conscious assistance.

You are the only person who can put a limit on your unconscious mind. Without your input your unconscious mind knows no limits. In the same way that your computer stores a file that you save, your unconscious mind stores exactly what your conscious think, and uses this information as part of your results – in how you act (your actions), in the words you use to express yourself (your words), and in everything that you feel (your emotions and feelings).

There are many quotes used that Earl Nightingale (1921-1989) said and the one that really helps you understand how you are living the life you are living today is *'We tend to live up to our expectations.'* When you think something and you store that thought in your unconscious mind; a thought which you later use to make a decision; you are truly setting your own expectations.

Ben Nevis is the highest mountain in Scotland and in the whole of the British Isles; standing at 1,344 metres above sea level. The north face (700 metres) provides classic scrambles and rock climbs of all difficulties for climbers and mountaineers, and if you were asked to climb this north face tomorrow; what would you say? In my experience, working as a coach and mentor, if you were not a mountain climber, your normal response would be 'no, I can't do that'. Your response comes from what you have, over the years, stored in your unconscious mind. It may come from your knowledge of your commitments for tomorrow – those commitments which you believe you cannot change. It may come from your knowledge of your level of fitness. It may come from your knowledge of the distance between where you are today and where Ben Nevis is on the western end of the Grampian Mountains in the Scottish Highlands near Fort William. Whatever triggers this negative thought is what drives your answer.

What would happen if you were to STOP and think 'OK although my diary is fully committed tomorrow and I'm unfit, I can do this but maybe not tomorrow'?

This stopping to allow yourself to challenge your automatic thinking allows you to start releasing the future you in your inner most heart want to be living.

'The mind moves in the direction of our currently dominant thoughts'. Earl Nightingale (1921 – 1989)

Your dominant thoughts are those that come from the 'information' that you have stored in your unconscious mind. Wallace D. Wattles (1860-1911) said *'A person's right to live means his right to have the free unrestricted use of all the things which may be necessary to his fullest mental, spiritual, and physical unfolding – in other words, his right to be rich.'*

Get Out of Your Own Way!

Isn't it interesting how many years ago authors like Wallace D. Wattles brought the spiritual into his writing?

If you take what both Earl Nightingale says and Wallace D. Wattles says, then working through how your thought process works with what I call the 'Universal Thought Process' gives you the opportunity to create and live the life of your dreams.

Now is your opportunity to stop your self-sabotage.

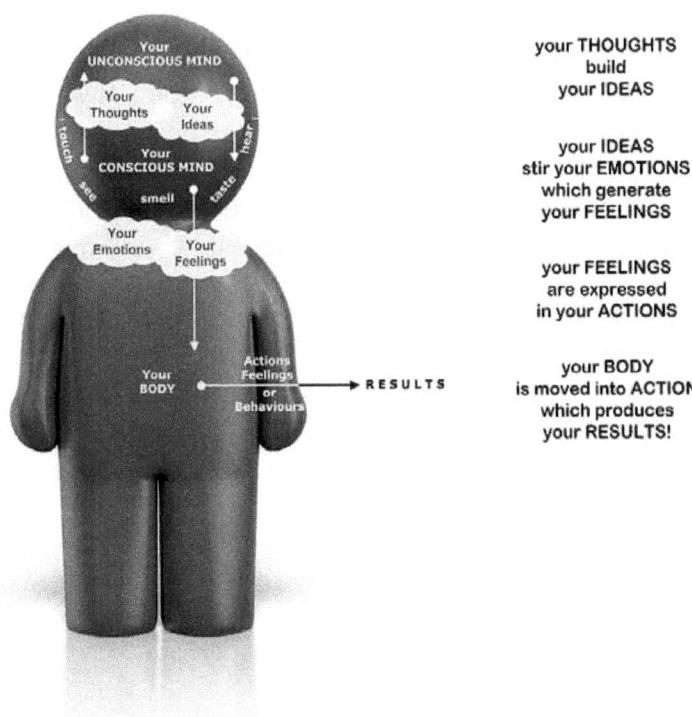

your THOUGHTS
build
your IDEAS

your IDEAS
stir your EMOTIONS
which generate
your FEELINGS

your FEELINGS
are expressed
in your ACTIONS

your BODY
is moved into ACTION
which produces
your RESULTS!

Your thought process is a simple four step process to create your results:

Get Out of Your Own Way!

1. Your thoughts create your ideas, which if these thoughts are positive will create positive ideas.
2. Your ideas will stir your emotions and create your feelings, which if the ideas are positive will stir positive emotions and create positive feelings.
3. Your feelings are expressed as your actions – verbal, physical, or emotional. If these feelings are positive, then your actions will be positive.
4. Your body is moved into action which produces your results. If these actions are positive your results will be positive.

The same is true of negative thoughts, ideas, emotions, feelings, actions and results. Positive doesn't always mean that you know what do to create that positive result, but something as simple as researching or learning what to do will create a positive result. The negative often comes when you let those negative thoughts dominate your thoughts.

Your dominant thoughts are those that come from the 'information' that you've stored in your unconscious mind. If what you have stored is negative, then more often than not your results will be negative; whereas if what you have stored is positive, more often than not your results will be positive.

Universal Thought Process

Before we look at how you can change what you have already stored in your unconscious mind, let us explore how the *Universal Thought Process* works with your Mind, Body, and Spirit.

What I call the *Universal Thought Process* is a major component of the *Law of Attraction*. Although there are many definitions of the *Law of Attraction*, what it really means is that you get what you focus your thoughts onto and into. Some describe the *Law of Attraction* as living the life of a *'living magnet'*. Others describe the *Law of Attraction* as *'like attracts like'*.

Bob Proctor (1934 -) in the film *The Secret* says that *'You will attract everything that you require. If it is money you need, you will attract money. If it is people you need, you will attract them. If it is a certain book you need, you'll attract it'*.

The *Law of Attraction*, in some ways, is like your unconscious mind; it is neutral. The *Law of Attraction* cannot differentiate between those things that you want and those things that you do not want. This is an important point; Bob Proctor goes on to say *'You've got to pay attention to what you're attracted to, because as you hold images of what you want, you're going to be attracted to things and they are going to be attracted to you'*.

Before I discuss the *Law of Attraction* in more detail, it is important to understand that the *Law of Attraction* does not work in isolation. It is your own *Thought Process (1)* that works closely with the *Universal Thought Process (2)* and the

Get Out of Your Own Way!

Law of Attraction (3) to release your own future to you.

These three elements create a combination of your communication with yourself and with the universe. These three elements help you release your future and attract your dream life to you. These three elements help you stop your sabotaging yourself.

Everything you have in your life today, or you want in your life has been, or will be given to you through your unconscious mind. As you have already read, your unconscious mind stores everything you think consciously: your thoughts, ideas, your 'I can do' and your 'I cannot do' attitude. Your unconscious mind stores what you are told by others, what you experience, as well as what you see, and feel. It stores everything!

Living the life of a *living magnet* means that often without being aware of it, you are bringing towards you the things that you need, or want as well as those that you do not need, or want.

Your unconscious mind also has another activity. Those thoughts that suddenly appear out of nowhere, often come as a result of listening to your *intuition*, or as I describe it, the *Universal Thought Process* and they are all captured in your unconscious mind.

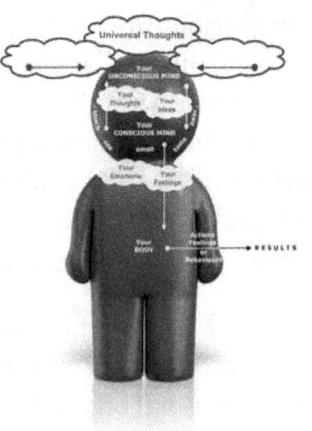

Although in the dictionary, intuition is described as *a direct*

perception of truth, fact, etc. which is independent of any reasoning process; it is in fact a sacred gift which each one of us has. Are you one of the people who are even aware of being in tune with their intuition? Whom else do you know who uses it? Whom do you know who trusts it? Who even questions this thing called intuition, which is often more commonly referred to as a *'gut-feeling'*? Yet our ancestors relied upon their intuition, sometimes described as *instinct,* as a key skill to keep them alive; they learnt to listen to, and act upon their thoughts.

Think about a time when you were in a meeting or a conversation, and you really wanted to ask a question or make a statement, but you didn't. What did you wonder as you walked away and reflected on what could have happened if you'd said what was on your mind? What stopped you? Now compare that to the time when you did follow your intuition, or your gut-feeling, and you did make the statement, or ask the question that was on your mind? Which scenario gave you the best result? Which felt the most authentic?

As an IT Project Manager working on a large project for a Blue Chip organisation, I once found myself in that position. I was in a meeting with the client Project Manager and all the project staff. The discussion was about a problem, which was stopping the software implementation moving ahead. A question popped into my mind. The question didn't seem to relate to the discussion. It didn't seem to make sense. What to do? Do I ask the question knowing that if it was inappropriate I would not look professional? After a few minutes of internal debate, I asked the question. You could hear a pin drop as the conversation around the table stopped. Twenty people stopped talking and all looked at me. Ugh! Then someone said *'That's just what we need to be asked. That's the missing piece'*. From a conversation that had been going round in circles, seemingly without a solution or way forward; to a conversation where suddenly there was an energy, a focus, a way forward, and all because I didn't let fear get in the way of my listening to and acting upon my intuition.

Starting to listen to your own intuition, gut-feel, or inner voice is one-step towards being able to release your future.

Spend some time now reflecting, perhaps with the workbook that accompanies this series, and write about all the times you wish you'd been brave enough to say what was on your mind. Now write about all the times when you were brave and authentic enough to make your intuition heard; when you did say what was on your mind. Exploring what you would have liked to have said is another successful way of releasing negativity you may be holding onto as well as recognising your progress.

Watching the film, *The Secret* I became fully aware of how *Universal Thought Processes* works. One of the people interviewed talked about how whenever he drives somewhere i.e. the shops he is mentally *asking the Universe for a car parking space close to the entrance* and that he usually gets one.

So one day I remember about a week before Christmas wanting to park in the centre of Canterbury, Kent, UK, I was shopping with a friend so we both asked the Universe for a parking space, not something easily achieved, but we got one. Now I always ask for a space or a gap whenever I approach a roundabout/traffic island and I get it.

Get Out of Your Own Way!

Having the positive thought about getting the parking place or space to cross the roundabout/traffic island, builds a positive idea, asked with positive emotion, which generates a positive feeling, and generates a positive result.

Universal Thoughts happen both as incoming thoughts and as outgoing thoughts. Not only do those thoughts pop into your mind from what appears to be no-where, but when you ask for something like a parking place, you are communicating with the universe.

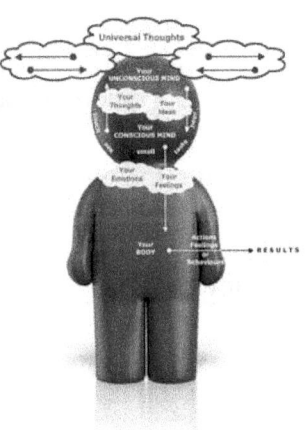

It is important to always converse through the *Universal Thought Process* with a belief that you will get what you are asking for. When you ask with a belief that you will get what you are asking for, more often than not the result will be positive; but if you ask with a belief that it will not happen, then more often than not the answer is a negative one.

When you are asking through the *Universal Thought Process,* you are invoking the *Law of Attraction*, which is neutral; *you get what you ask for.*

Bob Proctor (1934 -) explains in *The Secret* that *'most people have a goal of getting out of debt'*. He explains *that having a goal around the word debt will keep you in debt- forever - because whatever you're thinking about you will attract.* If in your conversation you use the word *debt* the *Law of Attraction* will attract *debt*. Bob's suggestion is that you *"Set up an automatic debt repayment program and then*

Get Out of Your Own Way!

start to focus on prosperity instead".

Releasing the future of your inner most dream comes from an understanding of how your mind (conscious mind), your body, and your spirit (unconscious mind using the *Universal Thought Process*) work together and in harmony. It comes from being fully aware of how you are consciously or unconsciously communicating with:
1.   Yourself.
2.   The Universe.
3.   Those around you.

But how?

This is achieved by learning how to releasing your future

Creating space to be still. One of the things that you don't often give yourself is space and quality time to be still. Releasing the future you dream about: a life full of happiness, health, wealth, love, friendship, true expression, and peace of mind; doing what you love doing does require you to create space and time to be still. Time is often the one thing that you don't feel you have enough of. It's no wonder when you consider that your mind has up to 65,000+ thoughts a day.

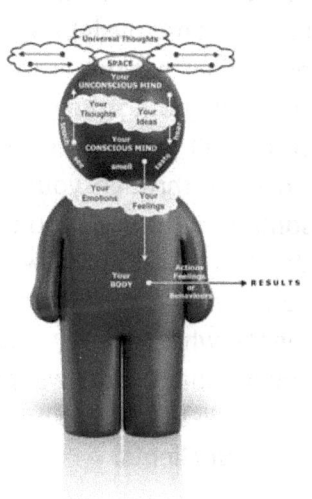

Your conscious mind is busy with the thoughts you want to focus on. Your unconscious mind is busy with everything else, including the assistance you need to live your life, achieve your goals, and many other things.

Creating space simply means finding a way to quieten your thoughts, calm your body, give yourself time, and allow yourself to be still. It isn't always easy, but there are a number of ways in which you can create the space you need to release your future.

Self-Talk. How many times have you said or heard someone say *"I can't do that"!* Too often probably. Releasing your future is all about becoming aware of your internal communication. This internal communication encompasses not only how you talk to yourself, but also how you listen, and interpret your intuition. It's about the questions and requests you are making to the Universe (more often than not, unconsciously), and how you interpret the things that people say to you. If through your internal communication, you truly do not believe that you can have something then you won't get it. The reason is that every time you ask the Universe through your *Universal Thought Process* to bring something to you, you are asking with doubt and disbelief. What you will get is what you are asking for but with the doubt and disbelief attached. For example, if you want clients who can pay you £150.00 per hour, but you only believe that clients will pay you £50.00 per hour then guess which clients will come your way – that's right, the £50.00 per hour clients.

Therefore, it is important you are absolutely clear about how to you talk to yourself. When you hear doubts, write them down, work on them, and most importantly, convert them into being positive thoughts. This is why a journal is a huge benefit and help in your on-going development.

Once you believe that you can have this thought, dream, aspiration, idea and/or future; it will start to come your way. You've heard the phrase *'seeing is believing'* which means that only when you see something changing, will you have physical or concrete evidence, to believe that something is true. The more positive your internal communication pattern is, the more you will believe in yourself, the more motivating it is and the more you will see concrete evidence of change happening around you.

Exercise 1 – Journaling

Journaling is the simple and easy way to allow you to clear space.

There are many definitions of journaling, but the definition that describes this exercise best is *using a tool and technique that allows you to capture your inner most private thoughts in your personal and private document.* Your inner most private thoughts include your conscious thoughts, fears, concerns, dreams, aspirations, and unspoken goals.

Find somewhere quiet where there are no disruptions, no interruptions, no phones, no one wanting to talk to you, where you can be at peace and quiet. This will give you the opportunity to capture exactly what is on your mind.

Often the thoughts on your mind are those your unconscious mind is trying to get your conscious mind to listen and be heard.

It is important that you capture your thoughts EXACTLY as you hear them, whether they make sense or not. Do not try to analyse them. Do not try to rationalise them. Do not think about them. Just write them down. This exercise of capturing your thoughts releases them from your unconscious mind. It gives your unconscious mind together with the Universe the opportunity to quietly, and without your conscious involvement, work on the things that you want in your dream life.

Although this simple exercise of writing down your thoughts

Get Out of Your Own Way!

has a number of benefits, not least your conscious mind calms down, this in turn, calms your unconscious mind, which in turn calms your body. Combined, this allows your mind, body, and spirit to work in harmony. The biggest benefit is that your unconscious mind now has the space it needs to continue working on your future, addressing your concerns, solving your problems, and materialising your requests, and/or your dreams.

You will find a lot more information about how to journal and the benefits of journaling when you visit this link - http://www.nyasa.biz/books/dial-a-guru/.

Fiona Harrold said *"The difference between who you are and who you want to be is the work you put in"*. This is very true. It is now up to you to:

1. Find a journal you will use on a regular basis.

2. Capture your thoughts: conscious thoughts, fears, concerns, dreams, aspirations, and unspoken goals. If you think something negative, it is important to write it down as you think it, cross it out, and re-write it in the positive tense.

3. Review what you have written and identify those ideas that truly help you move forward.

This exercise of regularly writing in your journal will soon help you realise that you have the opportunity to release your future and how step by step you are moving into it.

Exercise 2 – Meditation

Meditation is simply a skill that allows you to go beyond the busy *thinking* mind and move into a deeper state of relaxation and awareness.

One of the purposes of meditation is to relax your body, calm your mind (conscious and unconscious), and quieten your many busy thoughts. Quietening your thoughts gives you the space (and time) to honestly focus on what you want from your life.

There are many ways and techniques, which you can select to meditate, and these encompass a wide range of spiritual or psychophysical practices. Whichever way you select to meditate, the way or technique involves turning your attention inwards to a single point of reference: focusing on your breathing or waves breaking on the beach, or a candle flame, or listening to a meditation CD/DVD/piece of music, or something similar.

Your meditation may take you from the achievement of a higher state of consciousness, to a greater focus, to a place of creativity, to becoming more self-aware, or simply to a more relaxed and peaceful frame of mind. Whether you practice meditation now, or wish to learn more about how to meditate, the outcome of meditation is the same. You want to move your mind, body, and spirit from the busy place it is in now, to a place of quiet, and experience a deeper state of relaxation.

Meditation is a highly effective way in which you can create inner space to allow the thoughts, feelings and emotions of your dream life to come to you. You gain control of your thoughts, you become aware of the words you use, the actions you do, the emotions you feel and the experiences you have. You gain clarity of what you truly want from your life. You gain the peace and calmness that your dream life will bring to you. You develop a more relaxed frame of mind, which enables an inner stillness, which allows you to truly focus on the future life you choose.

Meditation gives you the opportunity to know that you can do anything you choose to do.

You have probably already experienced times when you have thought that it would be fabulous to have *something* and suddenly it appears. Sometimes what you wanted appeared immediately, other times it may have taken days, weeks, months or even years. Moreover, sometimes what you've experienced was what you wanted and other times it wasn't. However, when you have belief in yourself and you truly believe that you are entitled to a life of happiness, health, wealth, love, friendship, true expression, and peace of mind then learning *how to Release Your Future* by becoming aware of your conscious and unconscious thoughts is a major step in the right direction. Start by becoming more *consciously aware* of how you communicate with yourself, and the Universe, through your *mind* (conscious mind, the words you use, the thoughts you think, the feelings and emotions you experience), your *body* (your actions and results), and your *spirit* (your unconscious mind and your power centre of belief and achievement).

Changing you own communication patterns is something that will take time and practice. It is not a habit you will change overnight. Therefore, to help you build on your learnings feel free to share your experiences with me at http://www.nyasa.biz/books/dial-a-guru/ and I will send you a **complimentary copy of the** *Law of Attraction is a Two Way Street*. Alternatively, contact me if I can help you *Release Your Future* when I will take you through my proven **8-step process:** *Living your dream life is a personal journal of learning, self-discovery, self-realisation, positive communication, and achievement.*

Get Out of Your Own Way!

Barbara J Cormack - Biography

Barbara J. Cormack MNMC, AFC, AFM, CIAC, combines her extensive background and experience with a keen insight into the demands of balancing the personal and the professional.

Barbara founded The Nyasa Partnership Limited and through this works as a Spiritual Coach, Personal and Professional Development Mentor, Coach and Mentor Trainer, and Speaker.

Coaching is a wonderful journey of self-discovery and achievement.

Born in Southern Rhodesian (now Zimbabwe) and raised in Malaŵi; Barbara has travel extensively (Africa, UK, Europe, USA and Canada) through her different careers – Auditor, Accountant, Financial Analyst, IT financial software specialist, IT Project/Programme Manager and application trainer, Professional Development Mentor; and at the beginning of this century, another career change saw Barbara qualifying as a Master Coach.

Mentoring is a wonderful journey of suggestion, guidance, example, self-discovery and achievement.

Barbara's passion in life is to ensure that her clients, colleagues, family, and friends become the best they can in all aspects of their lives. Her style of working makes the knowledge of your future clear, inviting, compelling, and achievable. Barbara understands dream achievement, change, values, beliefs, and habits; and will work with you, using many different tools and techniques, to with inner confidence live the life of your dreams. After many years of transition, which included moving to her dream destination (her little piece of Africa in Europe; Madeira, Portugal); Barbara now has the ultimate 'virtual working life' living in central rural France.

Training is a wonderful journey of learning through shared information, guidance, self-discovery and achievement.

Barbara's clients hold her in high esteem. Her style of supporting makes the possibility of sustainable change compelling, exciting, and achievable. Author of two books, co-author of seven books, and previously a columnist; Barbara available to coach, mentor, train students, and travel to attend speaking opportunities worldwide.

Stop Dreaming, Start Believing.

To contact Barbara, click this link http://www.nyasa.biz/books/dial-a-guru/.

Get Out of Your Own Way!

Section Three
Powerful Public Speaking

by
Tina Sibley

"If you want to be a great speaker, you can. It is the most important skill that anybody with responsibility over others should master, and like all skills, it can be learnt". - Richard Denny

Get Out of Your Own Way!

What Public Speaking Will Do for You and Your Business

Speaking in public has been acknowledged as the number one fear in countless surveys, higher even than death! This is totally illogical; nevertheless, that is the experience of so many people. If public speaking seems so scary, then why is it worth the effort of doing anything about it?

Well, think about those goals of yours; will you achieve them if you continue to avoid speaking in public?

Think about it for a moment.

How many times have you been frustrated because you attended a networking meeting but no-one was ready to hire you, or your services? How many opportunities to shine have been given to someone else, because they were more ready to speak out than you?

How long are you prepared to fade into the background? What will it take for you to step out of the background and step into your spotlight so that you can spread the important message that you have? If you don't take action and step out of the background now, then when will you? How many more opportunities will you lose before you're ready to step forward?

In my humble opinion, public speaking skills are absolutely essential if you want to have any kind of successful business.

Let me make this absolutely clear – it's not an extra nice addition to your skills set – it's a resounding MUST to have. If you're happy to settle for an average level of success in

Get Out of Your Own Way!

your business, then fine, you will probably get away with not speaking or presenting at all, and if you do, you will get away with being adequate. But in order to be hugely successful, you need to not only get confident at public speaking, but you need to get good at it too.

Why am I so sure of this? Because I've seen both these scenarios so many times before!

There are certainly a number of famous business people who have made a great impact and a lot of money without necessarily having great speaking skills. You only have to think of the astonishing success stories of Thomas Edison, James Dyson, Bill Gates, Richard Branson, and more recently, Mark Zuckerberg.

However, unless you have an incredible new invention, the next super-product, the next software programme or social media platform, or an extraordinary entrepreneurial flair, you will need to make your mark, inspire and make things happen.

You can't possibly expect to motivate anyone to achieve great things unless you have the ability to communicate your message. You can't possibly expect to persuade or influence unless you can communicate your message. You can't possibly expect people to buy from you unless you can communicate to them how good your product or service is. You can't possibly expect to stand out in a crowded market place, get noticed and make a difference *unless* you have the capability (and passion) to effectively communicate your message.

In short you can't possibly expect to be hugely successful

unless you have great speaking and presentation skills. I'm including presentation skills here as you will need to use both to achieve success. The difference is that pure *public speaking* is simply where you *speak* without any visual aids whereas *giving presentations* usually involves you *presenting* information and most commonly uses a slide format such as PowerPoint.

There are many successful business owners who are not household names, although they are well known in their own fields. For example Wayne Dyer, Ali Brown, Brendon Burchard, not everyone knows them, but they are hugely successful. How have they achieved such success? They have quite simply set themselves up as an *expert* or a *credible authority* in their field.

To achieve this they have done two things:

1. Given great talks and presentations.

2. Written great books.

Who are the movers and shakers within your field of expertise? How have they become so well known? What are they like at speaking? What do you need to do to become recognised in your field? How will you build up your status as a credible authority?

Having talked about the good and the great, let's now explore how great speaking and presentation skills will help us mere mortals to climb that ladder of success.

Speaking to Sell

When you run your own business, or if you plan on starting

a new business, you will need to attract and sell to customers. Therefore, speaking is crucial as it can quite literally mean the difference between failure and success. The key goal is ensuring that your business has a steady stream of new clients who keep on buying from you. Without this stream of new clients, you have no business, no matter how good you are at what you do!

So how does speaking help you to attract new clients?

- As a speaker you set yourself up as a credible authority in your field, so you stand out from your competitors.
- As a credible authority you can raise your prices and earn more money.
- At networking events you're able to get your message across giving people a clearer idea of what you can do for them.
- Being the speaker at networking events, or giving talks to groups raises your profile and gives you the opportunity of persuading people they need your services.
- Delivering taster seminars is a great way of drawing new clients to you.
- You may be invited to speak on local radio to reach a wider local audience.
- People will want to partner up with you and these joint venture opportunities will help you to reach your target audience more quickly.
- Creating compelling web videos so reaching a worldwide audience and transforming the results of your website becomes easier.
- By standing out from the crowd, you make it easier for clients to find you, which means you're free to do

Get Out of Your Own Way!

what you do best.
- You will begin *attracting* clients to you instead of having to constantly seek for and chase them.

On top of this, of course, there is the sales pitch. Unlike sales-people who work for organisations in a specific sales role, many people who run their own business find sales difficult. Becoming good at speaking and delivering presentations is a key part of sales and will make selling much easier.

People buy from people they know, like and trust. Speaking goes a long way in helping your potential buyers get to know, like and trust you.

> Let me tell you about John. John was a distributor for a well-known multi-level marketing business and a member of a local business networking group that I used to belong to. This networking group held a big open morning and invited everyone and anyone who wanted to attend. At this meeting there were 4 other distributors from the same multi-level marketing business as John.
>
> Everyone got their chance to give their 40 second *elevator pitch* to the rest of the room. As we had five distributors from the same organisation, I watched with interest. John rose to the occasion and spoke brilliantly; he literally blew the other four out of the water! After breakfast was over, John was surrounded by a flock of interested people, the other four need not have bothered showing up.
>
> What was the difference? John had taken the trouble to learn about public speaking by being an active member of a local speaking club. The evidence is clear; good speakers get

> better results every time.
>
> Whose shoes would you prefer to be in; John's shoes or one of the also attended shoes?

There are so many reasons to speak up

Whether you want to make an impact professionally or socially there are thousands of different situations that will be enhanced by an ability to communicate what you have to say. "The way we communicate with others and with ourselves ultimately determines the quality of our lives". Tony Robbins

Throughout my life, I've noticed that the people, who've made the biggest positive impact on me, have been great communicators. Those I judged less favourable (and sometimes harshly), have lacked those same skills.

So it stands to reason that you absolutely MUST do what it takes to overcome any fears you might have about public speaking and develop the skills you do have.

Let's now start to relate this to *you* and *your* business.

Identifying *Your* Goals

This section is all about YOU. It won't take you long to *read*, but it will take you a long time to *do*. This isn't a standard section on goal setting – there is lots of great stuff around goal setting already available out there – instead, I am going to put speaking in the context of helping you to achieve your goals. Remember that the whole point of reading this book is so you can overcome self-sabotage, make positive

Get Out of Your Own Way!

changes and succeed in your personal and business life. It's time to stop being a detached observer and throw yourself into this experience.

Your Own Reasons for Speaking

You're obviously reading this book because you have a desire to improve your communication skills at home, and or in the workplace. Having a career, or a business are great reasons for developing your skills in public speaking and presenting. It will help at this stage to get really clear about your reasons for doing so. I suggest keeping a speaking journal, to keep your eye on the goal, and keep track of your progress.

Now would be a good time to list all of the reasons that prompted you to read this book. Start with benchmarking *where* you are now versus *where* you wish to be on a scale of 1-10 with one being poor and ten being satisfied. This will help you identify and measure your progress.

Where are you now?
1---10

Where do you wish to be?
1---10

List Reasons:

What do you want to achieve?

Just doing lots of visualisations isn't enough though!

To accomplish great results, it will help you to write down *exactly* what you want to achieve long term, *and the baby steps involved* in getting there. What are your overall objectives? I've already asked you to think about your goals but it's time to be more specific. Where do you want to be in 1, 5, 10, or even 20 years' time with your career and personal life? Make a note of all the steps or stages you will have to go through to get there and *what type of person will you need to become?*

Get Out of Your Own Way!

When you have done this, scrutinise these steps in detail. Then go back to the list above and write down exactly how and where the skill of being a great speaker will assist you in your quest.

By making a direct link between being a great speaker and achieving your goals, you will become more motivated to conquer any fears and do what it takes to become a confident and eloquent speaker.

The Art of Public Speaking

Public speaking is quite simply what you do when you talk to a group of people. This group may be small, or it may be very large indeed: hundreds, or even thousands. Speaking in front of small groups happens all the time, you do it every day. It's called *conversation*.

Generally, talking to groups in conversation doesn't cause problems as this isn't perceived as *public speaking* so the anxiety doesn't appear, even though while you're talking all eyes in the group are on you. Take the same group of people, formalise it by standing out front, instead of in the group, and suddenly it's a different story.

Public speaking actually takes many forms; informal conversation, and the more formal speaking occasions such as speeches, presentations, talks, report-delivery, keynote addresses and toasts just to name the most common. From this point onwards, I will refer to *speaking* but the principles apply equally to all forms of public speaking.

Art or Science: Born or Made?

There is an interesting and ongoing debate over whether public speaking is an art or a science. The debate also continues over whether good speakers are just born that way and are *naturals,* or whether it's a skill that can be learned.

Some research states very strongly that it's an art, while others state just as strongly that it's a science. I say it's both!

Get Out of Your Own Way!

I'm not sitting on the fence here, I believe that to be a great public speaker; you need to engage both the left and right sides of your brain.

The Science of Public Speaking

All great speeches start with a structure and follow a logical sequence. This is what makes it a science because writing a good speech starts off with a left brain activity. By following good rules for structure, sequence and method, any speech will go adequately well, even if the speaker has no artistic or natural talent.

The Art of Public Speaking

While writing the speech, art appears in the choice of vocabulary and how phrases are composed. The real art, though, comes across in the delivery which uses the right brain and is, in fact, a performance. It's how you say it that makes the difference between adequate and great. Delivery uses intonation, emphasis and dramatic pauses for effect. Delivery makes use of facial expressions and gestures. A speaker who does not have structure, but is artistic will also be received adequately well.

Both Science and Art

Some elements of public speaking are difficult to *pigeon-hole* as they are indeed both art and science. For example, great sentence structure can be argued as a science because it uses grammar or art because it is beautifully put together. Rhetorical devices such as alliteration can be labelled as science because they follow a rule, but they can also be called artistic because they add colour and enrich a simple sentence.

Born or Made?

No speaker is just *born that way*! Anyone can learn to be a great speaker, just as anyone can learn science or art.

Sure, some people do have a natural talent and find it easier to learn than others. The same goes for any other subject. I struggle with science, and some find languages easier to learn than others. Some are great at sports; others have to work at it. The same is true for public speaking. While you may never become a world champion, absolutely anyone can become both confident and competent.

It's worth mentioning here that some speakers are indeed very confident, sadly, that doesn't make them automatically good!

Learning the science and art of speaking and developing confidence will turn anyone into an incredibly good speaker. Throw in some natural talent and you have an orator who enthrals their audience every time.

We will look at what makes a great speaker in more detail later on, but for now, know that *you* can learn to be a great speaker too.

Overview of Public Speaking

Public speaking is as ancient as time itself. Centuries ago, speaking and storytelling was the only way to pass on knowledge and information from one generation to the next. Speaking was of great importance and influenced civilisations through debate, discussions and rousing calls to action. Speaking played a massive role in politics, war, religion and entertainment.

The first known public speaking training dates back to the ancient Egyptians, yet it's the ancient Greeks and Romans who stand out as the first great orators. The first public speaking trainers were *sophists* (wise men), who charged large fees for their training because of the need for great oratory in order to become successful in court, in politics, or in social life. Alternative theories were set up by Socrates, Plato and Aristotle and these ideas were developed and adopted by the Romans.

Heralded by many as the greatest of the Roman orators is Cicero, who was a lawyer, philosopher and politician. Cicero was a follower of Julius Caesar, and following Caesar's death, gave many great speeches attacking Mark Antony (for which he was made an enemy of the state and subsequently murdered).

Some of the best known speeches of the middle ages were given by leaders going into battle, such as Henry V and William Wallace. These have been popularised by modern films, but you may be sure that any battle was preceded with a stirring 'put the fire in your belly and be invincible' type of speech.

Some speeches have been life-changing and changed the course of whole countries, even on a global stage. Speeches have caused the start of revolutions and wars. They have also introduced peaceful campaigns and changed mass paradigms.

Great leaders from modern history such as Abraham Lincoln,

Churchill, John F Kennedy, Martin Luther King, Ghandi and Nelson Mandela attribute much of their success to their skills in public speaking. Barrack Obama is known for being the first African American US President because he shot to popularity through his charismatic speaking. Even Hitler led a nation and persuaded people to commit all manner of atrocities because of his ability to give compelling orations and to persuade through clever communication. (He also used fear, but initially he used persuasion to get into a position of power).

So speaking has always played an important part of public life – particularly by those wishing to be successful and become leaders.

What Makes a Great Speaker?

Take a moment or two to jot down in your journal who you think are great speakers. Then write down what it is that makes them so good.

The 3 C's: Confidence, Content, and Charisma

Being a successful speaker or presenter is all based on what I call the Three C's:

Confidence:

The Cambridge Dictionary describes confidence as *the quality of being certain of your abilities*. If you don't have confidence, your audience won't have confidence in you either and your message is unlikely to hit home. Deliver your message with confidence and you will be more credible and your message will be more believable. Overcoming fear and developing confidence is the purpose of this book.

Content:

Your content is your story, your message. No-one wants to sit through a boring speech. Work on getting your content right and you will captivate your audience from beginning to end and you will be more confident within yourself if you're confident about your content, we will be covering the basics of getting your content right in more detail later.

Charisma:

That indefinable quality used to describe great speakers. It's actually based around vocal tone and body language that accounts for the majority of the overall message and can be easily learned.

It's sadly impossible for me to cover all of these in great depth as well as put the case for speaking in just a few chapters. However, I will give you what you need to start.

Then we come to the fourth C - a bonus which is all about **Continuous Improvement**. I urge you to continue your speaking journey and learning wherever possible. Join a speaking club, learn to mirror the best of the best, read books, watch videos and webinar tutorials like those recorded in my 5 Star Speaker Academy, but most of all get out there and practice! When you do, you will be amazed at the difference it will make to you and the success of your business in a relatively short space of time.

So – let's get going with those three C's.

Public Speaking

The Number One Fear

There is something about the fear of public speaking that turns a person who is normally confident in most other situations into a quivering wreck. People who've risen to senior roles in their organisation; people who have successfully established a business suddenly take on the persona of awkward teenager asking someone for a first date. You know the one: the person that blushes, feels sick, trembles, breaks out in a sweat, feels that they're a fraud and that they can only stare stupidly at the faces in front of them, while their throat suddenly feels strangled and their voice comes out in a squeak.

I know this person; it used to be me.

It's a total myth that it's only shy people who suffer from the fear of public speaking. I couldn't understand why I did at all. I was never described as shy – I was outgoing – even described as extrovert, and I had no trouble at all interacting

Get Out of Your Own Way!

with people in general conversation. But something really weird happened as soon as I had to stand up and speak formally at the front of the room.

What exactly are you afraid of?

Identify all the things which worry you about speaking in public. Identification of these fears will help you to work on eliminating them. Make the list comprehensive as the more areas identified and eliminated, the more confident you will become.

Next make a list of the physical symptoms you experience when you are afraid. Don't put a label on them e.g. Fear or nervousness - just list the physical sensations - e.g. butterflies in my stomach, shaking, or dry mouth.

Where do you fall on the *scare-mometer*?

How do you feel about presenting in front of an audience? Be totally honest, are you nervous, afraid, fearful, terrified or petrified? Or do you feel totally comfortable and ok with the whole thing? You may find that you score differently for different situations and with different audiences.

Audience 1: _____

Fearful	1	2	3	4	5	6	7	8	9	10	Confident

Get Out of Your Own Way!

Audience 2: _____

Fearful	1	2	3	4	5	6	7	8	9	10	Confident

Audience 3: _____

Fearful	1	2	3	4	5	6	7	8	9	10	Confident

Unrealistic expectations

One of the reasons we are hard on ourselves is that we set ourselves such impossible goals when it comes to speaking in public, especially for the first time.

- We expect to be brilliant, even if we've never done it before.
- Only perfection will allow us to be satisfied with our performance.

Untrained but brilliant

How daft is it to expect to be brilliant when we're untrained and have never done something before?

Let me put this into perspective. If you had never ridden a horse before and I took you onto the moors, stuck you on top of a horse (even a placid, well behaved one) and said 'off you go then', how would you feel?

Get Out of Your Own Way!

My guess is that two things are going to happen:
1. Unless you're a bit of an adrenaline junkie, you would feel pretty scared. You would feel out of control, and be worried that you may fall off, and hurt yourself.
2. You most probably would fall off. You may hurt yourself and the likely outcome is that you would decide horse riding is not for you and utter something along the lines of 'never again'.

For some reason, we expect to be great speakers on stage just because we can hold a conversation, yet it's similar to the horse riding situation.

The same two things are likely to happen:
1. You feel out of control, and scared that it's not going to go well, resulting in your embarrassment.
2. Although you won't get physically hurt, nerves mean things don't quite go to plan, and you end up feeling embarrassed and utter something along the lines of 'never again'.

In both cases here, a few lessons before taking the plunge would make all the difference.

It's totally unrealistic to expect to shine at something without being trained and without having any experience. You can either learn the hard way; through experience built up by making mistakes, and learning from them, or by taking lessons, and having positive experiences.

Incidentally, I learned both horse riding and speaking the hard way.

I learned to ride competently, but not well by adjusting my

Get Out of Your Own Way!

technique every time I fell off (not recommended). I also learned to speak, competently, but not well by doing it and then assessing myself afterwards. Eventually, I got trained properly in both riding and speaking and went from being adequately competent to being good at both. If only I'd taken proper lessons first.

Expecting perfection

It's equally daft to expect absolute perfection! This is particularly true if you're a novice, but equally applies to those with experience. Perfection is rarely attained in public speaking even by professionals! Professional speakers do attain a certain level of polish and style, but that's because they develop a small number of talks over time and practice them until nearly perfect.

You just watch next time a professional speaks. You will notice mistakes. It's just that the speaker doesn't let the mistake bother them. Either they correct themselves, or they ignore it and move on so the speech flows with ease because they have practiced it. Even TV broadcasters who speak nearly every day for a living are not perfect. They mispronounce words, include lots of ums and errs and make other mistakes. They too move on without hesitation and most people don't even notice their mistake.

Remember you're not a TV broadcaster, and you're not a professional speaker, so you're not expected by your audience to deliver a performance equal to the professional. And you're certainly not expected to be perfect.

What is expected of you is to deliver a message that gives value, that's all, and you can be trained to do that.

What is confidence and where does it come from?

Write down what confidence represents to you. It is often different for different people. Where do you think you will get your confidence from?

Typically, confidence comes from being prepared. It's important to feel in command of the situation and what you're going to talk about. The first rule then is to prepare properly. Most people underestimate the amount of time needed to prepare for a speech. According to Wayne Burgraff, an 18th Century philosopher, good practice is 'one hour of preparation for one minute of delivery'. This has been adopted by many, including the great raconteur Bob Monkhouse.

Give yourself plenty of time to work on the content. When you know that your content is good, your confidence will increase massively.

However, even the most prepared of people still suffer from

nerves and a lack of confidence. So, although preparation is vitally important, it's not quite as simple as that.

Confidence is affected by our self-esteem which is our sub-conscious at work. Logically, there's no reason to be nervous, but years of sub-conscious conditioning can over-ride our conscious logic. The good news is that we can re-programme our sub-conscious using various techniques and by exploring what causes our nerves. As you read on, refer back to the list of fears you made earlier as you will be able to use the exercises to work on these fears.

Confidence is a *mood* or an *internal state* and your state comes from just three things:
1. What you focus on.
2. The language you use.
3. Your physiology.

Let's explore each of these:

Your focus

What you focus on is the difference between being terrified and being superbly confident. What you focus on is made up of a wide variety of *stuff*, a lot of which is going on in your subconscious. Your focus is determined by your attitude, your beliefs, and what you choose to dwell on.

A popular saying quoted by many authors' claim "What you think about, you bring about". This concept of a self-fulfilling prophecy is particularly true of public speaking. If you think about all the things that can go wrong, you will become so nervous, you won't feel able to think straight. Consequently, all those things probably will go wrong! On the other hand when you think about all the things that can go right, and visualise a wonderful response, then you will be calm and confident, you will be able to focus on your speech, and everything will go right.

Choose your attitude

You have a choice about how you approach each day; you can choose how you approach your work and you can choose how you approach your speeches and presentations. It's a bit like having a menu:

What would you like to choose off the menu?
- Sad
- Happy
- Nervous
- Confident
- Angry
- Chilled Out
- Terrified
- Excited

Notice the physical symptoms you experience when speaking. Where are they? These are typical symptoms of nerves. However, they are also symptoms associated with being excited. What would happen if you thought you were excited, rather than nervous?

Many of us lose sight of our ability to choose. If you don't know you have choices or don't believe you have choices, you don't. We all have difficult life experiences, but choosing your attitude, and acting like a victim are mutually exclusive.

Get Out of Your Own Way!

Choose what you focus on

People who are anxious about speaking report to me that they are worried about the following:
- Forgetting their words.
- Mouth going dry.
- Hands shaking.
- Dropping their notes or losing their place.
- The projector/technology not working.
- The audience being hostile.
- Being asked questions they can't answer.
- Hecklers.
- Mind going completely blank and freezing.
- Being absolutely terrible.
- Getting the feeling of wanting to die or flee.
- Feeling physically sick.

If you're focusing on all these things, then no wonder you feel anxious and would rather not do it! Instead focus on the following:
- I have a really important message I want to get across.
- This message is going to help a lot of people in the audience.
- They are going to love what I have to tell them.
- It's no problem if the technology doesn't work, I have a plan B.
- The audience is really friendly and want me to succeed.
- I know my stuff so any questions I can't answer will be unrelated to my topic.
- I may feel a bit nervous, but I'm going to be absolutely fine.
- A fantastic round of applause at the end.

- Interested people who want to know more.
- New clients!

Trust me; when you focus on list two instead of list one, you will begin to feel a whole lot better!

The internal language you use

"Words….. They've been used to make us laugh and cry. They can wound or heal. They offer us hope or devastation. With words we can make our noblest intentions felt and our deepest desires known". Anthony Robbins and again "As soon as we put words to an experience, it changes the meaning we experience".

Anthony Robbins has written extensively on the subject of transformational vocabulary and the amazing thing is that it is so simple to apply and it really works. In his book *Awaken the Giant Within,* he tells the story of three CEO's in a meeting (himself and two others) where they received some upsetting news about their companies.

He said he was *"angry"*, another said he was *"absolutely livid"* while the third was *"a little bit PEEVED"*. Who do you think was headed for the biggest stress levels? Tony found that by using the word *"Peeved"* whenever he was beginning to feel angry, amused him and transformed his emotional state into one which was a lot less stressful than the one produced by anger and frustration.

Next time you are about to speak in front of a group of people, which feeling would you rather experience:
a)   Terror because your stomach feels so nauseated you want to die? No of course not!

Get Out of Your Own Way!

b) A little nervous with butterflies, but they're under control. Getting better.
c) Confident and excited? Yes that's the feeling we want before we speak isn't it!

People who ask me to help them get over their fear of public speaking tell me that they are 'absolutely petrified', 'scared to death' or 'totally terrified'. Notice how extreme these phrases are.

When our brain hears these phrases, it translates the word into a life-threatening situation and the body produces adrenaline to cope with the flight or fight moment. But you're not in a life-threatening situation, so the adrenaline isn't appropriate, or necessary.

The first thing I do is to ban such expressions; they are unhelpful to say the least.

Some will tell you to tell yourself the exact opposite and, in the hands of a good NLP practitioner or hypnotherapist, telling yourself the opposite works for some.

However, if you're doing this by yourself the problem is that when you tell yourself you're supremely confident, the little voice in your head screams 'nonsense' at you! And so it doesn't always work.

The little voice will accept a modified statement though. Instead, tell yourself: 'I'm nervous, but that's OK I will handle it'. The voice inside your head will have difficulty objecting to this and as the language is less extreme, it won't have such a dramatic effect on your body.

When you do handle it, and you will, this is further evidence that you will be OK next time. So you can then modify the statement again to: 'I'm a little nervous, but will be absolutely fine'. Next time, you can modify the statement further: 'I'm feeling really excited (same symptoms as nervous) and this is going to go well'.

Gradually, you will come to enjoy that *buzz* you get from speaking, and look forward to the event, rather than dread it.

Your physiology

"Emotion is created by motion. Everything that we feel is the result of how we use our bodies". Anthony Robbins

Even the smallest of changes in our facial expressions, or gestures can affect the way that we feel at any given moment. Think about your posture for a moment. What is it conveying? Is it upright and alert, or is it slumped?

I want you to do something to show how powerful physiology is.

- Think about your posture when you are tired. Now adopt that physiology completely: posture, gestures and facial expressions. How do you feel? Tired?
- Now, keeping the same physiology, without altering it at all, try to feel really alert, wide awake and ready to go. Could you do it? I doubt it!
- Now think about your posture when you are on top of the world. Now adopt that physiology completely: posture, gestures and facial expressions. Now how do you feel? Great?

- Again, keeping the same physiology, try to feel really tired and down. Is it working? Again, I doubt it.

Have a go at changing your physiology to different moods and notice the difference in the way you feel.

Physiology and public speaking

When someone is extremely nervous when they take to the stage, they typically adopt a *closed* physiology; it's the subconscious desire to protect or hug your body. It's also common to adopt a *stand to attention* stance. This physiology is guaranteed to make you feel awful!

The closed and stand to attention physiology means that you are likely to be standing with your feet too close together. Your shoulders will be rolled forwards and down, your hands in front of you and possibly head down as well.

If your feet are too close together, you will feel unbalanced and wobbly, not great for instilling confidence. It's also more likely that you will shake which will be visible and this will affect your voice.

If your shoulders are forwards and down, which is likely to happen, particularly if your hands are in front of you to hold notes, your diaphragm will be restricted, which will affect your breathing. This will cause a number of side effects.

First, you will find that insufficient oxygen in your bloodstream will cause you to feel slightly sick and faint; it will cause a lack of alertness resulting in your brain going blank. Your muscles will feel weak so you will go wobbly at the knees. You won't be able to take a good breath to project your voice, so it will come out squeaky and wobbly.

When you become aware of all this, your nerves will increase and so a downward spiral of panic sets in!

Finally, if your head is in a downwards position, this seems to have a chemical reaction in our brains which causes us to feel more negative hence the expression 'I'm feeling down'.

So the wrong physiology will completely thwart your efforts at feeling confident!

A solution:

Stand with your feet further apart, in line with your hips in a relaxed, but grounded stance. This will make you feel more balanced and in control. Push your shoulders back and down and have your arms relaxed. If you need to hold notes then practice having your hands in front of you while keeping your shoulders back and down. This will open up your diaphragm, so you can breathe properly, getting oxygen circulating to your organs, your muscles and your brain.

These changes in physiology are within our control and offer us immediate improvements.

The head position is more difficult – especially when you're standing and your audience is seated, particularly if you're on a stage. The trick here is to look up when you begin and look up occasionally, if only briefly, to break the *down* position.

Get Out of Your Own Way!

Preparation

Preparation adds to confidence so it pays to allow enough time to prepare thoroughly.

Knowing your subject

If you are to speak with credibility and *from the heart*, then you need to know your subject.

Speak only about what you know and feel comfortable with. If you are to be confident, then it really helps to know what you are going to talk about. Stick within your subject and do not be tempted to stray outside it. If you're talking specifically about one project, don't be tempted to answer questions about another project, unless it's relevant and you have the information.

Do your research, back up what you are saying with statistics, quotes, testimonies, examples, stories and anecdotes. You can get useful relevant information from libraries, trade journals and from the internet.

Knowing your audience

Knowing who is in your audience will help you to build rapport with them.

Find out what type they are: Agreeable, apathetic, hostile, uninformed or mixed. Once you have this information, you can prepare for their reaction and add in whatever you need to counter it, or capitalise on it.

What is their background: industry sector, level of seniority, prior knowledge of the subject, mixed or unknown? If you have an audience from a particular industry sector you can build rapport with them by using trade anecdotes or jokes. A word of warning when using humour – it can backfire! Therefore, learn more about how to use humour in your speaking. Finally, it's also important to be aware of any cultural differences or etiquette.

Knowing your venue

If you're on home territory in a familiar room, you will always feel more confident than if you're *playing away*. If you're in different surroundings you need to get to the venue early enough to feel comfortable with the facilities, the layout, and who will be seated where.

Knowing your equipment

It's vital to feel comfortable with your presentation equipment. If you're using someone else's, then get there early enough to play around with it, and ensure you know how it works.

Having a contingency plan

There's always the chance that technology can let you down. When delivering a presentation, as opposed to a speech, the bulb in the projector may go, or the laptop decides not to connect to the projector. I've even faced one situation where a thunderstorm caused a total power cut. Ensure that you are able to deliver the presentation without the use of a projector; remember it's a visual aid and not the presentation itself.

If you have to refer to charts and graphs, print them out, so the audience can see them and use a flipchart wherever possible. If you don't have to rely so heavily on PowerPoint, then you won't need to feel so anxious about it letting you down!

Prepare yourself

This is common sense, but with the hectic lifestyles we lead, this often gets overlooked. Get plenty of sleep the night before, ensure you eat enough of the right foods so that you are nourished and alert, drink enough water so that you are hydrated, but make sure you take a comfort break so you're not fidgeting.

It also helps to pay attention to your appearance as this will influence your confidence. If you have a lucky shirt/tie/skirt or whatever, then go ahead and wear it (as long as it's appropriate), anything that adds to your confidence is good!

Public Speaking: Content & Charisma

Content

Every speech or presentation that leads to rapturous applause has been thought about and carefully crafted. Let's look at how to craft a great speech and the steps involved.

Your purpose

The first thing you need to do is identify the point of your speech.

What is the main focus? Is it to inform, educate, to entertain, to persuade or to inspire? Are you trying to sell something, get people to make donations, or recommend you to others? Do you wish the audience to go away and take action, or just to reflect and think things over? Do you want to make them laugh, or sit on the edge of their seats? Or do you simply wish to furnish them with information?

There may be more than one purpose for example, you may wish to be educational, but at the same time be entertaining. If your main purpose is to educate, then people should remember the information, rather than the jokes.

Your message

First of all what is the message you want to convey?

Secondly how will that message be received?

If you're delivering bad news, then you need to be frank and the style and content of your speech needs to be consistent. If possible, when delivering bad news, give some options or potential solutions and ensure you allow plenty of time for your audience to digest the information.

If your message is likely to be resisted, then you need to acknowledge that resistance and deal with it.

If your message is likely to be welcomed then build on the good feelings to motivate your audience which is a good opportunity to influence and persuade.

Your speech structure

There is no *best* way to organise your speech or presentation. There are several different ways and the method you choose often depends on the subject material, and your objective.

However, although you can organise your speech in different ways, you will still follow a simple structure:

Basic structure

There is nothing worse than a speech which rambles all over the place and doesn't make a point. This mistake is guaranteed to get your audience checking their watches, shuffling about, or worse, falling asleep!

This may sound silly or basic, but your talk needs:
1. A beginning: the opening.
2. A middle: the main body of your talk.
3. An end: your finale.

It's amazing how many speeches (and presentations in particular) don't set the scene with a proper opening, so many just give what is a cursory introduction to the middle or main body.

The time for each should be proportionate based on how long your talk is. You need to be looking at around 5-10% of the time for the beginning, 5-10% of the time for the conclusion and the remaining 80-90% of the time for the main body.

The importance of a powerful opening

The opening should immediately catch the audience's attention and tell the audience what you will be talking about. *It should give them a reason to listen to the rest.*

Examples of a good opening are:
- A startling question.
- A challenging statement.
- An appropriate quotation, illustration or story.
- A display of some object or picture.
- An attention-getting generalisation that ties in with your subject.

Avoid these weak openings:
- An apologetic statement.
- A story or joke that does not relate to your topic.
- A long or slow-moving statement or story.
- A trite question. For example: "Did you ever wonder if there is life on Mars?" (it's too easy to answer 'no' to this question and you've then lost the listener).
- However, asking "Is there life on Mars"? said boldly, looking directly at audience, followed by a long pause which asks the listener to think about the question will engage them.

Draft the body

The middle, or body, is the main part of your speech and consists of the facts or ideas you want to present. The amount of information you include in the body will be limited by the amount of time available to you, not forgetting how much the audience can remember. Most listeners will remember only three to five main facts or ideas. For a 10 – 15 minute talk, three facts or ideas are plenty.

It's worth noting that the body should also have an introduction (the link from your opening into your material), and a conclusion to sum things up, before moving into your grand finale. Your conclusion is your final opportunity to convey your message and main points in a manner that will help the audience remember them. It needs to reinforce your ideas, and leave listeners with a lasting impression, and hopefully wanting more.

Do your research in advance and make sure you have plenty of information from which to choose. Then arrange it into a logical sequence that leads your audience from your well-crafted opening to your dynamic finale.

Discard anything that's not relevant or doesn't fit into the time allowed.

The finale

The grand finale is your final opportunity to have your audience remember you; you want them saying 'Wow'!

After the conclusion, finish forcefully and confidently, too many talks end with a limp 'well that's it, are there any questions'?

You want to end with a BANG!

<u>Good endings will:</u>
- Link back to the opening.
- Deliver a strong call to action.

It's your opening and your finale that will make the greatest difference to you in converting your audience from passive listeners into active admirers.

Remember to pay attention to your timings; there is nothing worse than a talk which runs over time! Organise your speech so that you can easily cut things out if you find you're running over, and have some back up material in case you find you're running short. That said any additional material needs to be relevant and not there just for the sake of it. If you've planned and rehearsed well, you should avoid these problems.

How you work on putting these together

I have written the steps in the chronological order in which each part comes in the speech. However, when you're working on putting your talk together, it's actually better to work on them in a different order.

1. **Your purpose:** What do you want your audience to think, feel, or do by the end of your speech?
2. **Your finale:** Your purpose leads you to the result you want at the end, so work on this part first. As IBM said 'Begin with the end in mind'.
3. **Your opening:** What strong beginning will introduce your topic in a way that points to the end?
4. **The body:** The journey that leads from your beginning to your end and that fulfils your purpose.

Add the spice

This is where we add the magic ingredients that help you to really connect with your audience, set you up as a great speaker, and turn your speech into something that gets you noticed.

Get Out of Your Own Way!

Using rhetorical devices

Rhetorical devices add colour and depth to your speech, making it more memorable. They also make it much more likely that your audience will connect with you to the point they feel engaged enough to buy from you.

People will be able to understand your point much more easily when it is delivered in a fun and memorable way.

Consider using:
- Stories and anecdotes
- Similes
- Metaphors
- Analogies
- Alliteration

Using powerful vocabulary

Do you want *satisfied* customers or *delighted* ones?

Do your customers want to become more *efficient*, or would they prefer to become more *successful*?

Is your product *great* or *sensational*?

Can you help your customers to *improve* or to become *unstoppable*?

It's important to use the most powerful, evocative language. Be descriptive while avoiding the trap of using words that people won't understand, or words that will seem unnecessary and pompous.

Once you've drafted your speech in more detail, go back

through it and work out where you can add the *spice* to liven it up and make the difference between a *good* speech and a *great* one.

Charisma

The 3rd all-important C of being a great speaker is Charisma. Some dictionary definitions:
- **Charisma:** The magnetism and appeal that comes from having personality, passion and a certain delivery style.
- **Charisma:** Meaning "gift of or from thee divine". It is a trait found in individuals whose personalities are characterised by a powerful charm and magnetism, along with innate and markedly sophisticated abilities of interpersonal communication and persuasion.

Many people think you either have charisma or you haven't. Undoubtedly some have more natural charisma than others, but when it comes to charismatic speaking, it can be learned.

Charisma comes from:
- Confidence and content which we've already talked about. A confident speaker will always be more charismatic than one that looks ready to flee! Adding the spice to your content will also increase the charisma and lends itself to a charismatic delivery.
- Being authentic.
- Your delivery style.

Get Out of Your Own Way!

Your delivery

It's not what you say; it's the way that you say it!

Vocal variety

Your voice is the link between you and your listeners. It is the primary medium for conveying your message. There's nothing worse than a monotone voice that doesn't vary in pitch, pace and tone, and lacks energy.

A good speaking voice has several qualities:
- Pleasant conveying a sense of friendliness.
- Natural reflecting the true personality and sincerity of the speaker.
- Forceful conveying vitality and strength, even when it isn't especially loud.
- Expressive demonstrating various shades of meaning, never sounding monotonous or motionless.
- Easily heard as a result of proper volume and clear articulation. If listeners can't hear you, they will not pay attention and your message will be lost.
- Varied pitch moving up and down the musical scale.
- Varied rate not too fast, not too slow, but moving within a range of 125-160 words per minute.

Top Tip: practice reading out loud and play with your voice. Adapt it to show the qualities mentioned in the list above. Adapt it to portray different emotions or moods. Be as dramatic as you like - the larger the audience - the more important this is.

The role of breathing

A good-quality voice begins with good breath control. Your voice is supported by a column of air and the depth and steadiness of this air affects your voice. You'll find that breathing deeply from your abdomen, or lower chest will provide better vocal quality than breathing shallowly from your upper chest.

Silence is golden

At times, you won't want to use your voice. Well-timed silences or pauses add impact to your words and are a powerful speaking technique. They also give you time to think about what's next! Remember to maintain eye contact throughout pauses.

The power of body language

Body language is as important in public speaking as it is in everyday conversation. Imagine a speaker who is sincere about his or her topic, yet stands stiffly before the audience during the entire speech; not moving or even looking at anyone while speaking. The words imply the speaker cares about the subject, but the body communicates otherwise. The result? The audience doubts the message.

Not only does body language communicate confidence and power; it enhances your believability. It illustrates and emphasises the points you are making and helps to release any nervous energy you may have. Body language is expressed in stance, movement, gestures, facial expressions and eye contact; otherwise known as non-verbal communication.

Get Out of Your Own Way!

Stance

Although it's good to move during a speech, occasionally you'll stand still as you speak, usually during your opening and closing words, or as you make an important point. The stance you assume while standing still is important because it indicates your confidence and comfort level.

If you fix your eyes on the floor, and slouch your shoulders, your audience will think you're shy and weak. If you repeatedly shift your weight from one foot to another you will appear uncomfortable and nervous and your audience may be distracted by your movement. When you stand straight, feet slightly apart, your weight evenly distributed on each foot, and you look directly at your listeners, you will convey confidence and poise.

Movement

Appropriate movement during a speech produces variety for the audience. When you walk from one place to another you attract listener's attention and get them involved.

Any movement needs to be deliberate and purposeful. Avoid pacing, fidgeting, swaying from side to side, or bouncing up and down on your toes. Most definitely avoid putting your hands in your pockets and jangling loose change! These are nervous habits that distract the audience. Instead, deliver part of your speech from one spot, then move to another part of the stage. Movement is ideal when making a transition from one point to another.

Gestures

Gestures are what happen when we move any parts of our body to *talk* to our audience. These movements can be subtle, or outrageously obvious. They can literally bring our speech to life.

<u>Use basic gestures to show:</u>
- **Size, weight, shape, direction and location.** Use hand gestures, along with your voice to declare "It was THIS big"! Or "It's over THERE"!
- **Importance or urgency.** Slam your fist into your palm to show how important your point is or to indicate "NOW"!
- **Comparison and contrast.** Move both your hands together symmetrically to show similarities; move them asymmetrically to show differences.

For the best effect, your gestures need to be elbow height or above, but not in front of your face, and moving away from your body. They are either obvious and definite to show conviction and enthusiasm, or they are subtle to imply wry humour. However, whichever type you use they are always fully committed to and never wishy-washy.

If you're not comfortable with a gesture, do something else. Gestures need to be varied and appropriate. Beware; the same ones used over and over are distracting and annoying. If you're speaking on a large stage to a huge audience, your gestures need to be big and bold so that even people in the back of the room will see them, however this would seem mad and erratic on a small stage in front of a handful of people, so act accordingly.

Get Out of Your Own Way!

Gestures mean many things and these meanings will vary from culture to culture, so be sensitive to your audience. For example, while making a circle with your fore-finger and thumb means 'OK' for some (particularly those in the scuba-diving community), it's a very rude gesture for others.

Generally, clenched fists show power or anger. If you want your audience to join you in fighting some injustice for example, you could clench your fist as you urge them to take action. Opening your palms indicates generosity and caring, so you may display your open palms when describing how a kindly customer helped someone in need.

In **North America**, a forefinger pointed toward the ceiling means people must pay attention to what you are saying. Folding your arms across your chest projects strength and determination. Clasping your hands together in front of your chest conveys unity.

Your Energy

In order to convey enthusiasm and excitement, *you* need to have *energy*. You not only need to *have* energy, but you need to *convey* it to your audience.

In order to *have* energy, you need to pay attention to the following:

Look After Yourself

Don't expect to be full of energy if you neglect yourself. If you speak regularly it is important to pay attention to what you eat, and remember to drink plenty of water. Certain foods such as milk, chocolate, or cheese coat your throat with a sticky lining, and may lead to an irritating habit of constantly clearing your throat. Drinking water with a slice of lemon will cleanse your throat and keep you hydrated. Your voice is a tool, so look after it; it's not a good idea to go to a rowdy party and have a loud sing-song the night before! (I made this mistake once and discovered that singing loud rock music the night before gives you a gravelly rock voice when speaking the next day)! Don't expect to perform well if you have burned the midnight oil the night before practicing and rehearsing. That's just as bad as partying the night before!

Physiology

Remember what we said previously about your state being driven by your physiology. If you adopt an alert, energetic posture, you will feel alert and energised.

Movement

Energy comes from motion so one of the best ways to get energy is to move! How many times have you felt too tired to exercise, but when you get out of your chair and do it, you feel better and have more energy as a result? So don't sit around just before you speak, if you can help it. I know that sometimes you're required to sit in the audience waiting for your turn. If so, adopt a straight, alert posture in your chair.

Mental State

Your mental and emotional state will follow your physiology which you can enhance by thinking positive thoughts. Remember a time when you felt super-charged and buzzing with energy, now is the time to immerse yourself in that feeling and bring it with you to the present time.

Breathing

If you have been breathing shallowly, then you are not getting much oxygen to the brain which will make you feel sleepy! Take some really deep breaths and fill your lungs with oxygen, this will move to the brain making you feel more alert.

Just before speaking, go somewhere private and psyche yourself up by breathing deeply, moving around, adopting super-confident physiology, and filling your head with positive thoughts. Then go out there and *knock 'em dead!*

Being more charismatic

If you follow these guidelines, focus on delivering a competent and confident performance, you will be charismatic enough to deliver a speech that will go down well with your audience.

Later on, when you have got to grips with the foundations, you will go on to become a truly charismatic speaker by mastering the craft of oratory. Mastering this craft is done by paying greater attention to *how* you craft your content and *how* you stage your delivery.

It would be too overwhelming to put all it takes to master public speaking in these few pages. However, you now have the basic essentials to get started. The only way to become an accomplished speaker is to put into practice each stage one step at a time. I have given you *all* the tools required to become a confident and competent speaker.

Once you are practiced and have developed these skills, come back to me and we'll take you to the next level where you will learn more about mastering the art of public speaking with my *5* Speaker System* and when you do, quote **DAGFAN** in your e-mail to me at tina@5starspeakeracademy.com to claim your special discount of 25% for being a DAG fan.

Tina Sibley - Biography

Tina Sibley has been coaching and training for over 20 years and has been running her own business since February 2000.

When recession hit, Tina found it challenging to attract clients and struggled – *until* she mastered the art of public speaking and her presentation skills to sell *without* being sales-y.

Tina has been particularly successful at attracting clients through her online *wicked webinars series* and is well known for making sales totaling over £10,500 from just one webinar resulting in a regular monthly income.

Tina now inspires trains and empowers others to achieve similar success by sharing her webinar based speaking and presenting skills training.

Section Four
Be Healthy, Fit and in Flow

by
Susan Hay

"Until you can listen wholeheartedly to your own body and what it's telling you, don't even begin to listen to the myriad of marketing messages our food industry presents". - Susan Hay

Nutritional Health

Where to start? Do the damn exercises...

If you like me, and every other soul on this planet are looking for that quick fix, the easy way, let me help you out. It doesn't exist. You knew that though didn't you. You won't get the answers you're looking for from just reading. Real 'ah-ha' moments come from thinking then doing. I know you're worth the extra few minutes that the exercises take to complete, so grab your pen and read on.

Did you know that 79% of females in the UK have been on a diet of some kind for over 10 years, and that on average, women spend 6 months of the year counting calories, or that last year the proportion of women who tried to lose weight went up from 63% to an all-time high of 65%? Did you also know that nowadays 39% of men are said to be on a diet, and a third of 10-11 year olds, and over a fifth of 4-5 year olds are now classed as overweight or obese? *1

So, if the word 'diet' sends shivers down your spine, if you've tried the Duncan, ate the Atkins and drunk enough maple syrup to make you feel sick then you're not alone.

The word *diet* is so daunting and scary that just reading the word on the page has been proven to raise stress levels *and* cause an emotional reaction in the brain.

A diet mind-set is a deprivation trap. According to Institute for the Psychology of Eating, the word *diet* more commonly refers to a "regimented, restrictive way of eating for the goal of weight loss, or medical improvement." The Institute maintains that this "can really shift our mind and our body into deprivation mode, which is not a fun way to live. When our body and mind perceives we don't have enough, we start to live life in survival mode, rather than thrive mode". And so the cycle continues; deprivation = the want for fulfilment.

If you're like how I used to be - at your wits end and losing the will to live, sick and tired of being on a diet - then let's make a pact together, right here, right now, never ever to diet again! Why? Because for one, we both know that diets don't work. In fact, we often end up heavier in weight and lighter in pocket than we were before we started dieting at all. **'95% of diets fail and most dieters will regain their lost weight in on average just one year'.**

Instead, let's swap the don'ts, mustn't and shouldn't non-serving, negative words for healthy, nurturing, positive ones instead. Let's be *Healthy, Fit and in Flow.*

Healthy, Fit and in Flow work together. For all of us a healthy body starts with a healthy mind so we're going to focus on the holistic approach and work with your entire system. This will help you achieve a more relaxed, accepting mind-set, as well as help you to love, accept and cherish your body.

I'm here to help you to lose weight *without* the pressure. *Without* the worry and stress and *without* feeling as though you have to give up everything that makes you feel satisfied. So, ditch the diet, throw your arms in the air and shout "I'm going to become the best version of me that I can be".

Before I let you in on the secret of being happy with your body, your mind and who you are unconditionally, let me

Get Out of Your Own Way!

tell you my story.

Growing up I had a sweet tooth. When I reached my teenage years, I would even be known to eat half a pound of jelly sweets for breakfast. This insatiable craving for sugar didn't do me any favours. My skin suffered and I continued to pile on the pounds. I began to have problems with energy levels and was continually feeling sick and tired.

After a number of years of enjoying sugary-based foods and indulging in sugary alcoholic drinks, my body gave up on me. I began to have horrible stomach conditions and pain whenever I ate anything. I was working endless hours in a stressful job, and was eating on the go, and drinking to forget the work. Stress levels rose; energy levels dropped and I hit an all-time low. I felt depressed, and my life was consumed with negative thoughts about food, and my life.

I had tests and scans and more tests until finally my doctor gave up on me and actually said "I don't think that there's anything wrong with you". At that point I didn't give up. I got angry and determined to find the solution, and I did. Through changing the food I ate, changing the lifestyle I lived, and changing the thoughts that controlled my mind, I became a healthier me.

I knew that I wasn't alone in feeling like this; you only had to walk into any gym changing room in the country to hear quotes like "I lost 2 lbs this week, so I'll have a takeaway tonight". Or "I'm so tired I think I could sleep standing up". At the time we were in the aftermath of the recession and most people were working long hours and struggling to keep it together.

Get Out of Your Own Way!

I had no respect for food what so ever, I just ate as fast, and as conveniently as I possibly could. But my mind was constantly telling me there was a different way, a better way to be me.

If this sounds familiar, stick with me and I'll take you through my journey, and specifically how I found a more mindful, and empowering relationship with food. By following the steps I'm about to reveal, you too can make small easy changes to reach a healthier you. This plan isn't about being thin, skinny or slim, or any of those media style semantics. This is about creating a healthy relationship with food again, and about you feeling healthy, and confident.

Right, so this is where I expect this all sounds a bit familiar and now you are aching for me to tell you *how* to find the right direction, or make a change that actually works. Not just works in the short term, but something that lasts. Something that leads you to a way of eating that will improve your health and your zest for life. And that's exactly what I'm here to help you achieve.

After I hit my *all-time low* and realised that I couldn't keep treating my body, or my mind like the enemy, I found a way. By making *small* daily changes I turned my health around. I healed my mind, and I witnessed a new state of fitness, health and clarity of mind that I'd never known before, and believe me once you've felt this new way of being you'll want more of it. And now it's your turn; it's your time to thrive.

It all starts with getting naked!

That's right the first thing I'm going to say to you is 'get your kit off'. When you've done that, go and stand in front of a full length mirror - not necessarily right now - you may be reading this on the beach, but when you get home. I know this may be scary because I've done it as a first step myself, but please bear with me, as this is the turning point in how you think about your physical body. As I mentioned this *isn't* about dieting, in fact it's not a diet at all. It's a way of working with your body and mind to change your perspective and become in control of your choices again. It's about becoming *Healthy, Fit and in Flow*.

So undress and find yourself a full-length mirror. There's only one absolute condition to this; when you take a long look in that mirror you're not, I repeat, not allowed to look for the negatives. I don't want to hear 'my big bottom', or 'my flabby tummy'. Instead, I want you to look carefully and pick out all of the positive great things about your body. It may be 'I like my shins', or 'my legs are strong'. Look for positives; don't get distracted by the voice in your mind that is shouting out the negatives. I want you to repeat aloud all the positives you see, and then write them down. Really mean them too; when you unconditionally mean what you've written down, that's when you will start to notice a shift in your perspective.

Our society, the mainstream media and advertising are based on making us feel different, odd and outside of the norm. It relies on us striving to achieve a picture perfect perspective that doesn't exist; one shape doesn't fit all. So much so that we forget what aspects of our bodies *are* great just as they are! As a nation and as a species we have forgotten *how* to love our bodies and the diet industry has been capitalising on our negative thoughts for decades. Now it's time for you to step up, take the lead and decide that it's only you who can change *YOU*. It's time to be your own version of perfect; you don't need to strive to be someone else's.

> So, I'm going to help you to tackle three key areas:
> 1. Achieve a *HEALTHY* Weight
> 2. Improve your overall *FITNESS*
> 3. Create mental harmony; getting your mind to work in *FLOW*
>
> Which all equals being *Healthy, Fit and in Flow.*

So, read on and begin the first stage on a journey to the best version of you that you've ever known; a healthier you, in body, mind and spirit.

<u>Shrink your focus down – right down</u>
It's truly about taking small incremental changes. When you commit to changing just one thing each day, it quickly becomes a new healthier habit. Healthier habits will help you achieve long-term goals. Be committed; from this moment on make a pact with yourself and with me to do one thing differently, every day, for 21 days, that's all - less than one month - that's the minimum time it takes to form a new habit. That one thing could be to; drink a green smoothie for breakfast every day for 21 days. Or at lunchtime take a 20-minute walk every day for 21 days. Set an alarm on your phone or write it on your to-do list. Bring this change into your life one day at a time.

We live in a society of overwhelm, and that constant feeling of bombardment causes us to feel that things are just too hard, and so we quit. The key to achieving your goal be it health, fitness, or even in business is to shrink the focus of your goal down. I mean right down! Shrink your attention to what you want to achieve in the next 5 minutes, but be mindful about how that next small decision will influence you taking a step towards what you want to achieve, or a step away, then make your choice.

Diets are statistically proven to not work! Well, that's not actually true, they do work, but only as long as you are on them, and we all know that's just not sustainable. Deep down you already know this. Diets don't take into consideration that the initial results seen in the first few weeks tend to be a loss of fluid from the body, not fat. This then plateaus at week 3 or 4 at which point most of us quit. Sustainable success in any area of your life is about taking small, steady steps in the right direction, it really is that simple.

Making slight shifts in your perspective and awareness will really make the difference in your choices. It will bring you back to the present moment, and help you be in charge of everyday decisions, especially when it comes to food. I'll explain further about how you will start to become more aware, and how to notice the choices you have, *before* you make the decision.

The world we live in now is driven by instant gratification. That applies to weight loss, fitness and personal achievements too. We are all programmed to want to achieve results and when we don't get *instant* results, we feel as though we have failed. Taking diets as an example, with most diets the focus is on losing a set amount by a set time. The problem being that the timeframe is normally way off in the future and we don't consider the small steps and achievements we need to make to get us there - there's no plan – we're just supposed to hang on to the final goal. But when we don't see results, we give in.

The key to achieving a healthy future starts with making your health a priority today, making a decision to go for a healthier tomorrow (or even a healthier this afternoon). It's the small changes you make that over time add up and push you towards your goal, towards what you want to achieve. It's called the 'compound interest effect', small steps towards a bigger goal gets results.

Exercise One

Over the following week write down every single thing you eat and drink (yes I know you may be thinking *oh gosh what a pain in the bottom*), but this really works so download your copy of the free **Healthy, Fit and in Flow food** diary from my website at http://www.healthyfitandinflow.com or you can get your hands on a print copy of the gorgeously designed food diary from our website too.

You will find this easier if you keep your food diary near your bed and each night write down what you ate. Include everything, even that solitary jelly baby! Don't lie to yourself though; it will form your plan for change later on. Don't criticise either, or beat yourself up when writing down that blueberry muffin, you're simply writing it down (don't worry I'm not going to ask you to eat it after, so there's not even any paper calories involved), and what you write is totally private. You don't have to share it with anyone if you don't want to.

Get Out of Your Own Way!

You'll also find it useful to write down any physical or emotional symptoms you experienced each day. Write these next to the specific food that caused the emotion i.e. pizza = indigestion, guilt, pleasure, bloating, happiness, loss, anger.

From day three onwards you will see a pattern emerging. There'll be certain foods and drinks that form the basis of your daily diet. We humans are suckers for routine. If you start buying a certain product; it's not long before that product becomes part of our daily diet, good or bad.

After seven days, you will have collated a small journal full of your very own food habits. It will highlight everything you ate including *when* you're most likely to reach for that jam doughnut, or packet of crisps. More importantly, you'll also notice the times that your will power is like steel and you have stuck to eating healthy foods that nourish your body and mind.

Look back through your food journal to day one, but when you read back through it refrain from judgement. Read through your journal as if it belongs to someone else, and if you wouldn't judge them, don't judge yourself.

What have you written on day 1? It's a Monday right? How did I know it would be a Monday? People always start a new regime on a Monday. Monday is the starting point of anything new; it's called the *Fresh Start Effect*.

According to research carried out by *Wharton School at the University of Pennsylvania*;
"On certain days, called temporal landmarks, you just have a different view of yourself" says Jason Riis, visiting professor

at Wharton School at the University of Pennsylvania who went on to say "you become more forward looking and it's been shown to structure our memories and experiences". *2

Exercise Two

Read through your food diary and circle those foods that you'd prefer were not on the list. The ones that when you read them make you feel that pang of guilt or the foods that you expected to be on there. Circle them and then write them under one of two headings:
1.   trigger foods or
2.   treat foods.

It's important that you don't mark these as *can't have* foods. They are simply triggers or treats. Triggers are the foods that are your *go to* foods when you're eating in an emotional state. Treats; well their just treats and can be eaten as exactly that, occasionally.

Do this for each day of the week in your food diary. Circle the foods and list them under your headings trigger foods or treat foods. This is about becoming aware of what drives you to reach for certain foods. What foods are repeated more than three times? Is coffee your guilty pleasure, or is it that morning muffin? Pick out the three foods that appear more than once on this list and write them down in your diary. Identifying and acknowledging these foods are the first stages in you changing your food thoughts and quieting what we call your *'chimp voice'*. What we are doing here is identifying your treat foods and changing your mindset towards them. So instead of the thought 'I want it, but I'm not allowed' rephrase it to 'I can have it, but I choose not to

Get Out of Your Own Way!

have it just now'.

What is the *chimp voice* and why does it crave control?
You know that little voice in your head that says 'go on have another cake, it's just one; one makes no difference at all. It's just cake, you'll be fine. There aren't even many calories in that one'! Well that's your *chimp voice*. So we're going to do some work to shut that voice up. In fact, we're going to gaffer tape its mouth shut and put you back in charge. This little voice is known as your subconscious, and this voice will do anything that you let it. We just need to let it know that achieving what you want; whether it's goals around your weight, or health is now possible, and it will happen. In fact just by reading this you've already planted a new seed in your subconscious that things are about to change for the better, and soon.

Here are four simple steps to regain control over your *chimp voice* and reason with it when it comes to making decisions around food.

Step 1 The first step in quietening that *chimp voice* is to be aware of it. Acknowledge it and ask it a question. Ask 'Why'?

Step 2 Listen to your higher self, get details from it. Ask 'What does my body need right now to feel better in every way'?

Step 3 Make a promise to your higher self, if I choose X (this green juice) then I will feel Y (more energetic).

Step 4 Give it some positive examples of what you want to achieve. Study other peoples inspirational stories to reassure yourself. It's about mirroring the success of other people who have achieved what you aspire to.

Don't get me wrong this voice isn't all bad; it's there for a good purpose. Its purpose is driven from deep down in our subconscious and is based on the *fight or flight* mechanism. It's essential for our survival, but our needs have changed. The subconscious mind makes over 75% of our day-to-day decisions. It is more powerful than the conscious mind, but it's also there to be reasoned with, questioned and tamed too.

This is how we start to understand the psychology behind what we eat; what drives us to reach for fatty foods, and what changes we have to make to our thought patterns to help curb the habits that no longer serve us. I'm helping you to change your attitude towards these trigger foods so you will become aware of them, and ultimately remove them from your daily eating routine.

First let's look at how our food has changed over the decades and why we are driven to crave the fast, convenient hit of temporary fullness.

The right kind of nourishment

To better understand our modern day relationship with food it helps to understand how our food systems have changed, and how it has evolved into what's known as a *Western diet*.

Mass production of food began in the latter half of the 19th century, when corporations discovered that there were faster and cheaper ways to manufacture foods. It meant a faster way of getting products to market, and even faster profits. The importance of a speedy turnaround went up, and the emphasis on quality and nutrition went spiralling downwards.

Like any good journalist knows *you want to find the truth in a scandal, and then follow the money* and the food industry hasn't escaped the scandal one little bite! You only have to look at the plethora of stories over the past few decades to read about the short falls in food quality, in nutrition and in health & safety to recognise that companies focus is primarily about speed of processing and its resulting profit.

Of course there are some *good eggs* out there; food manufacturers that believe in producing good quality ingredients. So here's my first piece of advice; find those companies and buy fresh, buy local and know your suppliers.

My second piece of advice is to become more aware of what you're choosing to buy, always check what the ingredients are, then ask yourself:
- "Why is this ingredient inside this food"?
- "What does it do"?
- "How does it benefit my body"?

The science that goes into mass produced foods is a lesson in human ingenuity. In the interest of saving a buck or two, some food producers come up with extremely complicated ways of replicating flavours found in nature. It doesn't make sense to do this when the flavours from nature are already available, and are rich in minerals, and full of natural goodness. But cost is the driving factor.

For example nature makes strawberries. They grow wild without any human intervention, they are packed full of nutritionally rich ingredients and they taste delicious. Yet some food companies replicate this strawberry flavour by using over four dozen ingredients. If you choose to drink strawberry milk shakes, or eat processed strawberry desserts, chances are you're drinking and eating an artificial flavour concocted from over 50 chemicals beginning with amyl acetate and ending in solvent.

I'd like to turn the clock back to 1906 and the introduction of the *Pure Food and Drug Act* and present you to an amazing chemist by the name of Harvey W. Whiley. Whiley was the leader of the pure food crusade, he had quantified concerns about the various chemicals being put into our foods. Consequently, he formed the *Poison Squad*; a group of young men who would voluntarily ingest food additives, and chemicals to determine their impact to human health, and bring national awareness to the problems experienced *3.

Amongst his concerns at the time was: the use of saccharin, bleached flour, caffeine, and benzoate of soda all of which had previously been approved for consumption.

On March 15th 1912, Whiley resigned from the *Pure Food and Drug Group* due to the ignorance of the government in relation to the use of certain chemicals and the affects they have on human health. He went on to work for the *Good House Keeping* Magazine where he continued to highlight, and expose the dangers of using these chemicals in food, and continually asked readers to ask themselves **"How close is this food to its natural state"?**

The amount of choice we have these days is exhausting. How many times have you rushed back from work thinking 'oh gosh what on earth am I going to make for supper'?

Get Out of Your Own Way!

Think about the amount of choices available and how many recipes are free for us to try. It should be easy right? But it's not, it's absolutely overwhelming.

In the Western world we have become accustomed to the overwhelming abundance of food. With our super markets stocking thousands of options at various price points, our choice has become extensive. We live in a time of abundance, but we're under pressure, overwhelmed and under nourished. The choice of produce has become absolutely exhausting, and so we become perplexed, and no longer know what the healthy options are. So we reach for the easy, quick solution. It's just human nature; don't ever think it's just you. It's everybody.

If you think back to our early ancestors they didn't have this unlimited choice. They would have eaten what was available to them at the time; home grown vegetables, grains and meat, or fish freshly caught that day. They didn't say 'oh I'm going to choose a paleo diet today'. That's all they had and so their diet was simple, varied, locally sourced, seasonal and organic! That's not to say that some days they weren't under nourished, because they probably were due to the lack of calories (when the animals were just that little bit too fast to catch). They ate when their bodies told them they needed to, not when they became bored.

Skip forward to today's busy household and the scenario couldn't be more different. With the pace of modern life and how much there is to fit into a 24 hour period, it's no wonder that most parents are grabbing the nearest ready meal to try their best to feed a family, especially those on a low budget. This doesn't have to be the case. We seem to have lost our connection with food in our modern world, and so we've lost the ability to listen to what our bodies are telling us.

With all of the hustle and bustle and daily grind of most people's lives, it proves quite difficult to find peace to listen to what our bodies are saying.

When did you last truly stop and listen to what your body is saying?

If you do, you will hear that it's not telling you to eat three large meals a day, or to reach for that burger and fries each night. Your body is on your side and both your body and mind will strive to work in harmony with each other to get the best result for you. We just need to get them talking the same language again.

We're all so busy going about our daily existence that we have no time to sit, listen and reflect. That applies for both external events and internal reactions and feelings.

If we take for instance the simple act of eating a meal; our body goes through so many different stages: the initial lust and hunger when we read the menu, the rumbling belly, through to excitement and eagerness when we see and smell the food. Plus there's the satisfaction and contentment you have when you've finished eating. Eating really does involve us using most of our senses. But we eat so quickly and often we eat on the go, meaning we don't have time to consider and reflect on these stages of digestion. We just *feed the machine* and hope that the blend of fuel keeps us going the distance.

Get Out of Your Own Way!

Exercise Three

Take time out each day before the set times you would normally eat and listen to how your body feels. I'd like you to write in your food diary which day of the week it is and what emotion you are feeling. What you are worrying about? What plans do you have that day? All of the above will help you to identify the emotions you have surrounding food and it will highlight the reason why you choose to eat what you do.

The main problem with overeating in Western society is not that we have a collective will power disorder; yes many of us do eat too much, but that we are eating the wrong foods for our bodies and our minds to function at the optimum rate. The packaged foods on offer are predominantly nutrient deficient. They lack the vitamins, minerals and enzymes our bodies require. The brain senses these deficiencies and wisely responds to this absence of vital chemistry by commanding us to undertake the most sensible survival strategy; eat more food.

The key is to buy the most fresh, local and organic food that you possibly can afford. OK, I know that organic had previously meant more expensive, and not readily available to everyone, but these days you can buy local much easier. Find someone in your area who offers vegetable box schemes, not just the mainstream companies that are a bit pricy, but get onto social media channels and search for local deliveries from garden centres and smaller producers.

Rekindle your love for real food. Each one of us, on a subconscious level will have our own desires and cravings when it comes to food. Find new healthy recipes, follow your favourite chef's online, and download your favourite healthy options. Put them into a scrap book in your kitchen. Have five or six healthy options that become your quick to make, fall back recipes whenever you're in a hurry.

How to feel physically, mentally and spiritually full
So why do we seek that emotional satisfaction from our food, and what is it that makes us feel physically, mentally and spiritually full? As humans we want things now, not in ten minutes or two hours, NOW!

Our desire for this instant gratification is no different when it comes to the food we eat and what we expect to feel from eating it. This desire is hard wired into our neurochemistry. Let me explain. Have you ever watched a crying baby bawling until red in the face and then its mother comes along with a bottle of milk and that infant is promptly transformed into a quiet and peaceful little bundle?

Well, this is a pre-programmed human trait that has been in the human genome forever. Getting the food we want right now is internally driven, and it's still a challenge for us as adults. We let this demanding internal voice run the show.

It's the voice demanding instant gratification that directs us towards making poor choices, all in the name of speed and emotional satisfaction. So here's the bottom line; instant gratification has some clear short term benefits, but brings with it some longer term headaches. Do you silence the screaming toddler inside of you right now? Or do you take a rain check, press pause and think about the longer-term effect of where you want to be in the future?

When your mind says 'pick up that cream cake, eat it and

Get Out of Your Own Way!

you're going to feel great, you'll feel better and happy', I want you to physically step back and in your mind ask yourself 'If I eat this cake, will it take me one step towards my goal, or will it take me one step further away from what I want to achieve'?

You know the answer already, so the only tough part is asking the question. Just do it the next time you're in that situation, and when you say 'no' to that screaming toddler inside, notice how powerful and in control you feel. Each time you take time to detach, decide and feel in charge of the decision, you are strengthening your mind muscle, and it'll be easier the next time.

Summary - Remember how we talked about your *chimp voice?*

Steps 1 The first step in quietening that *chimp voice* is to be aware of it. Acknowledge it and ask it a question. Ask 'why'?

Steps 2 Listen to your higher self get details from it. Ask 'What does my body need right now to feel better in every way'?

Steps 3 Make a promise to your higher self, if I choose X (this green juice) then I will feel Y (more energetic).

Steps 4 – Give it some positive examples of what you want to achieve. Study others peoples inspirational stories to reassure yourself. It's about mirroring the success of other people who have achieved what you aspire to.

I'm not saying "don't ever choose the cake"; I'm not saying that at all. That's the *don't have* mentality that most diets

Get Out of Your Own Way!

are built around. What I'm saying is "you're in control here - it's your choice – it's always your choice", but making that choice becomes difficult when the marketing of these products is so dominant.

You may have walked past the bakery lately and heard the whispers of 'eat me', 'buy me', 'take me home' coming from all of the tasty cakes in the window. These voices are actually coming from the cakes (please don't think I've lost the plot here), they are actually coming from the incessant advertising and marketing that we are subjected to every second of every minute of every day. It's said that we are exposed to over 3,000 marketing messages every day*4. That's mass confusion for your mind.

From the strategically placed products on the supermarket shelves to the painstakingly designed packaging of the man-made items we buy, they all have one thing in common. They are all made with the motive to sell, to make money. There are very few items that we are sold in supermarkets these days which have not had a careful and cleverly planned design and marketing campaign behind them.

Even the bananas have not escaped the politically correctness of shape size and packaging. Did you know that half of the bananas grown are thrown away because they are slightly misshapen*5. Odd is good, natural is good. Let's celebrate the odd, the natural and the things that stand out as different and have a personality. Let's celebrate this in our food as well as with our bodies.

What about that word perfection, what does it really mean? Isn't it completely subjective because it means something different to all of us? So, striving towards perfection is a goal that we'll never reach. Perfection when it comes to our bodies is media driven and based on stereotypes. What you perceive as the *perfect body* is different to someone else's perception of the *perfect body*. What I'm saying here is "stop thinking about striving for perfection because a universal definition of perfection doesn't exist".

Think instead about improving your confidence. What weight do you need to reach to feel confident? What does your body shape need to look like for you to be confident? What's going to make *YOU* happy? This suddenly becomes a less pressured goal when you take that long deep breath of relief and start planning the next small steps towards your own idea of perfection. Be grateful for you, for your amazing body, and how it supports you in this life.

How do I know how these marketing campaigns work? I used to design them. Yep, I was once on the muddy side of the fence, and one day I woke up saturated in the marketing lies, and I suddenly knew that the grass was definitely greener on the other side. So I jumped over to *Mother Nature's* side of the fence. That's why I'm writing this for you because I want to help you to jump over the fence to the side of feeling awake, aware, healthy and confident with whom you are as well as being comfortable with what your body looks like.

So now that you have your *Healthy, Fit and in Flow* diary filled out for seven days, let's take a look at making the small changes to get you heading in the direction you want to go; to reach your goal of being *Healthy, Fit and in Flow*.

Get Out of Your Own Way!

Time to change how you think about food

Ever wondered how two people could cook the same meal, with the exact same ingredients and yet their meals turn out remarkably different? Time, care, love and attention are normally the difference. If someone has cooked that meal with a little love and attention, it normally tastes better. It's odd, as it's not as though the ingredients know this, or the carrots are thinking 'yep I'm going to be tastier in this dish because my cook has taken time to peel me slowly'.

It's beginning to be widely accepted that our intention has an impact on the physical things around us. American author, journalist and publisher Lynne McTaggart has run a number of lab based experiments to study the effect of our intention; good or bad, on plants. The results are remarkable and may go some way to explain why some people can create a tastier meal than others from exactly the same ingredients. It's much more than simply paying attention. It's about paying attention to your intention too.

Exercise Four

So, how do you really pay attention to food? What is your relationship with food?

Let's time travel again. I want you to grab your *Healthy, Fit & in Flow* diary and write down your full name and after your name write down the words *Age 15*. Spend ten minutes just thinking back to the 15 year old you. Draw a picture of yourself back then if you want to. What did you look like? What did you spend your days doing? Now write down in your diary what you ate back then, not specifics but what kind of food? Did you always sit at the dining room table to eat, or were you grabbing food on the run? Were you already hooked on pop-tarts like me? Write a short description of your relationship to food back then. Also include any feelings or troubles that you may have been going through.

Now skip forward to your 20's when you were more in control of your own lifestyle and food choices. What did you choose? Did alcohol play a large part in your diet? Did your social life overtake every minute of the weekend? Write down how you felt, again dig deep and spend 10 minutes thinking back. What emotions are you feeling? What worried you back then that may have led to poor food choices.

Hopefully, by doing this short reflective exercise you will see that where you are today is the result of a long journey with food. Each step on that journey has played a significant part in how your health and mindset is today.

Once you have written down your food journey, spend a little more time thinking back over what your food journey looks like. Take a big leap forward to today because this is where we change your story. As Einstein said "Insanity is doing the same thing over and over again and expecting different results". This is where we stick a great big crossroad sign in your life because now you are going to choose a different road going forward. It's time to point your health in the direction you really want it to go.

Think about this journey in a positive way though, because each choice and small step you take from this point on will determine what your future health looks like in 5, 10, 15 years' time. The choice is always yours. What do you want

Get Out of Your Own Way!

your future self to be writing down if you did this exercise in 5, 10, 15 years' time?

Now I want you to leap forward 5 years. Close your eyes and spend a few moments thinking about where you will be? Who you are with? Where you are living? What you are eating and what your body looks like? Picture yourself in the clothes you want to wear, doing the activities you love to do, eating the foods you know will enrich your health. Go on, spend a few moments visualising your future self. If you respond more to feelings or sounds then write about this instead, or describe it out loud and record it to listen back to later.

Feels great doesn't it! By doing that short exercise you've already created new neural pathways in your brain. Every thought creates a neural connection. Remember, our minds don't know the difference between visualising yourself being that version of you, and *actually* being that version of you. If you think a thought often enough, the neural connection will grow strong, particularly if there's an emotional attachment to it. It's time to change the conversation inside your head and form new pathways that direct you towards your health goal.

<u>It's time to start eating!</u>
What? Are you crazy I hear you say? Eating? 'But I'm trying to become healthier, lose weight, and become fitter'.

One of the best ways to achieve long-term sustainable weight-loss is to eat. But wait, the key thing here is to eat the right foods, and create a meaningful relationship with food. To receive pleasure from it, celebrate it; enjoy growing, cooking and sharing food. Trust your body and listen to what it is saying. Be willing to find your natural appetite and your inner nutritionist, your body will begin to find its way. It's that simple.

What's the first thing that comes into your mind when you think diet? It'll be a limiting word I bet like: restriction, reduce, low fat, the words that instantly put us in the mind frame of lack. But what actually happens when you choose not to eat?

<u>Let's talk about blood sugar</u>
Your blood sugar level is the amount of glucose that's circulating in your bloodstream. It comes from what you eat and provides energy to cells immediately, or can be stored for future use. There's been a lot of discussion recently around blood sugar levels, the peaks and troughs and how they influence the way that our body retains and absorbs sugar and fats. A well-balanced blood sugar level is key to your overall health, fitness and hormonal balance too. If you tend to eat based on your emotions, then I bet that your blood sugar levels are up and down like a rollercoaster.

The key when it comes to balancing your blood sugar is to eat in 3's. For the next week change your routine and try to eat something every 3-4 hours. Make sure you eat breakfast; maybe some fruit with natural organic yoghurt topped off with some sesame or pumpkins seeds. Drizzle a little maple syrup if you need that sweetness; make sure it's a 100% pure, high-grade maple syrup and not a pancake syrup which is normally made from high fructose corn syrup. Add a sprinkle of cinnamon too; cinnamon is fantastic for balancing blood sugar levels. Studies have shown that consuming just half a teaspoon a day can reduce blood sugar levels by up to 29%*6.

Plan ahead and pack yourself three healthy snacks to take to work with you; some whole almonds, an apple, cottage cheese and rice cakes. Think variety and don't think limits and whatever you do, don't think calories.

Are you a fan of mathematics? No, me either. In fact I don't like counting much at all and that goes for calories too. 400 calories of green veggies produce a significantly different result on your body to 400 calories worth of crisps. So don't get caught up in the calorie game, and if you already are, it's time to throw the calculator out of the window.

When you learn to listen to your body and what it responds to, then it's easier to balance out the essential requirements of your cells, the peaks and troughs in blood sugar levels will even out, calories become just maths and nobody really likes doing maths do they.

Let's talk about fats
Another key area that I'd ask you to pay no attention to is *low fat* labelled foods; low fat, no fat and anything that is marketed as fat free. This is another cycle of marketing that was introduced into our food system in the 1980's. It's true that saturated fat is a type of fat that is primarily responsible for clogging our arteries and increasing cholesterol levels. The food industry made a switch from animal fats in products to unsaturated vegetable oils. To enable these oils to be used in the place of solid fats they were hydrogenised.

Unfortunately, what wasn't investigated at the time, or before they were added to most of the packaged foods on the supermarkets shelves was how hydrogenated fats could increase levels of dangerous trans-fats. Trans-fats are both bad for the heart and our cholesterol levels. The other issue with low fat foods is that more sugar tends to be added to maintain the taste and texture.

"The most power you have as a consumer is knowing exactly what you consume".

As in everything though; in our mind, bodies and in life, it's about balance. Our bodies do need fats. Certain fats, like those found in nuts, seeds and oily fish provide essential fatty acids (including the omega-3 variety). These essential fats are important for maintaining healthy blood vessels, balancing hormones and for the correct functioning of our nervous system. It's about including the good fats from: avocados, nuts, seeds and oily fish and limiting the bad fats in saturated foods such as: cakes, biscuits, and refined white flour goods. But it's about more than just a list of good fats; it's about including this list in your daily diet and creating delicious, simple and healthy meals, which you're confident enough to cook.

So let's get back to changing your relationship towards food. When was the last time that you cooked or made some food while truly focusing 100% on the task you were doing? It's easy to get distracted in today's world, with all of the responsibilities we have day to day. But when you train your mind to shrink that focus down and take time to notice every single little detail in the task you are engaged in, things become simplified. When you start to focus in on the detail of what you're doing, and bring yourself into that precise moment things begin to flow, and your mind begins to thrive.

Physical Fitness

Let's not forget fitness.

Additionally, start to move your body more, small movements even. It's not about forcing your body into a state of recovery due to over exercising; it's just about moving more. Take a walk, do some stretches and start to focus on each body part as you are moving them. Slow, focused movement gets the metabolism moving. I bet you've a skinny friend who never seems to put on weight right? Have you ever noticed that she/he is always active, moves around a lot, or has an active job? Although your metabolism influences your body's basic energy needs, it's your food choices and your physical activity that ultimately determine how much you weigh.

Mental Flow

About this state of flow.

What does flow mean? We hear it being referred to in sport, dance and arts, but can it also apply to food and eating? Yes it can, and it does.

Our whole existence revolves around energy. We are a flow of energy, as are animals and plants. Energy is what we feel when we enter a room sometimes, or when we meet a person for the first time. The key to this is that energy doesn't just flow randomly, we all influence how energy flows, and whatever we focus our energy on will expand and grow.

Let me give you a simple example: you have an idea to plant a veg patch in your garden. That idea mulls around in your head for a while, then you suddenly start to research ideas and information on *how to*, suddenly you're thinking about buying a spade and 'voila' the next sunny day you find yourself out in the garden digging. You focused your energy onto one topic and have begun to make it a reality. It's the same with food. It's time to place your focus on creating a better relationship with food and getting in flow with food.

<u>Do you mind – I'm eating</u>
It's time to turn off your mobile phone, unplug from life and tune in to the enjoyment of eating again by becoming mindful. Mindfulness is defined as 'deliberately paying attention, non-judgmentally, in the present moment'. Mindful eating is described as 'using all your senses in choosing to eat food that is both satisfying to you and nourishing to your body'.

Get Out of Your Own Way!

So, how do you know if you are eating in a more mindful way? A simple exercise is to think back to your very last meal. Got it? Good, can you describe the texture, the flavour and the taste? When you are aware of the present moment whilst eating, you will notice the flavours and become aware of each taste in your mouth.

Eating more mindfully also allows you to release any previous habitual patterns associated with eating. It breaks the cycle of *eating out of habit*. It allows you to become aware of what your body responds to, what it enjoys and thrives on. It also allows your mind to hear when your body is saying that it's had enough. By taking steps to eat more mindfully you will be training your mind and your body to work in a closer relationship. Your mind will be able to respond to your body's reactions, and your body will start to thrive on the foods that also nourish your mind.

Eating mindfully also results in you eating more slowly. Eating slower allows digestion to fully take place. Also your body will recognise when it is full *without* feeling the need to finish every morsel on your plate. When we take time to chew our food we suppress the hormone *Ghrelin* a hunger hormone that stimulates appetite. By suppressing Ghrelin, we won't be as hungry and can feel full faster and are more likely to eat smaller portions.

Exercise Five

To bring you into flow and help you to eat more mindfully, I'd like you to really think about your next meal. Make it a meal when you have a little more time: like dinner. Now, think about what you'd like to eat, not just 'oh I fancy pasta'. Take a few deep breaths right now, breathe in through your nose for a count of five and then slowly out through your mouth for a count of five, do this five times. Now think about what you'd really like to eat. What flavours do you want to taste? Do you enjoy crunchy foods, savoury, or salty foods? Really think about the taste, texture and preparation of that meal. Has that made you crave for that specific food? When you start thinking about eating, the brain readies the digestive tract for nourishment. We're back to the fact that in our brains the very same neurons fire when we think about doing something compared to actually doing that task.

Every thought creates a neural connection. So to change the story and create healthier pathways, you have to change the foods you think about. Think about new, exciting foods that are nourishing, colourful and healthy. This will allow your brain to let your body trial these foods and once your body starts to adapt to these new healthy options, your brain will benefit too.

"Mindful eating empowers you to break old automatic or habitual chain reactions, and discover options that work better for your body and mind".

Eating more mindfully is part of becoming Healthy, Fit and in Flow. It is a holistic approach and will allow you to become more aware and focused in every way. Your journey with food up to this point has been a completely unique path. You've adopted habits and routines that may, or may not serve you going forward. The key is; if you are ready to make changes in how you eat from this point forward, then your health, your weight and your lifestyle goals will become a reality.

Slowing down and becoming aware of your decisions and habits is a key step. Once you become aware of the decisions you are making before you make them, then you're back in control. Once you're in control, you will be able to take a step back, pause and ask yourself the question 'Is this decision taking me a step closer to my goals, or is it taking me a step further away'?

That small decision will both empower you, and boost your confidence in making future decisions. These small decisions add up and over time will create real change. Once your body finds that state of balance and flow, it will find its own equilibrium of ultimate health and believe me; you won't want to go back to your old habits. Your newfound energy and optimism will become an addiction in itself.

Another key step is to start enjoying and respecting food again. Become curious, try new things and cook new recipes and share food with friends. Become aware of your relationship with food; notice what makes your body feel good and what doesn't. Ask questions about the ingredients in certain foods and find out if those ingredients serve you or not. Stop thinking from a place of lack and telling yourself that you don't, can't, or mustn't have that certain food. Make it a choice; it's always your choice. Involve your subconscious in the decision and decide that you don't want that food just now because it doesn't take you in the direction of your goal.

If you are ready to take a step in the direction of a healthier you, and create the future self you envisage remember, your next decision counts. So slow down, ask questions, and listen to your body respond; it talks the same language as your mind, it's on your side.

Get Out of Your Own Way!

I'd love to hear your outcome after implementing these exercises, especially what you observed from completing your food journey, anything at all you wish to share. Head over to **www.healthyfitandinflow.com** and click on *My Food Journey* to read even more of my top tips.

If you're looking to be *Healthy, Fit and in Flow*, but want that additional support to push you towards your goals, you may be interested in my online course offering guided support and weekly webinars with experts in health, nutrition and mindfulness. Plus, you get to join a supportive community that you are part of for life. Head over to **www.healthyfitandinflow.com** to find out more.

References

*1 (*http://www.dailymail.co.uk/health/article-430913/Average-woman-spends-31-years-diet-researchers-say.html*)

*2 (*http://papers.ssrn.com/sol3/papers.cfm?abstract_id=2204126*)

*3 (*https://papers.econ.mpg.de/evo/discussionpapers/2013-03.pdf*)

*4 http://www.digitaltrainingacademy.com/documents/DSC_%20Online_media-consumer_experiences_of_media_10.1.pdf

*5 http://www.theguardian.com/environment/2013/jan/10/half-world-food-waste

*6 http://www.ncbi.nlm.nih.gov/pubmed/19930003

Dr Steve Peters writes about the 'Chimp Paradox' being that voice inside your head – either it can be positive or negative

Susan Hay - Biography

After a high-pressured career in the corporate world and her own challenging journey with food, Susan escaped and went free range. After retraining in Holistic Nutrition with SNHS she set up her own publishing company aptly named *Thrive*. She now edits their in-house Health & Nutrition magazine available in hardcopy and on-line.

Thrive magazine focuses on sharing healthy, ethical and natural products and news stories worldwide. Susan says "Thrive exists to help everyone get that little bit healthier. We have some real champions writing for Thrive Magazine helping us to spread the word about clean, mindful and natural ways of living".

Health & Nutrition has become Susan's life mission and she also works as a Clean Eating Coach. Working with clients, she gets to the root of their food issues, inspiring change, as well as helping them to have fun with food again.

Susan adopted a plant based diet 4 years ago and is also a self-confessed juicing fan. She's also an avid mindfulness practitioner and practices the hemi-sync meditation technique from the Monroe Institute.

Get Out of Your Own Way!

Section Five
Escaping from Toxic Relationships

by
Tomasz Nędzi

"Once you learn to be happy, you won't tolerate being around people who make you feel anything less".

Get Out of Your Own Way!

In 2004 I found myself single. The reason being I had cheated on my then girlfriend with whom I had been living with for the previous four years. I was not especially happy in that relationship, but I experienced the type of inertia that held me there.

One day I met someone else and a romance developed. The problem was I wasn't free to start a new relationship; I had not finished my previous one. Consequently, when my girlfriend discovered what had occurred, she made the decision for me and ended our relationship.

When the end came, I was completely lost and I did not recover easily. On one level I knew the situation was my own fault; on another I couldn't understand why I wasn't happier to escape from a relationship I hadn't been happy in.

If you think that story is complicated then wait for what happened next.

I then found a new girlfriend on the Internet via a dating website. She was funny, strong and independent. It seemed as if she knew all the answers to the many questions in life, questions about my future, questions I could not easily answer for myself. I soon found myself to be in love, or at least that's what I thought at the time.

I invited her to join me for a few days break in Berlin where I was enrolled professionally to attend a conference. She agreed and all the arrangements were settled. However, the happy moment of our first meeting was spoilt when suddenly she had an uncontrolled panic attack in the taxi on the way to the railway station. She thought she'd lost her keys and started to behave in a difficult to understand (hysterical and aggressive) manner. The situation rang a little warning bell, but I ignored it putting it down to nerves.

Two months went by without any further issues when she suggested we buy and build her dream wooden house together. I responded that it may be too early in the relationship to commit to such serious plans. Added to which my financial situation was not strong enough for such an investment. I was finishing my MBA studies so needed all my money to pay for my tuition fees. I was working, but my contract was temporary, and I wasn't sure whether or not my employer would sign another employment contract with me.

My girlfriend wasn't working at all. However, she wouldn't listen, or accept 'no' for an answer. Consequently, as I couldn't refuse her (I didn't want to lose her, *or* be alone again), I agreed to her suggestion. I knew it was sheer madness to agree to buy and build a house with someone I'd only known for six months, but it was not my idea. Nevertheless I did agree to her plan.

She sold her flat and moved into my rented apartment in order save money for our new home. When my employer did not sign another employment contract with me she blamed me for the situation. I found myself to be trapped with persuasive feelings of guilt. I now know that guilt is a very strong emotion in people who feel responsible. It was this guilty emotion that kept me in this relationship far longer than I expected, or was healthy.

Get Out of Your Own Way!

How satisfied are you with your relationship?

The Personal Success Handbook: Everything you need to be Successful by Curly Martin says "A relationship exists whenever two or more people interact". Therefore, by definition we potentially have hundreds of relationships every year.

According to Maslow's hierarchy theory of needs we have to have relationships in order to live and satisfy our physiological and needs for safety. We need to exchange our services for money and money for products in order to satisfy our basic needs for food and shelter. When we talk about higher level needs, we are referring to our need to give, and be loved which in turn influences our self-esteem. A variety of our needs can be satisfied by a variety of relationships. Therefore, it's important we enter into good healthy, nurturing and mutually beneficial relationships.

Relationships are divided into categories according to the time and frequency of each interaction. The following table gives examples of some typical relationships:

	Minimal duration	**Medium duration**	**Longer duration**
Transient	Shop assistants	New acquaintances	Long haul flight staff
Short term	Course tutors	Repeat clients	Friendships

	Minimal duration	Medium duration	Longer duration
Mid-term	Childhood friends	Work colleagues	Employer
Long term	None	Lovers	Spouses/ partners

The table above shows that some relationships are transient and although they may positively, or negatively influence our life their duration is passing. So if for example a shop assistant is unpleasant to deal with; this could potentially spoil our day, but it will not ruin our life on a daily basis (unless we shop in the same shop each day). Fortunately, we have power to choose *which* shop to use, if we don't like one, we simply change *where* we shop.

On the other opposite side of the table we find the relationships which are the most important and have most profound influence on our life. These are the ones we live with every day and they do decide how we feel on a daily basis e.g. how secure and happy we are.

My experience of toxicity started with guilt. Then it became worse. Initially we were happy, but them my partner became disillusioned and dissatisfied with me. I was being offended then felt beaten and offended again. My self-worth was questioned with different humiliating comments and remarks. I was unable to escape because of the guilt I felt for not investing the same amount of money into our new home as she had.

Get Out of Your Own Way!

"You can either give negativity power over your life or you can choose happiness instead". Anais Nin

What is toxic a relationship?

A toxic relationship is one which undermines your self-worth. The one which makes you feel less worthy and which takes your energy away.

A toxic relationship can happen between different parties for instance:
- Couples
- Parents and their children
- Siblings
- Neighbours
- Work colleagues
- Employer and employees
- Professionals like teachers and their pupils.

First it's important to identify a toxic relationship then determine who this person is in relation to you. Doing so will help you adopt the most effective strategies for protecting yourself and your future dealings with them.

Relationships are divided into either *equal* or *unequal* relationships.

✓ Essentially equal relationships tend to be nurturing in nature, meaning *both* sides have and respect each other's similar rights.
✓ Unequal relationships as defined by hierarchy and occur naturally throughout society. One person is superior to the other such as: teacher and student, military superiors and their subordinates, employer

- and employee, parent and child and so for.
- × Unequal relationships that are toxic are those where one person *thinks and behaves* in a superior way to the other. They are not nurturing, respectful, or healthy relationships. One person is made to suffer which manifests in all sorts of physical and mental ways not least lower self-worth and increased anxiety.

When we stay in a toxic relationship we make our life miserable. We transfer responsibility for our health, happiness and safety into the hands of another, albeit unconsciously. This is especially true of romantic relationships.

Toxic characteristics differ from person to person so initially they may be difficult to detect. Also, we may find that there are certain characteristics in one person which we don't like, yet be able to justify the same characteristics *as acceptable* in another person depending on the situation we find ourselves in. For instance, we may witness aggression at work and call it *bullying*. Yet the same level of aggression in a personal relationship may be described as over-protective.

Therefore, in order to protect ourselves; we need to understand more about what constitutes a toxic trait. Knowing this will help to empower us because then we'll be able to not only identify *which* people make us feel worse than others, but also *how* we best to proceed with them (or not as the case may be).

The toxic trait I didn't like in my relationship was that my partner became aggressive. She started accusing me of being at fault for her financial situation. Consequently, she started to undermine my self-worth by using certain behaviours which made me feel worse or even bad about myself.

"You cannot expect to live a positive life if you hang with negative people". Joel Osteen

Toxic behaviours

We can identify toxic behaviour by analysing the way we treat each other. Toxic traits are insidious. Some are common place behaviours that we may see or hear in relationships around us. We may not actually consider, or recognise them as toxic, simply because we are seeing or hearing things in isolation. But for the person suffering, there is no doubt they are in a toxic relationship.

What we usually observe in toxic relationships are:
- Toxic words; these are belittling comments designed to undermine and hurt. They are rude, painful and designed to gradually erode self-esteem.
- Faux pas; these are the half-hearted apologies made to cover deliberate or accidental, mistakes by an insensitive person to hurt another.
- Ambiguous compliments; the compliment that gives with one hand and takes with another designed to give a false boost of confidence when in fact they are intended as a put-down e.g. "you look lovely in that old dress".
- Sarcasm; sarcastic or ironic comments showing the intended recipient some hostility and unfriendliness.
- Toxic self-talk; this is another form of passive aggression when the speaker makes negative comments about themselves in order to show others they have a negative attitude towards him/herself too.

These comments undermine the capabilities and skills of another by making them feel useless too.
- "It's only a joke"; usually anything but funny, and just when you are about to respond they blame you by saying "It's only a joke where's your sense of humour"? This situation is toxic because it has nothing to do with humour; the person is using humour as a cover to be cruel because they mean what they just said.
- Subconscious comments; this is how people show their *true colours* because their attitude and approach come through even when they don't realise what, or how they are saying. By listening to what people say *between the lines* you will discover this toxic approach.
- Toxic phrases; curses are obvious to ascertain, but there are other words which are less obvious. Phrases like: "You should…", "Why don't you…", "You'd better…", "Why can't you…", "You must…", "I don't believe you", "You always…", "You never…" and so on. These phrases make the speaker feel in control while making the other person feel attacked.

You will probably recognise some of these behaviours. You may even have used some of them yourself, or you may have been at the receiving end. Either way, reading about these toxic behaviours and language may act as a *wake-up call* in helping you identify and realise their potential for harm in your daily life.

I used to experience any number of the above scenarios in my personal relationship. It started with toxic comments like: "nobody likes you"; "don't you know everybody is laughing at you", "even your parents have left you". I

Get Out of Your Own Way!

sometimes heard comments which were rude and painful, they were usually followed by: "where's your sense of humour"? And "can't you take a joke"?

My partner succeeded in making me feel guilty with comments like: "you should be earning more money"; "you will never amount to much".

I also heard unpleasant comments which were directed towards other people. My partner thought they were simply the expressions of someone being truthful, but in truth they were nothing but faux pas, or ambiguous comments designed to humiliate.

"The company you keep not only defines you but binds you; strive always to seek the company of the truth". Panache Desai

What do toxic people do?

A toxic person is someone who wants to destroy you. They don't consciously set out to sabotage a relationship, they just can't help themselves. They quickly lapse into old habits and before long; they've made it their mission in life to thwart you. They expend a great deal of negative energy, and efforts into making you feel small, and insignificant at every available opportunity. This person will do whatever it takes to destroy your happiness and enthusiasm for life, even at the expense of their own.

Toxic Types

According to author Lillian Glass who writes about toxic relationships, there are 30 toxic personality patterns:

1. The Cut-you-downer; people who like to humiliate others in order to feel better about themselves.
2. The Chatterbox; people who prefer talking to listening to others.
3. The Self-destroyer; people who tend to annihilate themselves physically and emotionally.
4. The Runner; people who would rather escape from problems than stay and solve them.
5. The Silent but deadly volcano; these are people who tend to erupt like volcano and like volcanos, they eruption unexpectedly.
6. The Gossip; people who like to share private information about others, yet don't like to reveal the truth about themselves.
7. The Angry Pugilist; people who are constantly irritated, and or aggressive toward others, and *spoiling for a fight*.
8. The Gloom and Doom victim; people who enjoy being a victim, they are happy being unhappy.
9. The Smiling Two-Faced Backstabber; people who initially look and sound friendly, yet will use every opportunity to stab you in the back.
10. The Wishy-Washy Wimp; people who are indecisive and won't take their own destiny in their hands.
11. The Opportunistic User; people who take an interest in other people only *if* they can take advantage of them.
12. The Bitchy, Bossy Bully; people who are happy and feel superior when other people suffer under their control.
13. The Jokester; people who escape from reality into the jokes they create; they are not treated seriously by others.
14. The Unconscious Social Klutz; people who are clumsy and act lost in social relationships and situations.

15. The Mental Case; people who have mental problems and are unpredictable.
16. The Bullshitting Liar; people who don't tell the truth and *big up* everything that is going on in their own lives to impress others.
17. The Meddler; people who like nothing better than to interfere uninvited into lives of others because they think they know best.
18. The Penny-Pinching Miser; people who are so attached to their own money that they will try everything to fool others out of spending theirs instead.
19. The Fanatic; people who are so completely wedded to their own beliefs, ideas and ways that they are too close-minded to talk about different things.
20. The Me, Myself and I Narcissist; people who are so self-absorbed that they are their only source and subject of conversation.
21. The Eddie Haskell; people who pay insincere compliments in order to achieve their goals.
22. The Self-Righteous Priss; people who think they are perfect, and therefore, believe are always right even when they aren't.
23. The Snooty Snob; people who are pretentious and pay a lot attention to superficial attributes of status.
24. The Competitor; people who like to compete with everybody and everything in every single situation imaginable then take delight in winning and beating others less fortunate than themselves.
25. The Control Freak; people who like to control things and people by any means possible usually via manipulation and compliments.
26. The Accusing Critic; people who are difficult to please

> because they are always so critical towards everything and everyone.
> 27. The Arrogant Know-it-All; people who use their knowledge to intimidate and humiliate others.
> 28. The Emotional Refrigerator; people who use their lack of emotional reaction and communication to control others.
> 29. The Sceptical Paranoid; people who don't trust anyone or anything and view the world with suspicion.
> 30. The Instigator; people who enjoy provoking others to make their lives difficult and complicated.

This multitude of *toxic types* complicates the process of identifying a toxic relationship. People adopt different types based on each different situation they find themselves in. Therefore, no one person is ever only one type. Usually people display many different types for many different reasons. However, when you know what you are looking for, one type in particular normally makes itself known and that's the more dominant type people cannot easily hide even if they want to.

My partner seemed to be The Cut-you-downer as she seemed to be happiest when I was in misery. She used certain toxic and aggressive words to offend me which in her own mind made her appear stronger so it fed into her need to build her self-esteem. Studying for my MBA had the opposite effect; she couldn't be happy or supportive of me as this made her less educated.

What I also learned later was she was The Opportunistic User because she did not maintain relationships with other people if she couldn't take advantage of it. She kept her social contacts *only* when they were of potential benefit to her.

She was also Accusing Critic as she was never satisfied with what she got. As my colleague said later *he never heard any positive comment come from her about anything.*

I found it difficult to please her as well because she was quite unstable in her behaviour which made her The Angry Pugilist too. She wasn't afraid of attacking other people whenever they didn't want to do what she wanted or expected them to do.

I knew she was a difficult case, but with my belief that people are essentially good, and they can get better with help, I naturally tried to help change her toxic behaviour - several times - to no avail. In order to change the toxic person we need why they are toxic in the first place.

"Letting go means to come to the realization that some people are a part of your history, but not a part of your destiny". Dr. Steve Maraboli

Why are people toxic?

This is very good question. It's difficult to answer, but it's worth exploring. First, there is no one reason why people become toxic. Usually it's a combination of environment and genetics, truth is we don't always know the reasons why. Toxic people can be extremely intelligent, secretive and deceptive. Being toxic crosses all the boundaries of culture, sex, age, religion and education.

One expert suggests that toxic behaviours are caused by jealousy. People envy one another for all sorts of reasons.

In order for the toxic person to feel better about themselves they behave aggressively to compensate for their own shortcomings, perceived, or otherwise.

We usually envy young, beautiful, wealthy, intelligent people. Some of us may even aspire to become just like them and adopt their lifestyle. That doesn't mean they necessarily feel the need to do, or say anything negative about these people. Instead, they accept, as the majority of us do, that there will always be people who are younger, more beautiful, wealthier and more intelligent than ourselves.

However, toxic people are unable, or unwilling to accept this situation as reality. They do not accept their own limitations so set out to sabotage those around them by causing conflict and misery.

Unfortunately, toxic people don't tend to like or love others who are worse off than they are. In fact, they tend to hate and disrespect them. Therefore they hate and disregard poor, old, weak and ill people. It seems that toxic people don't even find satisfaction in knowing there are people worse off than themselves. They are completely without compassion for others.

One would expect that toxic people would at least love the people closest to them, but it seems that due to their unhealthily low self-esteem, they are be nicer to strangers than to their own family, even if it's only pretend niceness.

Toxic people don't appreciate or value themselves, so why would they appreciate or value others, even those closest to them who try to show love and respect. Toxic people can

Get Out of Your Own Way!

be so difficult to please or satisfy. There's only one hope and that is to rebuild and protect your own self-worth and to be happy regardless of others opinions.

When I met my partner she seemed happy to be in love with me. Perhaps it was because she had spent the previous five years alone and single that I was initially appreciated. In the beginning she was content to have a boyfriend.

However, it was only a matter of a few months before she became offensive. She started screaming at me and using toxic language trying to undermine my personal self-worth. This progressed into toxic behaviour where she would beat me with her fists and even used a chair to hit me.

Initially I was shocked and stunned. When I called the police to complain that my partner was using violence towards me, the policemen wouldn't take me seriously. They didn't want to listen or take my concerns seriously. Instead they tried to trivialise my problems as the guy who can't manage his own women. I was alone. I had to accept that there was nobody else who could help me deal with this.

Surviving Toxic Romantic Relationships

Why do we stay in toxic relationships?

We quickly learn to behave differently when we're around toxic people because their behaviour is unpredictable. We may choose to protect ourselves by withdrawing and being quieter than normal to *keep the peace*; or else the opposite occurs and we find we become aggressive back. Toxic relationships expose all of our worst characteristics, traits, behaviours and language. This is a lose-lose situation.

Believe it or not, we stay in toxic relationships because it is more comfortable than the alternative. It's the *comfort zone* that keeps us trapped. It may be unpleasant, even brutal to stay, but it's the reality we know. The relationship we are in is certain and we think we can manage it. Escaping is uncertain and may even be risky.

We also sometimes believe, and hope, that the toxic person who doesn't like, love or respect us will eventually change. We are waiting in vain for things to go back to the way they were at the beginning. This has something to do with the fact that by now, our self-worth has been eroded to the point that we allow another person to decide for us how much love and respect we do, or do not deserve.

It's only later, when we have escaped, that we are able remember the importance of respecting and loving oneself rather than trying to change somebody else's attitude towards us. After all, "a change imposed is a change opposed". We can only change ourselves so that's where our focus and energy needs to be directed.

Get Out of Your Own Way!

I was trying to get out from this unhealthy relationship. I went to psychotherapy to deal with it. I regularly attended group sessions to build a support structure in order to get out. Members of the group listened to my story. They helped me to analyse my situation. I grew stronger and even managed for a time to move away from this relationship, but like a lot of people, I was dragged back in. We had a newly built house, my daughter was born and it was to be a fresh start. However, as is often the way, things became even more complicated.

I created a successful training business and started earning serious money. I bought new appliances for the kitchen, electrical items, floor coverings, and was paying for all other expenses. I thought this would remove my guilt. It didn't. Apparently, I could never pay for more than she had already invested in the new house. To hear that everything I was doing wasn't enough kept me trapped in the guilt despite trying so hard to please her. The situation made me think deeply about my life.

How to escape with your life

End it now. Don't waste another minute dealing with a toxic, negative, energy-draining person. Don't waste valuable time trying to change them. Change yourself instead, change your circumstances and get a toxic person out of your life.

Don't say a word; leave all of your belongings if you have to; leave in the middle of the night, whatever it takes, just get out.

Then cut off all communication. Don't take their calls. You have heard all their lies before. They will not change. It is who they have decided to be. They don't choose to change themselves, instead they prefer to change and control you. So leave your job, move to another city if you must, just do what you need to do to start all over again because your life is worth it. You deserve to have peace of mind, a great relationship and an exciting life.

Undoubtedly, it can be difficult to get out and escape from such a toxic relationship, but if you don't make the move, what's the alternative?

Staying will only make your life unhappy and prolong the misery. Either way there is risk involved, the big question is: which of the two is the riskiest situation?

To help you safely extract yourself from any toxic relationship, you need to create an exit strategy. Also a plan B, both of which need to include *how* you are going to handle the toxic type you are escaping from to pre-empt all the *what if scenarios* that may happen. Preparation is always a fundamental key to successfully achieving a goal.

This is a sensible idea. Planning your exit strategy in your own time will build your confidence as well as give you a sense of control. Just knowing you have the tools and resources to implement your escape plan *when* the time is right, will help you achieve this as safely as possible. Considerations also need to include *how* and *when* you're going to end things. Don't forget to factor in *where* and *what* you will do afterwards, thinking ahead will minimise unforeseen issues.

Remember, if you are dealing with an angry, aggressive bully you do not need to break up with them in person, or escape alone. Part of your strategy may be to use any of the various communication mediums available today like text, e-mail, or phone. Alternatively, you may decide to call a friend, or a professional to be with you at this difficult time.

If the toxic person you are dealing with is a control freak, then your strategy may include giving them specific information and facts, so there is absolutely no ambiguity about your message. This can help them understand your rational for leaving them.

The key to ending any toxic relationship is to mean exactly what you say; don't apologise, don't get into a debate, don't proportion blame and most of all, mean what you say. This is not a time to show vulnerability.

Of course leaving someone, even a toxic someone, is going to be emotionally and possibly physically challenging. You must be prepared to experience a whole range of emotions from: guilt at leaving, to sadness over the loss of what you initially had, to the grief for what could have been in the future.

Whenever I would leave the house in the morning feeling angry and upset, I would stare at the nearby hotel across the road. I promised myself that one day, I would escape, because staying in this relationship was destroying me. It was literally stealing my energy, my money and my self-respect.

I tried to communicate this to my partner verbally in personal and by writing her letters, but she would not respond. I even scheduled a relationship therapy session for us, but my partner was not interested in receiving help of any kind. Thereafter, I finally understood and accepted that I was not able to fix our relationship.

I was still being supported by my psychotherapist who said I needed to clearly state *I'm leaving* in no uncertain terms to my partner. That way she would have to understand and accept that this relationship was finished.

During the morning of Sunday the first of November we were all lying on the floor; my partner was absently-mindedly playing with our daughter. I suddenly realised that I was no longer prepared to be invisible. I got up and unexpectedly started packing my things. I then said "this relationship is over" and left. I moved into the hotel across the road.

How to stay out

The exit strategy you planned was about implementing the *how* and *when*. The next stage is about *where* you go from here, and *what* you do, and hopefully *who* will be supporting you. This is important because on the one hand it's a liberating stage in more ways than one. Yet it's also a potentially lonely and anxious time, hence the support, be it from personal, or professional means, we all need someone on our side.

This is the time to nurture your own needs. I decided to go shopping for personal items the same day I moved out. Unfortunately, due to festivities, the shops were closed so instead I went to the gas station to buy something good to eat. I spent one month in hotels travelling to courses I was teaching. When I was staying in hotels I used the opportunity to comfort and pamper myself by utilising the

Get Out of Your Own Way!

SPA facilities.

To stay away from toxic relationships one needs to create a certain support structure. This includes the need for safe and nurturing relationships in healthy environments. Both will help you survive the most difficult times. What you've known and were familiar with is now gone. The future is unknown and may be uncomfortable. Therefore, it's all too easy to retreat back to a previous relationship. It's natural. It's commonplace to go back. I did. A couple of times! This time was different. I meant it. I wanted my toxic relationship to be over, finished for good, so finally, I decided not to go back.

One month later I rented an apartment nearby in order to stay close to my daughter. Those first days in that empty apartment were quite difficult, there was nothing personal inside. I went to the florists to buy flower to brighten up my new home. I saw a bamboo tree and I realised that was a good symbol for my situation. This bamboo could show me how to survive, stay strong and yet be flexible all at the same time. This small tree helped me to go through my most difficult times.

The friends and the family of an ex-toxic partner are not the best people to go to for support after the relationship is finished. Therefore, it's important to find new friends and to create new acquaintances. New positive and supporting relationships are supposed to show new life perspectives as well as broaden the vision for a new life ahead.

I had to leave everything known to me behind in order to accept an unknown future. I had to *learn to stand on my own two feet* so when my father offered to support me, I declined because I needed time to adjust and understand my situation as well as re-organise my life.

I went online to find new social contacts. I joined one of the dating websites, and after browsing for similar interests, I found my current wife. I had carefully examined her approach and attitude via on-line chat before engaging further. I couldn't afford another mistake. Therefore we spent two weeks talking on-line and over the phone to understand each other. When we met in real life I was surprised by her calm and warm nature. It was like discovering a new world and being anchored in a safe harbour after a long time of stormy seas and bad weather. I am still a father for my daughter and I have not forgotten about her, but this new friendship and love helped me to become happy again.

It's important to concentrate on the positive aspects of any situation. Remember, a toxic person is happiest when someone else is worse off than them. Therefore, reframe from engaging in language or behaviours which is likely to satisfy them. Instead, let the past go and concentrate on own successes future.

It was obviously not the end of the story because I still had my daughter living with her mother where I had left my personal and household belongings. Therefore, I needed to maintain contact with my previous partner. It has taken about seven years to unravel the situation in the courts. I have lost the case over my money and belongings so walked away with nothing. I had three court cases to achieve regular contact with my daughter. That process took time, money and energy but it was worth it. I was free from this toxic relationship and free to live my life again.

Get Out of Your Own Way!

Strategies for dealing with toxic parents

What if the toxic relationship is with your parents?

While entering into new relationships we usually don't wonder about previous relationships which may influence new bonds. However, the one important relationship we need to take into account is the relationship we have with our parents.

I understood that there must be something stronger than just being in my own *comfort zone* which kept me in my toxic relationship. I realised as a client of psychotherapy, that the *cause* of my behaviour could be traced back to my relationship with my parents.

Some parents do support and love us. Sadly, there's also some which do the opposite. Therefore, the relationship we have with our parents can also be toxic. Consequently, they can also negatively influence future relationships with significant others in our adult life.

I was raised by a single parent, namely my mother. My parents separated when I was just four years old. My father was living some 300 kilometres away. Therefore, I couldn't see him more than three or four times a year. While my mother remained single, my father decided to remarry and have another child (daughter).

Toxic parents come in all guises. They may simply be inept, or addicted to some stimulant, or they may deliberately be inadequate. Regardless, they all put themselves and their needs first. Sometimes, parents simply repeat what they learnt from their own parents; so they may turn out to be control freaks, verbal and or physical abusers.

When I was young my mother relied very much on my opinion. She would talk with me about subjects too difficult and complex for a youngster. She was a working mother and because she worked shifts, she wasn't at home the majority of the time I was. I would call her an inadequate parent because she left me alone and expected things from me which were not appropriate for a child of my age.

My father on the other hand was a controller. Whenever we met he always tried to impose his lifestyle and values onto me. For example: he wanted me to be sporty despite being a fat child. He wanted me to attend the church and be religious when I was not convinced about my faith.

He was also an inadequate parent. When I met my father's fiancée she was quite nice and tried to gain my acceptance. But when they were married she changed her approach and I couldn't visit my father at his home anymore. When I did, his wife made an aggressive scene, even throwing canned food at him. My father was explaining that we couldn't see each other more frequently because his wife is against it. He wanted me to accept this situation, but the truth is, he was expecting me (his child) to solve his own problems with wife and he couldn't deal with it.

Susan Forward in her book *Toxic Parents* suggests that forgiving parents is not necessarily the most straight forward solution to moving forward. Apparently, when we forgive others we're likely to absorb the blame ourselves. Therefore, it's better to apportion the blame to the parents for their inadequacies.

Get Out of Your Own Way!

My parents deserted me emotionally. I was either left alone by my single working mother, or indoctrinated by my father to live his one and only acceptable way of living. No wonder I couldn't be alone for even a shorter time. I was afraid of being on my own. Hence it was exceedingly difficult for me to leave my own toxic relationship as an adult. I was alone most of my childhood and youth, so I would rather accept being with somebody who hurt me, rather than stay alone.

We often feel we are still under the influence of parents as if we were still little children, even into adulthood. We still expect their acceptance and want to deserve their acknowledgements. This makes it easy for them to continue controlling what we do: either we do what they want, or they don't accept and acknowledge us. As adults we need to understand our beliefs in order to know what is generating our behaviours. We will be then able to regain control over what we do, think and feel.

When I had introduced a new girlfriend to my mother she would be usually nice, but when she met my wife for the first time she behaved rude and was not nice. It took some time for my mother to learn to accept my wife as my choice. They now have good relationship, but in the beginning it was difficult.

It is also important to remember that as an adult we do not have to think, feel or behave in the same way as our parents. When we are determined to think, feel and behave as we choose, we also need to accept that our parents might not be happy or approve of the decisions we take, and that's fine, we do not need their approval to be happy.

I was a child when my father expected me to be religious. He used to go to church and expected me to believe in God as he did. In order to satisfy his expectations I would attend church even though I wasn't convinced it made sense. When I was 14 years old I decided not to go to church anymore. It has taken me the following 20 years to stop feeling guilty about it and understand why I stopped.

I've realised it's also quite acceptable to take care of myself first without taking my parents into consideration. I've learnt that if we don't treat ourselves with respect and care it's a real possibility that others will not treat you with respect either.

Growing up I felt incredibly responsible for my mother. She had been responsible for me when I was young, now it was my turn to be responsible for her. I was even escorting her to the ATM so that she could withdraw her money safely. I was overprotective for her. It has taken me a number of years to realise I need to be looking after my own interests first.

Therapists suggest confronting inadequate parents, virtually or in person, may be a useful way to break negative cycles with them, there's the option to rebuild relationships if that's what you wish, and to *clear the air* about whatever happened, then describe what you want, need or are willing to accept moving forward.

A popular cathartic tool to instigate healing is to write the toxic person a letter. Writing a letter creates a structure for you to say what you want to say about what they did to you and how it's influenced your life choices. Also how you felt / feel and what you expect in future. It doesn't matter if the person is alive or dead, whether the letter is posted or burnt, it's the act of saying what you need to say that's important. Of course if the confrontation occurs in person, a safe neutral place with a mediator is recommended.

I realised from my therapy session when I was almost hitting the pillow, which symbolised my father, that I held a lot of anger towards him. As a result, I found it quite difficult to deal with older men in authority positions. There were times when I had no contact with my father for years. With the help of my therapist I decided to write him a letter. It took me three hours of constant writing to fully express everything I've ever wanted to say to him. I gave this letter to my father personally and asked to him to read it. When we met next time he said he had read the letter and agrees with many points and disagreed with others, but he never commented more than that on what I have written.

It's important to accept that the reaction of our parents can be different to what we expect. They can use various defensive mechanisms to preserve the status quo and maintain their authority image. The most important thing is to define new rules for your adult to adult relationship. Know what your rights are, be strong enough to assert them and be confident enough to honour your boundaries so your individuality is respected. Parents can accept them or not, but this is never more important than it is in a relationship with controlling parents. You have to be the one who is controlling the situation. You decide if you continue the relationship, or if you want to abandon it in the event your rules are not respected.

When I met my wife I decided to involve my father in our relationship. He was invited to our home. We asked him to come to our wedding and for the birthdays of our children.

We tried to involve my father in our life again and again but he was never certain if he could make it. He was still so under the influence of his wife and accepted that he could only come when she didn't know about it. We couldn't visit him at his (and his wife's) apartment because she would not allow it. My father was denying our existence and was able to sacrifice our relationship in order to satisfy his relationship with his wife. He was above all very attached to his catholic religion. Although he was not officially divorced from my mother, so living with his second wife, he was constantly presenting himself as fiercely catholic. He was living in denial of his sins and when he tried to indoctrinate our children with religion we took control and discontinued the relationship.

What is most important for us to recognise is that being an adult means we are responsible for our own happiness. That means our primary responsibility is to love and accept ourselves even though our parents did not, or do not meet our needs for love and acceptance.

Toxic In-laws

Toxic in-laws can also make for a miserable life. When we fall in love we think we are entering into a new relationship with our partner. We are in fact entering the social system of our partner's whole family where the roles have already been defined, and where the status quo is well established. We are happy when we are welcomed into a family with loving acceptance by understanding in-laws. What happens when we aren't?

When I met my current wife for the first time she was calm and quiet for a reason. That was because she was still dependent on her mother. This was yet another toxic parental relationship to take into consideration in our daily life as new partners.

> Susan Forward in her book *The Toxic In-laws* defines toxic in-laws as following:
> 1. *The Critics:* these parents critique anything and everything you do, whether you ask for their opinion or not.
> 2. *The Engulfers:* these parents think because they raised you, they own you as if you were an extension of their personal property.
> 3. *The Controllers:* the alpha parents who dominant you, your partner and your children, if you let them.
> 4. *The Masters of Chaos;* these parents are often self-absorbed by their own issues, as a coping mechanism, they project their issues onto their adult children.
> 5. *The Rejecters;* are parents who tend to love conditionally; if you don't follow their rules and ideals, you are rejected as unsuitable to partner their lovely child.

These definitions are based on couples. Of course one in-law may fit one category, while another fits another category, further complicating what is already a complex situation.

My new girlfriend was 29 years old and obviously heavily under the influence of her mother. She tried to control everything her daughter was doing by shopping for her groceries, her clothes and doing her cooking. It wasn't unusual for her to call her daughter a couple of times each day, and if she didn't get a response, would think nothing of phoning around to enquire where her adult child was.

My in-laws may have been divorced for many years, but the ex-husband was still very much dependent on his former wife. He always listened and obeyed whatever she said. Even her other daughter to lives in France was controlled over the phone.

So when I have entered into the family dynamics I was treated as the stranger and foe who wanted to take away the eldest daughter. I was initially renting my own flat, but as the relationship grew closer, I moved into my girlfriend's apartment. I was then accused of wanting to steal the family's money even though I was paying half the rent. My in-laws become *rejecters* critiquing me in a bid to scare me away.

I was not so easy to scare away. Before long the unannounced visits started from my soon to be mother-in-law, her behaviour was unpleasant and designed to undermined our relationship.

The solution to our problems is in the way we treat ourselves and others which reinforces how we want to be treated in return. Therefore, we have to start from a place of self-reflection and self-love in order to be able to face toxic in-laws.

Typical problems experienced with toxic in-laws are exacerbated by being:
- A victim and there's nothing we can do to release the control our in-laws have.
- Too reactive and responsive to what in-laws are who may make us look ridiculous, if the response is not adequate for the situation.
- Unreactive which gives the in-laws the perception

we've accepted the situation as it is.
- Unrealistic about how you will be when provoked by in-laws.
- Unrealistic about your partner's ability to shield and protect us from their parents.
- Unrealistic about in-laws willingness to accept and love us when they don't even have to like us.

What is important to remember is we all have rights and we have the right to protect them.

Eventually we left my partner's family flat and moved to my smaller flat and started a new life completely on our own. I proposed to my partner and she agreed to marry me. We started planning our wedding. My mother-in-law proposed to pay for it in order to decide when and where the wedding will be and how it will work. We refused and organised it according to our own plans. It gave us control over what we wanted. It also released us from any future feelings of reciprocity.

What we need to do is speak to our partner and:
1. Set new boundaries; defining concrete rules which you both agree on will define how you operate in your relationship with in-laws.
2. State your position by expressing factually, without blame or other emotion your perception of the current situation.
3. Communicate without being defensive what is important moving forward.

After we were married my mother-in-law started treating me as her own personal property and tried to make me comply with her rules as she did the rest of the family e.g.

she organised Christmas a week early just to make all her grandchildren spend more time with her rather than their grandfather. I spoke to my wife about it stating that I did not want us to be part of this spectacle which makes only my mother-in-law happy. We discussed this and decided not to take part in her plans. Instead, took part in family gatherings on our own terms.

It's crucial to involve the partner in any discussions about situations arising, rather than repress emotions, because they may prove to be your most important supporter of our rights. Situations like these are difficult tests for any partnership as they prove how resilient a bond is. There could be two results:
1. our partner will support us, or
2. they will take the side of their parents.

It could even be necessary to consider divorce if the partner continues to refuse to respect our rights because it turns out they are more attached to their parents than they are to their new family. This result is a sad one, but this could be better than staying in unsupportive and toxic relationships. We have to take into consideration that our most important obligation is to love and respect ourselves.

We have discussed the situation and my wife has accepted my position. Consequently, we confronted our in-laws together at my psychotherapist office where we felt comfortable to do so in a controlled environment. As a result we now limit the amount of information we share with my mother-in-law so she can no longer conspire against us with my father-in-law. We have finally succeeded in separating both relationships with father-in-law and mother-in-law. Now we have decent relationships, at least, with one of them; my father-in-law was fortunately able to spend time with us without any controlling influences.

Conclusion

"Pause and remember — you deserve peace! So, don't feel bad for one moment about walking away from people, jobs, and situations that keep you from having peace of mind".
Jenni Young

In our wildest dreams we may want to escape from a toxic relationship. However, in reality running away is not always an option. Escaping from what is wrong can also undermine our self-worth because it suggests we are unable to deal with our problems. Therefore, it's important to deal with toxic relationships no matter how challenging. Doing so could even help raise our self-respect and confidence. If we do, we need to take certain factors into consideration.

It seems there's much more important action to be taken and it's not about others. It's about us. We need to focus on self-love and self-understanding because this is self-acceptance which will help us to deal with difficult and toxic people.

It's important to understand that people will do to us whatever we allow them to do. Therefore, defending our rights to be happy, respected and loved is important. When we accept these rights as our own, fighting for them will be much easier.

Utilising the support of professionals to help us understand how our past influences our current behaviours and emotions is proven to be helpful. Therapy can really help us get back in touch with what, why and how we feel. It can also help us to analyse our responses to the toxic situations we are experiencing as well as help us find appropriate responses. This specialised help can also help us navigate the difficulties of facing toxic people and transforming our approach towards them.

There's another important factor we should take into consideration too when dealing with toxic behaviours and people, and that is love of others. Obviously it's difficult to face people who don't like, or even hate us. However, it's important to use emotional support from those who want us to succeed and win. Love is one of the strongest human stimuli and this is the key element which can save us.

Thank you for reading my story and I wish you very happy ending of your story as well. Take care and love yourself.

Get Out of Your Own Way!

Tomasz Nędzi - Biography

Tomasz Nędzi has been involved in managing change since 1993. He started his first enterprise at 19 years old while studying at Management Faculty of Warsaw's University. After graduating, he joined IBM to consult and project manage national telco operator NASK.

He graduated from Executive MBA (Warsaw University of Technology, London Business School, HEC, NHH) and started his own training and consulting enterprise *Skills®* in 2004 which continues to thrive under his management. Consequently, he has trained thousands of project managers, risk managers and program managers as a PRINCE2® / Agile PM® / MSP® / M_o_R® / P3O® / OBASHI / Facilitation Approved Trainer.

He added coaching to his skill set in 2009 and graduated from Noble Manhattan with a Practitioner Coach Diploma and an Executive & Corporate Coach Diploma. He is an Accredited Practitioner Coach with the International Institute of Coaching & Mentoring (IIC&M). Tomasz is also the Head of Country representative for IIC&M in Poland.

Tomasz is a sought after public speaker and writer for national and international publications. He promotes best management practices including coaching, mentoring and facilitation for professionals. He is also a successful project/program coach helping organizations to better manage their investments during periods of change.

Having successfully overcome many obstacles to achieve a happy work-life balance with healthy relationships at home, and in the workplace, Tomasz is ideally placed to help clients overcome their own obstacles, self-sabotage and escape toxic relationships. To find out exactly how he helps clients achieve happier, healthier lifestyle goals and habits, contact him here www.skills.pl

Get Out of Your Own Way!

Section Six
Reflexology for Health

by
Danielle Lindsay

"If you're feeling out of kilter, don't know why, or what about, let your feet reveal the answer, find the sore spot and work it out". - Eunice Ingham

Get Out of Your Own Way!

The Healing Power of Reflexology

I have a new sense of purpose which is to write about alternative health; the options available to us, *and* the benefits of utilising them for our well-being. My areas of expertise are: Reflexology and Homeopathy. I'll be writing about Homeopathy in the next *Dial A Guru* series, in the meantime, let's discover the healing potential of Reflexology.

We totally take our feet for granted. Every day we expect them to take the pounding we give them without question. We rarely give them the attention they deserve. There are not many people who don't appreciate and enjoy a really good foot rub. The reason why? Well, on our feet we have a map of the body reflecting all of the organs, muscles, bones, and tissues which are stimulated by touch and bring about a healing response.

Reflexology was developed many thousands of years ago in Egypt, India, and Russia and further developed in China. This is explained at greater length under my history section. Although it is not actually pin-pointed where it originated from, all of these nations enjoyed its benefits.

Dr William Fitzgerald was the first known person to bring Reflexology to modern times, and Eunice Ingham brought it even further forward into the 20th century. Many adaptations have been discovered by practicing on the face, ears, hands and even the tongue!

When you receive a Reflexology treatment, the Reflexologist will use a thumb walking procedure to detect any imbalances in the body. Depending on where an imbalance is found on the foot, it will correlate to that part of the body (charts are provided further down for your information).

The Reflexologist will feel several different sensations when they are working from: cold or hot areas, to pinheads, crystals, bubbles or gristle. This can mean many things. However, the main point is these sensations signal an imbalance in that part of the body. The client may also feel certain sensations too: a tingling, or pulsating feeling, either in their feet, or in different parts of their body.

Apart from the fact that Reflexology is highly relaxing, working on correcting any imbalances will bring greater health and well-being. One such imbalance is caused by stress, which is becoming a major factor in our lives today due to the pressures of juggling work-life balance. Consequently, there is an increasing need to unwind and de-stress.

As I glance up from writing these words, I see from my window people rushing around due to their busy lives and schedules. These same people do not give themselves enough ME time. These people are also the ones that tend to find it hard to *switch off*, or *let go* of all their stresses at the end of a hard day.

The question I have for them is 'Do you live to work or work to live'? When we finally achieve the right balance, stress is no longer a factor in the equation. I am lucky, I live to work and I very much enjoy what I do.

Get Out of Your Own Way!

> Q. What's your answer to the question "do you live to work or work to live"?
>
> A.

I ask so many people "Are you happy with your life"? Many answer with "I get by", "I would love to be", "But I don't think it's possible", or "I can't afford to" and so on. You'll find more space to answer these insightful questions in the accompanying workbook also available on Amazon.

> Q. What's your answer to "are you happy with your life"?
>
> A.

Inspiration about issues and how best to address them tends to come up during a treatment, especially when there is a good connection between the Reflexologist and the client; even more so when a client brings a certain self-awareness, clarity, and a focussed approach to addressing those concerns. The rapport between Reflexologist and client is just as important as the treatment itself.

Get Out of Your Own Way!

Reflexology provides you with the time out needed to relax and focus, and when we do we can regain clarity, it sometimes feels like an epiphany. At the end of a treatment clients say things like: "I have just figured it all out"! Or "I need to change this or that to allow me to move on, why didn't I do this before"? And "I feel like this is where I fit in. I love what I do". So many times we *settle* so do not exceed, or strive to do more than we are capable of.

When I am working on a person's feet, I kind of tune into that person's energy and intuitively know what to work on. After being a Reflexologist for fifteen years, you really get to understand someone's feet just by looking at them. For instance, when the feet are particularly dry and cracked with a *yellowy* build up on the balls of the feet I am usually able to tell if they were once, or still are, a smoker. This is showing me there is a toxic build up in the lungs; the dryness indicating a lack of nutrients being absorbed, and probably dehydration too.

I have worked on people who have very ticklish feet and even though I always reassure them that it will NOT tickle, they are sceptical, but as soon as I start working on them, they tend to melt into a state of relaxation. Some people simply cannot stand anyone touching their feet, or even have other people looking at them. I explain just how important and precious their feet are and let's give them a bit of love! However, if it is a real major problem I always offer Reflexology on their hands instead.

> **Mini Case Study:**
> Client J had terribly deformed feet and he was incredibly ashamed of them. He suffered with a lot of nerve damage to his toes and balls of his feet. His wife encouraged him to

> come and have a few treatments with me as it had helped her in the past. He came very reluctantly and at first was not sure if he enjoyed it. After his first treatment he went away still feeling ashamed of his feet and said that he would call me and book again. He took a little while, in fact, two weeks went by before I had heard from him again. He booked for the following week saying he would give it another go. The reason he came back was that he had experienced a new sensation in his right little toe. He duly had his second treatment and again the next day he had further sensations. He continued to have 6 more treatments and by his 10th could move his toes independently. This was a huge experience for him as this had not been possible for many years. He still comes to me for treatments every now and then when he feels the need.

I have worked with people on a variety of issues; one issue being **infertility**, three clients have since gone on to carry through a successful full term pregnancy.

Also working on children who have been diagnosed with **Attention Deficit Hyperactivity** Disorder (ADHD) and Reflexology has produced great results in calming them down in helping them to learn to relax when they feel angry or anxious, in fact, Reflexology helps immensely with anxiety (see my mini case under the stress section) regardless of age or gender.

Reflexology can rebalance each and every bodily system: from the nervous, endocrine, lymphatic, circulatory, hormonal, reproductive and digestive systems. Working on all these levels brings increased mental, physical and emotional well-being benefits. Many of my clients report experiencing much better sleep patterns that continued to improve *after* regular therapy treatments. As good quality sleep is essential for healing, this is an important step in aiding the body's ability to recover. Reflexology is great for relieving the symptoms of **Chronic Fatigue Syndrome** and increasing energy levels in general, especially the days following treatment.

The feet constantly take a pounding every day and they are our shock absorbers, the amount of pressure that they have to undergo is beyond imaginable. For instance, when we are running we are placing approximately 3-4 times our own body weight of pressure on each foot step. Even at our optimum healthiest weight it is a huge pressure on our feet! This can show in the foot by hardening of skin and blistering for instance. Bunions are also a sure sign of pressure on the body and quite often it shows up in a related problem with the neck and upper spine; build up on the balls of the feet can show signs of stress on the chest.

The working mechanism of the foot consists of 26 little bones, tendons and ligaments. Each tiny bone does such an amazing job of keeping us upright; it seems impossible that our comparatively tiny feet keep our tall bodies standing and walking (which is great exercise for keeping our skeleton strong).

Whilst having a Reflexology treatment the Reflexologist will work on the lymphatic drainage area contained in our calves. This will help with the bodily water distribution system. Having worked with people suffering with the effects of water retention such as bloating in the lower abdomen and leg swellings, this has proved to be of huge benefit as Reflexology aids in balancing fluids in the body.

Get Out of Your Own Way!

Here is a list of the many ailments Reflexology can help with:
Allergies, Arthritis, Asthma, Back Problems, Blood Pressure, Bowel Disorders, Constipation, Eczema, Frozen Shoulder, Gynaecological Disorders, Hay Fever, Insomnia, Knee Problems, Multiple Sclerosis, Muscle Tension, Neck Problems, PMS/Hormonal Problems, Respiratory Problems, Sinusitis, Stress Disorders, Thyroid Imbalance, Aid in Circulatory problems, Lymph Drainage, Water Retention and Relaxation.

The Balance of Reflexology

From a young age I always enjoyed writing. I loved to read too and would make up stories about what would happen next following on from famous fairy tales. I have recently rekindled my passion for writing, and little did I know that this opportunity would present itself in the form of being published within the *Dial A Guru* series. When I was approached to write about Reflexology, I was thrilled to be able to use my writing skills to share the benefits of this amazing therapy with a wider audience.

Sometimes you just have an urge to do something completely different, especially after doing the same thing for a long time which can make you become stagnant. I always knew that I was supposed to work in the healing world and wanted to help people in any way that I could. As my mother was a Reflexologist, she was my inspiration to become one too. Little did I know that it was just the beginning of my healing journey.

At this point in my life I was a single mum of one and found it hard to balance work and life. However, with the loving support of my family, I found the time, and money to retrain. I trained at the *Kristine Walker School of Reflexology* in Brighton, East Sussex qualifying in 2000.

"A leap of faith is sometimes really scary, but also sometimes the best decision in your life. As a big believer in fate I just knew this was a path for me".

Whilst training to become a Reflexologist, I found I had a natural rhythm when learning the different techniques. What I loved the most was discovering the differences in each person's foot: the shape, instep depth, and also the colour and textures.

The different sensations I felt whilst working on the feet could be: hot, cold, pulsations, pinheads, crystals, gristles and bubbles. Sometimes you can feel the energy flow from point to point which is really something special. This is known as *Linking*. It is as though the energy bounces backwards and forwards until it becomes balanced. For many clients this experience is quite extraordinary.

The Theory part of training really intrigued me. We learnt the basics in Anatomy and Physiology. I have always craved knowledge and have been interested in Biology from a young age. I once considered the idea of becoming a Doctor. Little did I know that later in life I would effectively become a Doctor of natural medicines! I loved learning about the intricacies of how the body works. How all of the tiny synapses in the body make a connection to deliver a control or impulse. How each and every muscle in our bodies contract and relax.

The Human body is truly amazing and its ability to self-heal

Get Out of Your Own Way!

once given the necessary environment and nourishment is nothing short of a miracle.

History of Reflexology and its development

Not many people know that Reflexology was used in Egypt in 5000 BC; there are hieroglyphics and paintings in caves of Egyptians working on each other's feet. However, it is extremely difficult to pinpoint *who* actually discovered, or invented Reflexology as the Chinese were also practicing Reflexology around the same period.

The Sanskrit inscriptions on Buddha's feet stand as evidence of its use in India, and The Native Americans also included Reflexology as part of their health care. Having been used in China approximately 5000 years ago which developed alongside acupuncture (A.D. 1027), it is recorded being used as an energy-balancing procedure.

Over centuries of time Reflexology has been developed immensely. The Chinese developed the meridian zones and was later called *Zone Therapy*. The first recorded book based on zone therapy was written in 1582 by Dr Adamis and Dr A'tatis.

In the 1900's a team of Doctors led by Dr William Fitzgerald began using *reflex points* for pain relief. Dr Fitzgerald and Dr

Get Out of Your Own Way!

Edwin Bowers re-discovered and wrote about zone therapy. They also developed and described the 10 vertical zones from the tip of the head spreading down to the hand and legs to the tip of the toes. From this work it was found that zone therapy also has a therapeutic effect beyond pain relief.

Also in the early 1900's Eunice Ingham, a physiotherapist, working alongside Dr George Shelby-Riley, who also worked with Dr Fitzgerald, felt that the feet should be the specific area to work on for zone therapy due to their highly sensitive nature. She charted the feet in relation to the zones, and their effects on the rest of the body, until she evolved with a map of the body on the feet.

She also found that by applying alternating pressure, rather than constant pressure, she achieved remarkable results beyond pain reduction. She also discovered that working on these painful sites, over a period of several treatments, that a state of *normal* function could usually be restored. Being so successful, her reputation spread as a foot therapist.

In 1938 Eunice Ingham wrote *Stories the Feet Can Tell* and *Stories Feet Have Told*. Consequently, she is now recognized as the founder of the National Institute of foot Reflexology. She went on to lecture in many medical schools across the United States and Canada. The International Institute of Reflexology was established in 1973 to promote her technique which is now known as the *Original Ingham Method*. She taught Doreen Bayley who in 1966 brought Reflexology to England.

Reflexology is a *holistic therapy* working on the physical, emotional and psychological levels taking many things into consideration, for instance *how* a person is feeling, the circumstances they are dealing with, and the pressures it has on their lifestyle. Reflexology allows the person to relax and the treatment stimulates and removes blockages that have built up, giving them energy releases and allowing the person to heal physically and emotionally if needed.

Modern medicine treats the body like a car where you replace bits that don't work, or use drugs that are toxic for the body to re-correct a problematic *symptom*. Little attention is given to what is *causing* the problem in the first place. Our bodies are actually incredibly able to heal by themselves. If you cut yourself, the wound naturally heals by itself, and given the right conditions it will heal internally as well.

There are various theories as to why Reflexology works: one is that it stimulates senses from within the brain which has a knock on effect throughout the body. Another is that it works on chi energy as in acupuncture.

"I believe that when you train to practice Reflexology, your intuitive natural gift blossoms to help people. You help people to help themselves. They begin taking control back for their health and feel empowered in the process".

Our hands and feet have special functions other than just being tools. They are our first indicators to safety and danger. Our sensory preceptors are continually working to tell us that 'something doesn't feel right'. That feeling is expressed with a thought like: you're *treading on eggshells*, or when you put your *best foot forward.* All are instincts that something maybe a potential threat.

Get Out of Your Own Way!

If the client is unable to have Reflexology on their feet for any reason e.g. they are an amputee case, then hand Reflexology is a good alternative. Amputees have even been known to report that the sensation is still felt from the energy of the missing limb which can be of great benefit for phantom limb pain.

> **Mini Case Study:**
> Client G had his left leg amputated due to health reasons and was referred to me for relaxation and to help with phantom limb pains. I worked on his right foot as normal and then worked by using gentle strokes around the area of the missing limb. He was surprised that he still had sensations in response to my touch. He received great benefit from the treatments and the phantom limb pains greatly reduced.

Our brains have a blueprint of the body as a whole. Even when limbs or organs are missing, a client can still report experiencing sensations with that part of the body. Reflexology can bring great relief in this situation mentally as well as physically.

The body is such an intricate vessel, and with holistic treatments it can work wonders, sometimes beyond our belief. When you work holistically with some people, little miracles really do happen. Have you ever tried Reflexology? Are you intrigued? The benefits are sometimes astounding and working together as a complimentary therapy, alongside many other therapies can bring results to a beautiful healing journey.

Treatments and what to expect

Reflexology can be done in a treatment room, in the comfort of your own home, on the beach, or even in the park! The beauty of this means that the Reflexologist comes to you!

In a traditional holistic treatment room tranquil and soothing music can be played to create a relaxing atmosphere, the room will be warm and inviting and usually there would be candles burning to create a nice ambient light.

As the body needs to be fully supported and relaxed for a treatment; most Reflexologist use either a massage couch, or a reclining chair to provide the most comfortable position for the client's relaxation and they are covered in a warm soft blanket for that essential pampered feeling.

When you first visit a Reflexologist you will be required to give a detailed medical history, your lifestyle, occupation and sleep patterns. This is to help the Reflexologist work on past imbalances and for you to point out problems you feel needs attention.

A first appointment will last one to two hours following which, the Reflexologist will determine how many treatments you will need. Additional treatments will last anywhere between 30-40 minutes. A course of treatments will be on average one per week for approximately six weeks to experience real results. However, many clients enjoy Reflexology and feel the benefits so much they just keep coming back again and again.

Get Out of Your Own Way!

The Reflexologist will study the feet before starting the treatment to evaluate any problem areas, and get an overall picture of the person's health. Once settled into the couch or reclining chair the Reflexologist will massage with either a little grape seed, wheat-germ oil or baby oil when there is intolerance to the other oils, this helps move their hands across the feet with ease. They will then work systematically over each foot, ankle and calve to seek out and treat any problem areas. This is done with a compression technique known as *thumb-walking*. This is a caterpillar like movement, generally using the thumb or index finger which clears congestion in those parts of the body corresponding to congested reflexes by improving lymphatic, nerve and blood circulation.

A Reflexologist can tell so much from just looking at the feet: how they fall, their colour, their shape and structure are all vital indicators of what is going on in the body. For instance: red areas below the little toes could indicate inflammation in or around the shoulder. Yellow areas on the balls of the feet could show problems with the lungs. Inflexibility in the ankle could relate to inflexibility in the hips. So when a Reflexologist is working on these areas the client may experience a slight sensitivity which would indicate an imbalance in their energy system. The Reflexologist would recognise this and pay extra attention to them allowing the energy to flow freely once again.

As the body begins to relax, the client becomes more clear headed and able to view their life from a different perspective which leads to an improvement in their general well-being.

As I said, whilst Reflexology is mainly carried out on the feet,

Get Out of Your Own Way!

when this is not possible it can be done on the hands because they have the same reflex points. In fact, hands are just as sensitive as feet, sometimes even more so and healing has been reported to be faster when done on the hands.

A side effect of this wonderful therapy is that the client feels like *they are walking on air*, in fact often these are the very words they say as they leave the treatment room.

"Each and every person is different, but giving yourself permission to have time out for you and only you, is a huge part of the treatment too".

As I explain during my stress section to find quality *me time* is increasingly difficult and to acknowledge the importance of this is an absolute must in today's society. At some point in our lives we end up saying:
- "I need to put myself first, and if I don't look after myself, who will"?
- "I NEED time out and I need it NOW"!
- "I need the space and time to switch off from everyday life".

"If you feel burnout setting in, if you feel demoralised, or exhausted, it is best, for the sake of everyone, around you to withdraw and restore yourself". His Holiness the Dalai Lama.

When we start to put ourselves first, it allows us to value our lives, our health and well-being. To enable yourself to re-charge your batteries is an absolute necessity!

Mini Case:

Get Out of Your Own Way!

> **Client F:** Frozen shoulder. Client F was a 46 year old male who had a frozen right shoulder and was told that he would need to have surgery and further pain medication to correct it. He was not happy with this decision as he was a big believer in holistic therapies. I worked on the shoulder reflexes on both feet and after 7 treatments he had a huge improvement on movement and reduced pain in his shoulder.

Here are some charts which show you where the maps of the organs reflex points are on the feet and hands:

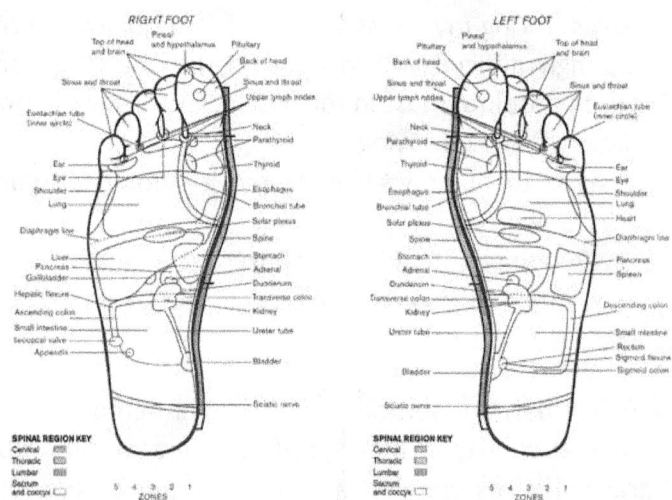

Figure a:

Get Out of Your Own Way!

Hand Reflexology Map (palmar side)

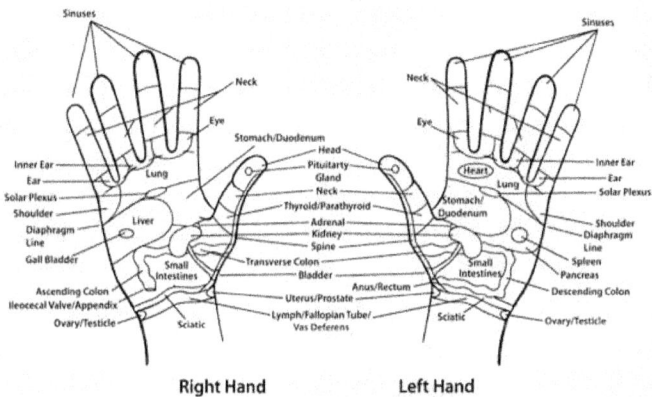

Right Hand   Left Hand

Figure b:

As you can see from the above charts the reflex points are very similar in both the hands and feet. There are mainly two reflex points, one on each side. The only difference is that the heart reflex point remains on the left sides, also the liver reflex point is only on the right sides. The only other difference is the large colon which as you can see flows from the right hand/foot, starting at the Ileocecal valve to the ascending colon then the transverse colon across to the left hand/foot to the descending colon and sigmoid colon.

When there is congestion, the client may have a possible reaction / side effect after a Reflexology treatment, in that they could have cold like symptoms such as a runny nose. This is due to the toxins and congestions being released. Tiredness is a common side effect due to toxins clearing from the body and rest is needed to continue healing. So it's a good idea to drink plenty of water after a treatment to help the body eliminate toxins quicker. Experiencing any symptoms is a great sign as it shows that the treatments are really working.

However, after having continued treatments you could also find that your side effect includes an increase in energy. Revitalisation is one huge benefit due to balancing of the body's Chi.

Stress and what happens to the body:-
Each and every one of us will at some point in our lives reach an uncomfortable level of stress; whether it is low, or high, we cannot avoid it. Each person will experience stress differently: *Anxiety, headaches, tension, neck pain, shoulders and back pain, raised blood pressure; eyestrain, migraines, constipation, indigestion, hypertension, hyperventilation, asthma, pre-menstrual tension, painful periods, and insomnia are some of the more common physical, mental and emotional signs and factors of stress.* They also deal with stress in different ways.

The most common cause of stress is as a result of how we perceive and experience life; we may feel upset that we aren't doing everything we ought to be doing because we haven't got enough money, time or energy. An example could be that a child asks his mother for a pair of Reebok trainers that everyone else is wearing, but at that moment in time the mother does not have the funds, but the child keeps on and on about them and the mother gets stressed because of the pressure and persistence of the child.

A person once said to me "I'm so stressed out, I can't eat, I can't sleep, I'm so fed up, and I just don't want to do anything anymore, what's the point"? Her stress was due to depression amongst other things, she'd broken up with her long-time partner and seemed to have totally lost track of things. She hated her job and was generally very unhappy. So she sat down and wrote a list of things she needed and wanted to do to change her lifestyle. She worked her way out of her stress level and reached a happier, calmer state by focusing on the things she could to be grateful for.

A positive mental attitude will do wonders and changing from a negative thinking pattern will change your whole mood to a positive one and your physiology in a second.

On the other hand stress is a useful necessity to us. It's what empowers the mother's spirit to save her child from the oncoming traffic, or it can also spur people on to achieve great things. It heightens our senses and awareness. The *fight or flight* response was lifesaving in the days of man eating animals where you either attacked, or were attacked! Today we are not often found in that situation; yet the mind and body may still feel threatened in other ways. Any perceived (actual or imagined) threat or danger will produce a *fight or flight* reaction. For example: if someone says something hurtful or insulting, the reaction includes a tensing of the muscles as well as biochemical (hormonal / other) changes; these could simply be bottled up and remain as an extra degree of muscular tension.

Physical effects of stress
Once alerted, the pituitary gland (situated in the brain) releases hormones into the bloodstream which induce the adrenal glands to secrete adrenalin, noradrenaline and cortisone to prepare the body for the emergency or challenge facing it. Sugar production is increased to aid in

the repair of any damaged tissue. Heart rate increases, blood pressure rises, the process of digestion stops and acid secretion is increased in the stomach, breathing quickens as the lungs attempt to take in more oxygen and the body temperature rises significantly. Our nerves are highly charged and our reflexes are sharpened.

If the body is repeatedly put into this *stressed* state, or kept that way for a prolonged period of time, various symptoms begin to appear. If ignored they can turn into painful and unpleasant conditions e.g. if the heart rate and blood pressure are continually being raised, and maintained for long periods, (due to being under stress) the blood is likely to clot, the arteries will harden which could result in strokes, angina and heart attacks.

Stress obviously has a detrimental effect on the immune system, rendering it less effective against disease. Continual stress prevents the body from fulfilling its normal functions of repairing, regenerating and subsequently protecting itself. The energy needed for this process is used up instead by the stress, so acid secretion in the stomach increases; therefore, irritation of the stomach lining follows which leads to gastric or duodenal ulcers. Other serious side effects of stress are: alcoholism / drug addiction and severe depression which can spiral out of control.

Although stress may start in the mind, it inevitably manifests itself in the emotions and body as well. An example of this is what is commonly referred to as a panic attack. A panic attack initially begins with the person feeling an acute stab of fear; this causes the person to suddenly stop and freeze up. Everything is tensed. The lungs and diaphragm can't expand to take in enough oxygen. Feeling that their breathing is restricted increases the panic, which in turn, causes the breathing to become even shallower. Then the person feels out of control, heart rate increases, chest and throat feels tight and closed, temperature goes up and hands begin to sweat. Although this may seem an extreme example, it serves the purpose to illustrate how stress affects the whole of you.

Uncertainty is a high stress factor too. A study in American college was carried out on some students. They were warned that whilst listening to a voice counting to 15 they could get an electric shock on the count of 10, depending on the card they drew from a pack with the words printed shock or non-shock. Both groups had a 20 card pack to pick from. For one group the pack contained 1 shock card and 19 non-shock cards equalling a 5% chance of receiving a shock. In the other group there were 10 shock and 10 non-shock cards, therefore, a 50/50 chance. The group with the 1 shock card suffered more stress and anxiety than the other group who reconciled themselves to receiving the shock; they hoped for the best, but expected the worst. This goes to show that everyone is susceptible to varying levels of stress and coping mechanisms.

Stress or arousal states can be stimulated by alarm, excitement, worry, sorrow, even joy. The same physical process takes place whether arousal is caused by a pleasant, or unpleasant experience, or factor. Stress is acceptable and harmless in small amounts for short periods of time *if* we:
- Don't suppress, or hide our feelings about it.
- We diffuse, or relieve it by relaxing.
- If we're able to let I go.

On the other hand, stress is potentially dangerous when we

hide or deny it.

Simple ways to relieve stress
1. **Deep breathing.** One of the simplest most effective ways of controlled breathing is the following exercise. Sit with your back straight, concentrate on the sound of your breath in and out. Breathing in through your nose, and out through your mouth. As you breathe imagine a feather being held a few inches away from your nose and concentrate on breathing in and out slowly so that the imagined feather hardly moves. The slower and deeper you can make the breaths the better. Count the number of seconds it takes to inhale and exhale, and then try to increase gradually to the count of 7 in and 11 out.
2. **Hot Baths.** 5-10 minutes in a hot bath has a sedative effect and is a useful means of muscle relaxation. A long hot bath has the opposite effect. A warm bath with 10 drops of an essential oil (i.e. aromatherapy) like chamomile for instance encourages relaxation.
3. **Meditation.** A controlled meditation will help to relax the whole body and if used daily, will provide you quality me time, even if only for ten minutes to rejuvenate.
4. **Reflexology.** A most relaxing and balancing therapy, proven to help people unwind and enjoy the valuable *me* time. Atmospheric music and the gentle touch, gives the whole person a holistic therapy.
5. **Walking.** Frees your mind, bring clarity and helps you gain fitness while enjoying *being at one with nature*. The permission that you give yourself to break away from the stressful situation gives relaxation.
6. **Creativity.** To be lost in your writing, painting, reading,

Get Out of Your Own Way!

listening to music (or composing it), craft work etc. is as they say 'tranquil and therapeutic'. Each and every time we are creative in whatever field we choose is allowing us to express ourselves; allowing us a release if you like, from our stressed lives.

> **Danni's Ten Commandments for reducing stress:**
> 1. Thou shalt not be perfect, or even try!
> 2. Thou shalt not try to be all things to all people.
> 3. Thou shalt leave things that ought to be done.
> 4. Thou shalt not spread thyself too thin.
> 5. Thou shalt learn to say "No".
> 6. Thou shalt schedule time for thy self and thy supportive network.
> 7. Thou shalt switch off and do nothing regularly.
> 8. Thou shalt be boring, inelegant, untidy and unattractive at times.
> 9. Thou shalt not feel guilty..... and especially,
> 10. Thou shalt not be thine own worst enemy.
> 11. Thou shall schedule regular Reflexology treatments of course!

> **Mini Case:**
>
> Client H came to me as she was recommended to see if Reflexology could help with her anxiety levels and mild depression. She had seen her doctor who had prescribed some anti-depressants. She did not feel that they were right for her. However, she wanted to try and see if she could cope by herself and try something alternative.
>
> Reflexology has been such a huge benefit for many people

Get Out of Your Own Way!

who suffer with anxiety and panic attacks, so I tried to reassure her that we will work together and try some relaxation techniques first with mini treatments at first.

She said I am willing to try anything! I taught her the 7-11 breathing technique and also showed her the adrenal reflexes in her hands to press on whenever she felt anxious.

Not only did she learn how to calm herself down, but she managed to relax more each and every time she came for Reflexology. She thoroughly enjoyed her 'lunch break' as she called it and talking was a huge part of her treatments as she felt locked up inside and not heard in her society. By talking she managed to lift a huge weight off her shoulders and felt that she was more able to cope with everyday life.

Case Studies and Coping Strategies for a wide range of illnesses

Case 1: Multiple Sclerosis, spasms and pain.
Client A is a 42 year old woman who is a married housewife with one teenage child. She was diagnosed with Multiple Sclerosis 1985. At the moment she is in remission and has been for the last three years. She is suffering mainly with leg and bladder spasms. Her other presenting problems are: tiredness, forgetfulness and she sometimes gets depressed.

She moved to East Sussex a few years ago from London and has been waiting to get physiotherapy help. Her medications are Detrusitol, Dantroline and Baclofen; she was recently taken off Oxybutin as she felt that they were not helping her anymore and so Detrusitol has taken over.

On first inspection her feet were very clammy, yet cold with a blue tinge, she then informed me that she had a problem with circulation due to lack of exercise. Her feet seemed to turn in on themselves and all of the toes were scrunched up.

I did not carry out a full treatment and I only worked on her for 20-25 minutes. I felt that it would be more beneficial to help her to get into a relaxed state as she seemed quite nervous, so I held both solar plexus points. She in turn seemed to calm and relax which afterwards she explained that she has a real difficulty in achieving this.

On her second appointment, I carried out a gentle full treatment, she explained to me on this occasion, that she was very embarrassed that she would sometimes have 'little accidents' (even though she was catheterised). I noticed that her bladder areas were red, puffy and tender. The only other areas that were tender during the treatment were the kidney and adrenal areas.

By the third treatment, she said that she was able to relax quite quickly and she also said that she really looked forward to each treatment as she felt less depressed and slept better after her treatment. Her feet were feeling much warmer, much quicker now and she said that for the first time, she experienced some tingling sensations as I worked on her, something she hasn't felt for a very long time. Her disposition was much more positive and brighter. A full treatment lasting 40 minutes was now a pleasure for her and very much looked forward to.

She informed me that her medication had been changed.

On her fifth treatment she experienced some leg spasms as I worked on the knee points, thoracic and also chest area. She had been having spasms since the change of medication. Her body was adjusting to the change of medication and on her ninth treatment her feet warmed quickly and were more sensitive, her leg spasms were less frequent.

By her fourteenth visit she seemed more positive and relaxed in general, the bladder spasms were still consistent and were her main concern, so I worked on the bladder areas for a little longer.

But on her eighteenth appointment, she called me for an emergency appointment as she was in pain that day and she felt I could help her to calm the pain down. Once again after the treatment she was much more relaxed and less tense. Although she suffered the occasional spasm, the benefit of

Reflexology aided her management of pain, and gave her respite whenever it was needed.

> Her Testimonial:
> "Danielle has introduced and converted me with her Reflexology treatments. At first I was a bit wary and sceptical that it would not make any difference to my pain levels and spasms. However, as each treatment went on I started to have feelings in my feet! This has not happened in a very long time so for me was a great experience. I am very grateful for the patience of Danielle, she has a very comforting and professional manner, and her relaxing treatments to me are heavenly. I would definitely recommend her to anyone".

***

Case 2: Breast Cancer and Lethargy

Client B is a 30 year old woman who is married with two children. She has suffered two bouts of breast cancer and has recently suffered menstrual problems and has undergone an operation to save her having a hysterectomy, but this has brought on early menopause. So respectively, she has been menopausal for six months having dizzy and fainting spells along with hot flushes and a painful lower abdomen.

On first inspection I found her feet to be quite dry with lots of dry skin around the big toes and heels. She found it hard to relax, mainly because she doesn't spend a lot of time on herself, or by herself. I used a lot of massaging movements to help her relax and I also found a lot of the reflexes to be tender: eyes, ears, eustation (inner ear), the shoulder areas were grisly, small intestine area seemed congested and the reproductive system as a whole seemed unbalanced. She told me that after the first treatment she felt tired and lethargic. However, that night she slept like a baby.

On her second treatment the previous areas were still tender. When I was working on her small intestine area I felt a movement and her stomach grumbled.

By the fourth treatment she seemed to have more energy. She had been sleeping much better and had a more positive outlook. She reported less abdominal pain which she said was *miraculous*.

On her seventh treatment there was some tenderness in the chest area, she explained she had been having some pain in her scar tissue. I gave her extra attention to the chest area in general and on returning to the same points appeared much smoother and less tender.

By the eleventh treatment she felt no more niggles and much more balanced, her reproductive area also felt much more in harmony. I included some hand Reflexology which she found fascinating and I showed her some points to work on by herself should she need too.

> Her Testimonial:
> Danielle is a very warm caring Reflexologist and has helped me not just with her relaxing treatments, but by listening and recommending relaxation techniques. She is a great confident and has become a good friend. I would like to thank her for her support during a very testing time in my life. For me Reflexology has been a great learning experience not only is it a relaxing therapy, but also an insightful journey to caring for myself by giving myself some

pampering time, we all need a bit of that!

***

Case 3: Arthritic knees and Stiff Shoulders
Client C is a 38 year old man who suffers with stiff shoulders and also has problems with his knees. He is due to have an investigatory operation on his knees shortly which is a double arthroscopy to detect whether he has Arthritis or water on the knees. He is married with one child. He cares for his disabled wife 24 /7.

He was quite sceptical as he said he has very ticklish feet, however I reassure him that the Reflexology treatment uses continual movements and even the most ticklish feet can cope with that.

On his first treatment I found that his feet were very dry around the little toes and also the sides of his feet, the shoulder areas on the feet were very tender, but on working on them they eased in pain. The knees were also tender but again with a little extra attention seemed to ease up. He has his operation date for next week.

On his second appointment, he has had his operation and this has shown that he has got mild arthritis. His knee areas are quite tender obviously due to the operations. I worked very gently on them and also advised him how to work on his hands to aid his healing. His shoulders were still the same as before.

By the third treatment the knees were less tender, but the shoulders felt gristly and congested, which seemed to be the same on the next treatment too.

Get Out of Your Own Way!

But by the sixth treatment his knee points seemed to have stabilised in harmony, and also the shoulder areas were a lot less congested, and more palpable. He feels much more relaxed and is being proactive towards his arthritis.

> His Testimony:
> Danielle was recommended to me by a friend and at first I thought I'm not sure about this, but I'll give it a go. Having very ticklish feet I thought that I would not enjoy it all, but was very pleasantly surprised. The heat that came from Danielle's hand when she was working on my feet was amazing, and I truly believe that her treatments have really helped my knees and their healing process. I don't feel as though my shoulders are as tense either. I would definitely recommend Reflexology for anybody.

***

Case 4: IVF and Infertility
Client D is a 29 year old woman who has suffered with bad menstrual cycles and also infertility. She has had 3 courses of IVF sadly; none have gone through to a full term pregnancy. She has been quite depressed and full of grief from her losses. She had heard that Reflexology can help with balancing hormonal and menstrual cycles and wanted to try the alternative route. On taking her case history it was clear that she had been on quite a journey and desperately wanted to start a family.

On her first treatment I found her feet had a good pink colour and were quite pliable. However, the reproductive areas for both ovaries and womb were red and tender to touch. Her adrenal points were also tender. So I worked gently on all the above points giving them extra attention. I used a technique called linking which allows blocked energy to clear and flow freely.

On her third treatment she had told me that she slept better after her treatment than she had done in ages. Again I worked very gently on her reproductive areas.

She had been having a stressful time at work lately and was finding it hard to relax, so I taught her the 7-11 breathing exercise. I also told her where to work on her hand to help with relaxation.

On her fifth treatment she told me that she had been relaxing much easier and that the techniques were working.

I noticed that her ovaries and womb were less congested and she had said that her cycle was not as heavy as normal. She was feeling much more positive about her work and seemed less stressed.

On her ninth treatment she had told me that she had some slight abdominal pains, so I gently worked on the areas needed and again gave her advice on which areas to work on.

She came for her thirteenth treatment with a huge smile. She had some news to tell me, she was pregnant. She had had an early scan and was 5 weeks gone. She went on to have a 39 week gestation and a beautiful baby boy.

She had regular treatments right up to the week before the birth, and she also used Reflexology points during labour which she said really helped with the pain levels so only needed gas and air.

Get Out of Your Own Way!

She still comes for regular treatments to this day.

> Her Testimonial:
> Danielle has been such a support and I totally believe that had I not met her and had Reflexology I wouldn't have our beautiful boy with us today. We had been through such a hard time with IVF and totally lost faith in us ever being parents. With all of the techniques Danielle taught me, I truly believe it gave us the hope that it might happen, and it did. I would rate Reflexology on a high scale with anyone who has had difficulties with their cycles as it really does help. To just learn how to relax again is a huge benefit. The breathing technique really helped me and I could re-focus and de-stress. I think that Reflexology has been a healing therapy for me.

***

Case 5: ADHD
Client E is a 3 year old boy who lives with his mother and 1 year old sister, his presenting problem is Hyperactivity. He is *always on the go* explains mum and *he doesn't stop, it doesn't matter how many times I tell him to do something he just ignores me. I don't know what to do?* His mum asked me if Reflexology could help to calm him down a bit to which I replied *the only way we can find out is to try him with a short treatment to start off with and see how it goes*, so that is what I did.

I asked him to sit down on mum's lap facing her and to poke his feet either side of the chair to which at first he was not compliant, but when offered him a reward at the end if he did, he didn't seem to have a problem.

Get Out of Your Own Way!

I did not give him a full treatment, but worked on the solar plexus points to help balance him and also the adrenal glands which I could actually feel were buzzing.

By the end of the short treatment he said that was *nice* and I said *can we do another treatment tomorrow* and he said *yes*.

He came back the next day and was ready to have the treatment straight away. I did the same and took a little longer on each point.

By the fourth treatment he was looking forward to having his treatment and mum had told me that he had calmed down for two and a half hours after his last treatment. He also went to sleep better and for longer through the night.

By the eighth treatment I was able to give him a full treatment and he actually fell asleep on mums lap.

I found out on the ninth treatment that he was much calmer during the day and has been listening to and co-operating my mum much better.

On the tenth treatment I felt that he had done so well that he could came once a week instead of every other day. We continued to do so for three weeks. After that I said to mum that I think he has had enough treatments, however, I was happy to see him anytime if needed. He came for a further two weeks and has continued to stay calm.

***

Mini Case Study:

Pauline came to me suffering from a very painful ear

problem that had started a year ago. After having caught three colds one after the other, Pauline's sinuses became intensely painful, and then her ear became very painful. After several visits to her own doctor and a private specialist, Pauline still had no relief from her excruciating pain. The pain stemmed from her left ear and ran down the side of her neck limiting the movement in the neck. Pauline received a couple of treatments from an acupuncturist and found this did give her some relief from the pain, however, treatments were expensive and Pauline could not go regularly.

After Pauline's first Reflexology treatment she found that the following day her nose was running continually and felt as if fluid was draining away from her ear. Whilst working on the left foot I found the eustaction reflex was much tenderer for Pauline then the ear reflex itself. I also worked carefully around the neck reflexes and found some tenderness also in the coccyx.

After the second treatment the same thing happened, however, this time it was the second day after the treatment. By the third treatment the pain had subsided considerably and Pauline was absolutely thrilled with these results, she also had far more movement in her neck. Pauline continues to preach the benefits of Reflexology to all she meets.

***

Mini Case Study:

Sue's job involves staying awake all night and she often gets very little sleep during the day. Sue suffers from varicose veins which are very painful at times. Also Sue's digestive system caused her discomfort at times.

The job Sue does is very stressful and one of the first things that Sue noticed after treatments commenced was that she felt much calmer and more relaxed. Over the following three or four weeks Sue's varicose veins had become less painful and visibly less pronounced and a small blood vessel which had become raised and a deep reddish-blue became smaller and turned a much paler pink colour.

Sue helped this process by working on the referral areas on her arm and hand at home in between treatments.

***

Mini Case Study:

Graeme reluctantly allowed me to treat him with Reflexology whilst I was still training. Being very sceptical of the whole idea, he was very shocked by the strong reaction he experienced after the very first treatment.

Graeme had a family history of heart conditions and circulatory problems and he found that on returning home after the first treatment he had severe pain in his legs. However, on waking in the morning Graeme found his legs felt better than they had done for years.

Suitably impressed he arranged for weekly treatments. During these sessions I worked on the kidneys, which were particularly tender in the early sessions, the heart and lung reflexes on both feet, the adrenal glands to enhance muscle tone of the heart and regulate blood pressure by controlling sodium and potassium levels. I

I also found Graeme felt a lot of tenderness in the large and small intestines. He confirmed that he suffered with difficulty in bowel movements from time to time. This improved considerably over the next couple of weeks.

The left hip to knee area was also very tender for Graeme, as he had quite bad varicose veins on his left leg. Also the lymphatics in the chest and groin areas of the feet were again tender whilst being worked on.

Over a period of seven weeks, Graeme's general health improved considerably. His circulatory problems were greatly eased and his permanently cold feet became warm and comfortable. The digestive problems also improved as did the pain from the varicose veins which had visibly decreased in size.

Graeme now has monthly treatments to maintain his new found good health.

If any of these cases relate to you or you would like to know more about Reflexology, I will always be happy to answer any questions. I hope that you have enjoyed my contribution in this wonderful book about *getting out of your own way* and achieving your health goals. I will leave you with a **poem for inspiration**.

When you feel that it's not going your way
A change of direction presents each day
If you look you will see
All around chances will be
A glimpse here and there

Get Out of Your Own Way!

A door opens somewhere
Hearts racing with excitement
Feelings of enticement
That's where you are meant to be.
Many times we miss the clues
Stuck in ruts of the blues
Look hard and things will appear
Your visions will become clear.
A sense of this feels just right
Grab with both hands and tight!
A warm fuzzy feeling inside
Something you just cannot hide
To scream out with such glee
This is happening to me
Take your leap of faith into the unknown
Go on try, just pick up the phone
Be inspired to live once again.

For more information about Reflexology and its benefits, or how it could help you, please send me a message here at http://dialaguru.eu/contact-us/. I will also be writing about Homeopathy in the next series called *Heal Your Life Holistically and Thrive!*
So until then, take care.
Love Danni.

> You have BRAINS in your HEAD
> You have FEET in your SHOES.
> You can STEER yourself any
> DIRECTION you CHOOSE.
> ~Dr. Seuss

Get Out of Your Own Way!

Danielle Lindsay - Biography

Danielle is a married mum of two beautiful boys. After being an estate agent for many years, she decided to do something different so followed her vocation and retrained in the complementary field. Now she offers alternative medicine therapies.

She choose to start with Reflexology having always been told she was good at massage and had *healing hands*. So she put them into action and successfully completed a year-long course which included basic anatomy and physiology in March 2000.

Her family supported her wholeheartedly throughout her training; not least they enjoyed being guinea pigs for the practical element of her course. Danni said *"I loved every minute, and to be able to help people was the greatest feeling ever"*.

Since then, Danni has established her practice and is pleased to note that all her clients come as a reference from a previous client, so word of mouth works for her.

Consequently, she has worked with many different people, from children to old age, with varying different needs and problems. She has even found that the treatment is successful for children suffering with A.D.H.D. Not only is the treatment so beneficial for so many 'dis-eases', it is great for relaxing and taking time out just for yourself!

Danni continued her training by adding Homeopathy to her skill set. She now offers both treatments and believes she has found her *true calling and now helps people with their issues at a much deeper level.*

Seeing remarkable results happen with Homeopathic remedies makes practicing a real pleasure, not least knowing four years hard work paid off for the benefit of her grateful clients.

Sadly, many people only use Homeopathy as a last resort due to the lack of education and choice. Therefore, her mission is to educate people about the complementary and alternative routes available in an entertaining and memorable way.

Consequently, she's already penned a study book aptly named *The Storybook of Remedies* which will help students and the public alike who are interested in this amazing practice. It also explains why it's so much more than just herbs!

Practicing from a beautiful and tranquil treatment room in Herstmonceux, East Sussex, Danni also offers a mobile treatment service so invites you to contact her so you too may benefit from these treatments.

Get Out of Your Own Way!

Section Seven
Breaking the Change Barrier

by
Jennifer Rahman

"To exist is to change; to change is to mature; to mature is to create oneself endlessly". - Henri Bergson

Get Out of Your Own Way!

Creating positive change to reshape your destiny

Thought you knew all about positive thinking and how it influences us? Well, think again! Recent research is pushing the boundaries of our understanding of positive thinking and why some of us find it so hard to change *despite* our best efforts.

Imagine today is the first day of the rest of your life. Whether you bounce or drag yourself out of bed, there are changes afoot. We have often been reminded of the cliché *change is constant* and whether you decide to partake in change or not, one thing is certain; change is inevitable. Even if you just lie in bed, change is happening within and around us. We refer to this as *action through inaction*.

Not all change is bad though. Change can also be good especially when *planned.* Albeit, we cannot control a lot of things in our lives, like the economy, politics, or natural disasters there are things that *are* within our control: for instance, how we view the world around us, how we react to circumstances, which job is good for us and where, when and what to eat.

The key question you will need to ask yourself is *"How happy are you with the life you are living"*? If the answer is *"Not"* then you need to consider why are you continuing to live a life that makes you miserable, that continues to add to your daily pressures and if prolonged, could eventually make you ill from chronic stress?

So why do you keep on doing what you're doing to yourself? Unless you are a masochist, and enjoy feeling disillusioned, and frustrated, surely the simply solution is to change the way you live your life.

A simple statement indeed, but as they say "easier said than done", not impossible though. When you have the focus, determination, and purpose to improve your life then the direction of change is in your hands, and not in someone else's.

"If you don't make decisions about how you are going to live in years to come, then you have already made the 'decision' to be directed by environments instead of shaping your own destiny". Anthony Robbins

How many times have you heard yourself say "I need to change, but I do not know how or where to begin"? If you begin your journey by perceiving change as a challenge, as an obstacle and more to the point, hard work, then it will be a self-fulfilling prophecy. However, when you perceive change as taking back control of your life, of being something positive and directional, then *you* are dictating the change you want to see in your life. Yes, it may require some effort on your part, but when you can visualise the outcome you choose for yourself, and then it is worth the time and effort. Martin Luther King, Jr. summed it up eloquently when he said "You don't have to see the whole staircase, just take the **first** step".

Design your destiny

I'm a life coach and as such adopt the mantra: *design your destiny by choice, not chance*. Consequently, I know and believe that everyone has the inner resources and resolve they need to move from a *problem state* to a *solution state*. I just need to get *you* to believe in yourself! Remember, a

Get Out of Your Own Way!

happy person is not a person in a certain set of circumstances, but rather a person with a certain set of *attitudes*. So learn to trust your instincts!

To answer the question "Where do I start"? You may like to utilise the accompanying workbook, also available on Amazon, to work through these questions in your own time and in more detail. For now, here are some questions that will get you thinking about what, or who is driving your need for change.

Q. Are you the person you want to be right now?

A.

Q. Are you leading the life you want right now?

A.

Q. What is motivating your decision to change?

A.

Q. Who else is involved with your decision to change?

A.

Q. What do you want to change?

A.

Q. What is preventing you from changing?

A.

Q. Who else can help you achieve your goal?

A.

Q. What will be the benefits of achieving your goal?

A.

Q. How will you measure your plan in terms of it being realistic, timely and measureable?

A.

Q. What else can you do to achieve your goal?

A.

Q. What other alternatives can you think of?

A.

Q. What are you not considering?

A.

Don't change because:
- ✗ Someone told you to, not even your life coach!
- ✗ You feel you have to.
- ✗ It will make others happy.
- ✗ Nothing else works.
- ✗ You have to salvage something, or someone (there might be other factors in play).

Get Out of Your Own Way!

**Remember *"A change imposed, is a change opposed"*.
Charles Handy**

Do change because:
- ✓ You really want to.
- ✓ You can see the higher good in it.
- ✓ You want to improve and contribute to your self-awareness and self-development.
- ✓ It will be good for you and you only.
- ✓ It will enrich your life in a positive way.

"Nothing splendid has ever been achieved except by those who dared to believe that something inside of them, was superior to circumstance". Origin unknown.

Knowing that you want to change and actually seeing it through are two different activities: one requires no effort at all, just verbal expression and day-dreaming, while the other requires focused, directional actions. Merely changing your behaviour, habits, relationships, and attitude towards life is a choice that you make for your better good, and because you want to, NOT because you feel you have to.

People seek to change their lives because they are not happy with one thing or another. No-one seeks to change when all is well in their world. We act like magnets, drawing people and experiences to us that resonate with how we think about ourselves, and what we wish for ourselves. We attract exactly that which agrees with our unconscious needs, desires, doubts and fears. But is there more to this than just making the *right* choices in life? I personally don't think that this is sufficient. You need to know what your *life's purpose* is to know what you want out of life. And no-one can determine your purpose in life other than you.

If you don't know what your goal is in life, then how can you create and attract what is right for you? How do you know what path to take? Without direction your life is *like a ship without a rudder*. A directionless life can have an enormously destructive effect on relationships, as well as drag others down without intending, or even noticing.

Having said that, I believe that you don't have to have a life purpose to live life on your terms, but if you want to create new beginnings, new successes, new relationships now and in the future, and then you need a *life purpose*. Why? Because you need to know what you could focus on, and how you could direct your energy to achieve whatever it is you wish to achieve. After all, your goal determines the direction of your change.

So whether you are searching for inner peace, looking for love, or trying to be healthier, your search will begin with the inner belief that *you are worth it*, and that you rightly deserve this greatness, and abundance that the Universe has to offer. There is nothing more beautiful and exciting than thinking you can achieve your dreams through endless possibilities.

Intention to succeed and to claim success *begins* with the intention to change. Having a clear *intention* means having to make a conscious decision to focus all your thoughts and inner energy towards your goal. Without a goal, your intention to change will not amount to the desired outcome.

"It is not the destination that counts, but the journey". I have heard this mentioned so many times, but truthfully it is both the intention, and how we go about changing that really matters. What is the point of going on a journey of self-discovery if you don't have the end in mind? If you don't have a goal (destination) then you could go on an endless, mindless journey, and perhaps never even reach your destination. So, in my opinion you need to appreciate, learn and discover both the highs, and lows of your journey, and celebrate success when you have reached your destination. It makes all your hard effort, time and personal sacrifice more meaningful and worthwhile!

Interestingly, we largely create our present world from our inner world; our self-image is often our fate, and also a marker of our choices; good, or bad. Depending on our self-belief and self-perception, the life that unfolds before us exactly mirrors the value of our self-worth. For example, when we have too little self-esteem our thoughts, conscious and unconscious beliefs will be negative, and destructive. Both will cause us to attract more negative experiences and events. However, when we have a strong sense of self-esteem our thoughts will reflect this. They will be positive and constructive which will attract positive circumstances into our life.

However, you can't sit back on your laurels just because you have the *right intention* to succeed. Being true to your intention stems from your heart's desires; meaning you need to dedicate your entire being, all your energies, breath and will-power to achieving these desires. *"Don't just dream it, be it"*! Rocky Horror Picture Show

To visualise, or not to visualise, that is the question

The Secret a powerful bestseller from Rhonda Byrne set the world abuzz when she drew our attention to *The Law of Attraction*. Many believed that you can create what you visualise. Consequently, sales of notice boards soared, and magazines disappeared from hairdressers as everyone, and I mean literally everyone was cutting glossy pictures from these magazines to attract their *vision of their dream life*.

If it was so easy why did a high percentage of people, just a few years down the line, give up in exasperation and disillusionment when they still hadn't attracted whatever they'd asked for?

Did Rhonda Byrne get it wrong? Was the Law of Attraction hocus-pocus? No! She was right, but people oversimplified the *achieving* factor for themselves, and misunderstood what Rhonda Byrne was really telling us; *positive visualisation is only a tool*; it is *not the source of creativity*. In the same way having a strong will, motivation and a healthy ego are merely tools. To achieve the end goal you need to also to take ACTION to achieve your heart's desire.

The power of your heart's desire.

"The important thing is to use your heart to decide what you want, then use your mind to empower your will and put it to work". *The Deeper Secret* by Annemarie Postma.

Vision boards and heaps of positive thinking were not enough to bring abundance and success to those who practiced these tools. I am guilty of subscribing to this *blue sky thinking* movement, but I soon realised that positive thinking alone, was not the answer.

So much of what we do is motivated by **FEAR** (**F**antasised **E**xperiences **A**ppearing **R**eal): fear of lack of something or someone, fear of inadequacy, fear of losing control and the

Get Out of Your Own Way!

list goes on. When you suffer from a lack of self-esteem and self-confidence you will always need to prove something to the outside world. Even the most positive thoughts can never reach further than the boundaries of self-interest. However, intention from the heart allows you to act from within, giving you direction and strength to achieve your goal.

We all want to experience success. No one starts out in life with failure on their mind, but failure is what we *create* in our minds. We believe it because it has become our marker of what we are currently experiencing because it is based on past outcomes. Failure consciously or unconsciously has become our *comfort zone* and clouds the decisions that we make. But we all *want* a better life. We say we do, but only the brave will do something about changing their current circumstances to achieve it. Isn't it easier to say "if only.... we could, we should have etc."? Isn't it less painful to say "See, I told you it would fail"!

Merely wanting something is meaningless. We can spend all day *wanting* to escape from it all, without taking one step towards changing the outcome. *Wanting* lacks the crucial element of decision-making!

"The world around us is a world of effects. So if you only change something in **that** world, you actually change nothing". Marianne Williamson.

Laws of the Universe

So if *wanting and wishing* are not enough to achieve meaningful and lasting change in us and our world, what other forces are at play? We are familiar with *The Law of*

Attraction which simply states that you attract what you wish for in your life. But there is other not so well known Laws of the Universe that need to be operating in tandem with the Law of Attraction to achieve our heart's desires. For instance:

1. **The Law of Belief** states that whatever you believe, with conviction, becomes your reality. Think of self-limiting beliefs and these will limit your opportunities. Believe in opportunities and these will find their way to you. "Whoever you say you are, you are". Henry Ford
2. **The Law of Substitution** states that your mind can only hold one thought at a time, be it positive or negative. However, you can learn to substitute one negative thought for a good thought and vice versa at your choosing. "All that we are arises with our thoughts". Buddha.
3. **The Law of Habit** states that any thought that you repeat over and over will eventually become a new habit, and the environment in which it exists, will become your new *comfort zone*. "If you always do what you have always done, you will always get what you have always gotten". Origin unknown.
4. **The Law of Creation** states that you must use your heart to decide what you want. The *will* and *ego* are there to act on what has been decided by the heart. It stems from creativity and possibility. "The best and most beautiful things in the world cannot be seen or even touched. They must be felt with the heart". Helen Keller.
5. **The Law of Inverse Relationships** states that there is a connection between your level of self-esteem and your fears. "The difference between a successful

person and others is not the lack of strength, nor the lack of knowledge, but rather in a lack of will". Vince Lombardi.

We know from the autobiographies of successful people that they dreamt about the outcome of their goals from an early age and developed an obsession with it. They could picture themselves achieving success, the acclaim that came with it, and could even feel the sense of satisfaction and excitement when they succeeded. Many of them were mocked for having dreams beyond their means, but they believed in themselves, and they eventually triumphed. Where they came across more successful people than themselves, they copied their strategies, stance, body language and verbal cues *mirroring* their rivals. These are patterns of successful people who have taken positive and pro-active steps towards creating well-formed goals and outcomes in their lives. They had a *life purpose* including the *will* and *motivation* to succeed, often at all costs.

Making a decision to change, means taking:
- Responsibility for your actions.
- Being accountable for your choices.
- Setting a goal that will focus all our energy on the outcome.
- Belief that you will achieve your goal.

In her book *Feel the Fear and Do It Anyway*, the late Susan Jeffers talked about "taking responsibility" for our actions. In her bestseller she said that *we all have to take responsibility not only for our actions, but life.* Taking responsibility also means not being too hard on yourself (self-blame), but equally taking ownership of your actions. We also have to silence our inner critic (self-criticism), and be aware that we have many options, or paths that we can take in any given situation. Whether you chose to take action, or not, these are the choices open to you. Doing nothing is also a choice, remember that.

But there is more to be said about taking responsibility. Sometime back, I came across a self-help article in a magazine that described our inner unconscious as *no-current* and *yes-current*. A *no-current* is unconscious negative energy that is self-destructive while a *yes-current* is positive conscious energy and thoughts that aid self-development. Sometimes, when we have to do something that takes us out of our *comfort zone*, even with the best intentions, we somehow manage to self-sabotage our efforts. This is due to the fact that while at a conscious level we *want* to take action to change, there is an inner unconscious voice, our inner critic, which tells us *not* to embark on this journey. The only way to silence this *no-current* or inner critic is to acknowledge its presence and learn how to overcome fear. It is acceptable to feel fear when we are forced out of our *comfort zone*, but the key is not to let fear overshadow and limit our life choices. By the latter, I mean that we can all learn to change our *no-current* to a *yes-current* and embrace self-discovery and self-development. It may take effort, but it is not impossible.

However, it is a mistake, and one of the biggest misconceptions of self-help development to think that acknowledging your destructive patterns is a bad thing. Having a positive attitude doesn't mean that you need to ignore the negative aspects of yourself. You can only set your potential for change in motion *when* you learn to hear *how* and *why* you unconsciously say "*no*" to the things you long for.

Get Out of Your Own Way!

It is a fact, not myth, that we cannot be happy all the time and in all situations. Life is not like that. Life throws us obstacles, problems and challenges, yet those who overcome these issues successfully, are those that have learnt the secret of *flourishing*. This is the precise science of building up positivity in your life so that you can deal with negativity *without* drama and self-destruction.

How will you become aware of unconscious negative traits? One method is *journaling* which is keeping a written account of your thoughts and reactions to people and events. When you write about your difficulties with life decisions and relationships honestly *without* censorship you will at some point discover a pattern; a common denominator such as: an emotional trigger, a self-criticism, or even a particular phrase that repeatedly shows up in your notes. These trends are indicative of your unconscious thought processes which points you to the long-held ideas and incorrect *conclusions* that probably formed early in life. This is your starting point for dealing with them constructively.

So don't just change for change sake. Instead, make change a positive and fulfilling life-long learning experience. The key to success is not mere knowledge. Knowledge alone is not power. It is the implementation of knowledge that is power. "Be the change you want to see in the world". Mahatma Ghandi

Get Out of Your Own Way!

The positive power of negative thinking

Are you kidding? Someone pinch me! Surely this can't be right? In 12 years of life coaching and holistic therapy training, I have been told that negative thinking is bad, and is the cause of all that is wrong with a person. So when I read an article by Adam Grant, author of the New York bestseller *Give and Take* as featured in the USA edition of The Huffington Post, I soon had to eat my words.

Increasingly research into human behaviour and emotions is throwing light onto what we feared most; that having a negative attitude, or outlook on life, is not so bad after all. In fact, it may even be good for us! So powerful are these new emerging research studies that many psychologists, holistic therapists, life coaches and even GP's have had to re-think their strategies, and their previously entrenched beliefs about the importance, and impact that emotions have on our mind, body and spirit.

I have long been a firm believer of the *think positive* movement. Conventional wisdom and my training told me that if I wanted to achieve any goal in life, I had to be positive. Interestingly, recent research into positive and negative emotions has raised some exciting, yet controversial findings. Strategic optimists and defensive pessimists succeed under different circumstances. Psychologists, Julie Norem and Nancy Cantor in the USA, studied personality traits in strategic optimists, and defensive pessimists. They believe that strategic optimists envision the best possible outcome, and then eagerly plan to make it happen. However, defensive pessimists are more anxious and set lower expectations for themselves in analytical, verbal, and creative tasks. In spite of this, defensive pessimists did not perform any worse than strategic optimists.

Most people assume that strategic optimists outperform defensive pessimists *because* they benefit from high confidence and expectations. Yet new research showed that while defensive pessimists exhibit negative thinking, they are able to transform their anxiety into action! Psychologists Julie Norem and Nancy Cantor, authors of *The Positive Power of Negative Thinking* believe that even die-hard pessimists are capable of success-driven actions and favourable decision-making skills *because* they intentionally use their negative thinking to transform their inner anxiety into action. By imagining the worst case scenario, defensive pessimists motivated themselves to try harder than the strategic optimists. In other words, negative emotions and thoughts *empower* the individual indirectly, and directly though action. The key though is not to let the negative emotions rule our lives.

Where did it go wrong? There is no right or wrong answer to this question. A lot more understanding into the human psyche and what empowers us to do the things we do is needed. Does it mean that because you have negative emotions, that you are to be condemned? No, it does not. I am not referring to the extremes of human emotions at the end of the emotional spectrum which are polar opposites whereby at one end you have absolute happiness and at the other you have depression. I am referring to the *in-betweens*.

Some researchers say "to be constantly happy is to be in denial of reality". We cannot be happy all the time. Life is not like that. Every day we all have our ups and downs. It is *how* we react to these fluctuations in emotions that are a reflection of how we live our lives. Just being aware of our personal negative emotions helps us to interpret and make sense of the world around us. So surely, negative emotions cannot all be bad, can they?

Whether you subscribe to the absolute realm of positive thinking or not, I am not here to criticise. Rather to shed some light and remind ourselves about the power of both positive and negative emotions. One is *not necessarily* better than the other, but perhaps it is time for us to ponder on what this new research is really telling us. At polar ends, extreme pessimism makes us fatalistic, while extreme optimism is toxic as it removes us from reality of the situation. The key is to find a balance between the two.

Gaining direction

In all the psychology practices, which includes amongst them: Cognitive Behavioural Therapy (CBT), Neuro-Linguistic Programming (NLP) and Linguistic and Behavioural Profiling (LAB), practitioners need to firstly identify the *problem state,* and secondly, move towards a *solution state*.

But we have always assumed that if you want to improve your life then you need to change the way you think. Haven't we been told in the media, self-help books, and by parents and teachers that we need to have a positive disposition in order to succeed in life? In principle, this approach sounds perfectly reasonable. However, in practice the approach often proves surprisingly ineffective, with research showing that some people struggle to continually think happy thoughts that employees remain unmoved by imagining their perfect careers, that diets fail to create perfect figures, and that those dreaming of endless wealth fail to make their millions. So what is wrong with this picture?

Psychologists studying the *happiness factor* believe that being happy with our life is so crucial to our well-being that it is difficult to imagine that there are any down sides. Although happiness is generally good for us, it can make us too gullible and trusting. Dan Pink, author of the book *To Sell is Human* believes that positive fantasies discourage achievement and should be saved for the Silver Screen. For instance, he disagrees with people who claim they can lose weight simply by thinking positively. He also says that people perform worse when they say "I will" rather than asking themselves "Will I"? He claims that when people are overly happy, their status quo interferes with their ability to attend to detail. Therefore, people tend to lose sight of their reality. Many may adopt the *let the good times roll* syndrome and find it incomprehensible that there is any bad in their world.

Psychologist Martin Seligman, author of *Learned Optimism*, believes that *searching for high-octane happiness can make us have a lop-sided perception of our reality.* Just as seeking out only the positive and avoiding all negatives is not just a waste of time, it also means that we are likely to fail at what we desire most; personal success. He believes that when things go wrong, pessimists view negative events as personal, permanent and pervasive whereas, optimists view the situation as an opportunity to learn from their mistakes, practice and do better. Seligman feels that it is time for people to re-think their quest for the *happiness grail* and instead learn to tolerate and appreciate what they already have.

Get Out of Your Own Way!

Our reality is vital to our emotional architecture, offering vital information. We need to feel the prickle of fear in situations where physical harm is possible. We want to feel the thrust of anger when we need it and we need to feel frustration when we fail to make adequate progress in our goals. Every emotion, even the negative ones are useful. Without them Martin Seligman believes that "we will be living in a world devoid of fully functioning human beings".

Being different can be healthy too!

"You have got to make the choices that make sense for you AND only you, because there's always going to be someone who'll think you should do something differently". First Lady, Michelle Obama

Just because you may have a different point of view, or opinion, don't isolate or punish yourself. Everyone is different and so are you. Instead, learn to embrace your individuality. Learn to pat yourself on the shoulder and more importantly, know that you have something to unique to offer, and embrace that difference!

It is not about whether you have positive or negative emotions, it is about *how* you use them to react to a situation or circumstance that matters. For instance, flying into a rage will not help matters much, but learning to acknowledge what triggers rage and how to manage rage will be to your advantage. That is the key to harnessing the positive power in negative emotions.

Instead of getting angry:
- Learn not to have an *emotional hangover* which is simply allowing your negative emotions to spill from

one scenario to the next, from one environment to the next. Intense emotions linger for a long time, and so are likely to spill over and manifest itself into other areas of your life.

Most people have regular emotional cycles, for example, not liking Mondays. When you are aware of these cycles, then you can prevent them spilling into your home life and leisure time. These spill-over effects also occur when different aspects of your life become blurred.

- Set clear distinctions between different emotions (work, home and so on).
- Take a moment to reflect on the emotional events in your life as and when they occur (or as soon as possible afterwards), without blaming yourself. Instead try to learn from the experience and put a positive spin on it.

Many believe that affirmations are powerful tools in changing mindsets. Dan Pink in *To Sell is Human* says "affirmations only make you feel good for the moment. It does not prompt you to summon the resources and strategies to actually accomplish the task. Action rather than affirmation is the key".

If you are a defensive pessimist, or are attempting to motivate one, the strategies that prove effective are often the reverse of what you expect. For example: it is proven that positive mood impairs the performance of defensive pessimists making them complacent. Lack of anxiety actually makes them lazy and lacking the energy that would usually be used to mobilise their effort and actions. So if you are the kind of person who's always telling other people to look on the bright side, you might want to reconsider because whether people succeed is not a matter of thinking positively or negatively, but choosing the strategies that match their thinking styles. "It's the *fit* that counts" says Heidi Grant Halvorson and Tory Higgins, Psychologists who write in *Focus*.

Emotions under the microscope

All emotions are useful, even the negative ones. There is a reason why we are what we are, and our emotional selves are a reflection of childhood, adolescent and adult experiences, values and social backgrounds. We are the sum total of our experiences, blue sky thinking, warts and all. This is what we call our e*motional palette* and like the artist, we dip into this range of emotions, good and bad, to help us cope with the rigours and pressures of everyday living.

ANGER

Anger is neither good, nor bad; it's what you do with it that matters. Psychologists Todd Kasdan and Robert Biswas-Diener, authors of *The Power of Negative Emotions* believe that only 10 per cent of angry episodes actually lead to some sort of violence, which suggests that anger rarely equals aggression. Anger usually arises when we believe that someone or something has treated us unfairly, or blocks our ability to accomplish meaningful goals. We have all been hurt or offended by someone before, no one is immune to life's negativity. However, positivity alone isn't enough to help us navigate every social interaction and relationship that we encounter.

Anger or feeling angry is a tool that can help us when used

properly. Anger can help us become creative and effective in our performance. Being angry may motivate us to work harder to achieve our goals by doing something to prove ourselves to others like Martin Luther King, Jr. said "The supreme task is to organise and unite people so that their anger becomes a transforming force".

How to use *ANGER* to your advantage

Our initial tendency when we get angry is to jump into a situation and react to what is threatening us. Instead, when angry give yourself permission to pause for a moment, even if someone is standing there waiting for a response. Slow the situation down mentally, take a few deep breaths and think through your choices. Choose good decision, not fast ones. A few moments of reflection of the situation is more effective and allows you to take control of your responses. Before you react ask yourself "Will my anger help, or hurt the situation?

GUILT

We have all come to think of guilt in much the same way as we think of fat being unhealthy. Now we are being told that fat is good for us so shouldn't we relook at guilt as well? I am not saying that it is always good to feel guilty, but at times it certainly conveys benefits; one of which is that you are more motivated to improve your behaviour than your less guilty peers.

Guilt adds to our moral fibre, making us more sensitive and caring citizens than we otherwise would be. Feeling guilty about something or someone should not destroy us. Instead use this moral emotion of raw introspection to change any self-destructive ways and make it the cornerstone of change.

> **How to use *GUILT* to your advantage**
>
> When you are overcome with guilt about some incident, or about someone harness the raw emotions of what you are feeling, and use a few moments to reflect on what is happening, and what you can do to improve the situation.
>
> "Make bold choices and make mistakes. It's all those things that add up to the person you become". Angelina Jolie.

ANXIETY

Much has been written about the effects of anxiety. Too little suggests a situation that is boring and lacking in stimulation. Too much anxiety paralyses a person. As long as the experience is brief, performance will take a dip, but in the end, you will be fine. So the idea is to experience just the right amount of anxiety; experience the motivational butterflies without the out-of-control panic attacks and chronic stress.

In anxious moments, our perception is heightened including amplified vision and hearing. We also experience a lapse in our ability to solve problems. It all stems from the primitive part in our brain which is primed for survival, giving us three courses of action: fleeing, fighting, or freezing. This process takes place unconsciously and much has been made of the way it can cause undue stress. But missing from this discussion has been how anxiety can *help* drive our success.

Get Out of Your Own Way!

> **How to use *ANXIETY* to your advantage**
>
> Obviously I am not talking about chronic anxiety, but a little anxiety is good for us. Anxious people are sensitive to the slightest change in their environment which means they can actually be motivate look at the problem, assess the issues, and work harder to overcome them.

ENVY

Does another person's success or good fortune sometimes leave you yearning for more be it a bigger house, more money, a successful career? We have all experienced this at some point. It's called *the grass is greener* syndrome. Consequently, we fail to appreciate what we already have. Envy is one of the seven deadly sins, but it seems to be thriving more than ever thanks to the advent of reality TV shows. An increasingly competitive and consumerist culture is fanning the flames of increased envy and frustration to the extent that some people want to trade in their perceived mundane lives for others that are perceived to be more fulfilling.

Mindfulness is growing in popularity too because the people who are sick of *keeping up with the Jones's* have realised that money cannot buy happiness. We are learning that what makes people happier is being actually to do with being content with what we already have. What they need to be happy and feel self-fulfilled in mind, body and spirit is acceptance rather than greed. It's the mantra of practitioners of mindfulness and many have said that it has helped them lead more contented lives.

Get Out of Your Own Way!

Having said that, to be envious of others is not always bad and in fact can be a positive and powerful tool driving change.

How to use *ENVY* to your advantage

First, we have to be aware that there is a difference between extreme envy, which is self-destructive and mild doses of envy, which is good for us.

Rather than spend your life feeling inept, unfulfilled, frustrated over what others have, use envy as a motivational tool to work harder and become more determined to achieve your goal in life.

Instead of letting envy destroy you why not take a few moments when the emotion strikes and ask yourself "is this what I really want? Will it really make me happy"? If the answer is a resounding "Yes" then seek a way to make it happen because it makes you happy, not just because you want what you can't have.

What is the right balance of emotions?

I first came across the concept of *flourishing* two years ago, and to me at least it seems to be the best method to take the good with the bad. I always wondered how some people seem able to overcome whatever life throws at them, and why others have such difficulty in keeping it together. The key is to know the *flourishing formula*.

Flourishing: *How to achieve a deeper sense of well-being, meaning, and purpose* is according to author Maureen Gaffney a sort of intuitive sense we have *when* we know that we are at our absolute best. Especially when we are using all our capacities: intellectual, emotional, positive and negative.

Believers acknowledge that some element of negativity is inevitable as we go about our lives. Negative emotions can be our best friends, protecting and helping us survive by making sense of the world around us that may be less than perfect.

The magic formula of flourishing is to have a 5:1 ratio of positive emotions to every 1 negative emotion. So to be in a state of flourish Gaffney believes that we need positive and negative emotions, not one or the other. People who have a tendency to worry, to ruminate, and to be afraid of life and who always see the negative side of things, must work harder to overcome adversity. We cannot just expect life to balance out for us. If we are not aware of what pulls us down, then we have no chance of rectifying the balance. Having a 5:1 ratio is to accumulate more positive feelings and emotions so that when we face negativity, our positive mind-set will act as a shock absorber and get us back on our feet. Gaffney states that the 5:1 ratio is a uniform law that when observed, will bring us back to a state of balance and fulfilment.

Most prejudices against negative emotional experiences are because people confuse extreme, overwhelming, problematic emotions with their benign cousins. Suppressing these emotions is psychologically destructive because it divorces us from the richness of life. Don't repress, ignore, or hide your darker gifts. Instead, become more aware of them and appreciate what they have to offer.

Get Out of Your Own Way!

DON'T:
- ✗ Confuse guilt with shame.
- ✗ Confuse anger with rage.
- ✗ Confuse anxiety with panic.
- ✗ Repress your negative emotions.
- ✗ Dwell longer than you need to on them.
- ✗ Avoid emotional hangovers.
- ✗ Let negativity define who and what you are.
- ✗ Let negativity overshadow your inner beauty.

DO:
- ✓ Acknowledge and become more aware of your negative emotions. Keep a journal.
- ✓ Learn to extract the positive strengths in your negative emotions and build on them.
- ✓ Learn to appreciate what these emotions are telling you about yourself, your behaviour and your reactions.
- ✓ Learn to accept, love and respect yourself for whom you are.
- ✓ Learn to empower yourself with a 5:1 ratio of flourishing.
- ✓ Surround yourself with people who will love and support you, no matter what.
- ✓ Let your inner strengths define who you are.
- ✓ Reflect on the emotional events in your life without blaming yourself.
- ✓ Learn to put a positive spin on emotional events and view them as life learning experiences.
- ✓ Embrace the sum total of who you are; positive and negative aspects of self.

Get Out of Your Own Way!

People who are able to use the whole range of the emotional palette and are comfortable with both the positive and negative within are the healthiest of all, and often the most successful.

"The gem cannot be polished without friction, nor man perfected without trials". Confucius.

Changing your past story to create a better future

What's your story?

We all have a story to tell. Our life is made up of stories we hold dear about our transition from childhood to adulthood, about our experiences, our jobs and those that we love and hold dear. No two people can have the same life story because we all learn, experience and react differently to the events, circumstances and experiences (even when you are one of twins), even if you are in the same place, the same time, the same event as someone else.

Two people will experience the same situation, but each will react differently and in accordance with their life skills, education, intellect and past experience. We each also have different learning curves and our brain processes information differently. Sounds simplistic enough, but why do we react so differently?

This is due to the fact that we each remember certain events differently, or don't recall others because we accord different values, meaning and rationale to some events above others. We also accord a hierarchy in terms of happy and painful events. This is part of the natural human response to process information so we are better able to understand the range, quality and substance of its meaning. How we do this is personal to each individual.

Researchers at the *University of Florida* have studied how we rank our feelings, according to their meaning to us. For instance, two people can attend the same wedding and while one remembers it as a joyous occasion, another guest will remember it as nice, but not the greatest. The reason for this is that we see, hear, and feel differently, or in neuro-linguistic terms, we use our sensory, auditory, olfactory and emotional modalities (and sub-modalities) differently.

One interesting outcome of their research indicated that there is a strong correlation between people's lives and their personal narratives. For example, people who are prone to a variety of negative emotions tend to react negatively to stimuli, whereas those with a positive disposition react to any given situation with a more positive attitude.

The most revealing aspect of our life stories is whether we can see past events as contaminative or redemptive. When we get stuck on a negative episode of our life we view it badly, and sometimes reminiscence with sadness. This is called *contaminative* behaviour, and in some cases it can emotionally cripple us, and prevent us from moving forward with our lives. On the other hand, response to a negative life story is *redemptive* because we look at what has happened, and take some learning experience from it, hopefully never to be repeated.

People with a redemptive outlook on life believe that something good has come from our suffering and are able to *bounce back* and move on with their lives. Many take to finding support from self-help gurus, personal growth sessions, life coaching, mentoring, mediation, hypnotherapy and the list goes on. Surrounding yourself with a support network of experts, friends and family is crucial to whether or not we are able to get over our hurdles and move on stronger.

Life is never easy and our happiness to sadness ratio changes from minute to minute. In fact, we cannot unless we choose to, remain in just one mood all the time. We may be happy one minute and sad the next. This is human nature and no one is above it.

Some naturally happy people will always adopt the *blue sky* approach and will see the bright side of any event, even negative ones. Pessimists on the other hand, will always look at it from a *yes but, no but* approach.

We all have our own life stories to tell and while we cannot change the course of our history, we are able to change our perception of past memories. Whether we are conscious of it or not, most of us view our lives as stories. This is after all how we originally started communicating with each other! Reminiscing about our life stories makes it possible for us to discern a series of distinct chapters, select our main characters and classify them either as heroes or villains. For example, what our experiences were of a good teacher who believed in us, a loving parent, an empowering boss, or the reverse. We like people that support us emotionally and who are more like us, our mirror image. Or we hate because of the hurt or sense of abandonment we felt regardless of whether the experience and memory is perceived as *real* or not. But who defines our reality? No one else but us!

As children, we are not emotionally, or intellectually adept at that stage to make sense of the world, so manufacture our dramatic personal myths by selectively mining some experiences and neglecting, or forgetting others. As we grow older, our intellect helps us decipher various stimuli and we learn through experiences and mistakes. However, if we have experienced an extremely traumatic episode, the memory of it will be ingrained in our unconscious until we recognise it as a self-sabotaging problem and learn to heal it.

Get Out of Your Own Way!

Furthermore, the main difference between optimists and pessimists is how they select their life memories and play them out. Repetition of such behaviour actually becomes a habit and over time transforms into either a constructive or destructive *comfort zone*. *Comfort zones* are those states of mind, or behaviour that makes us feel safe, comfortable and reluctant to leave. In the daily madness of the world our *comfort zone* becomes our *oasis*, and who can blame us if we choose not to leave it!

What's holding us back?

There has been a lot of research about the *pros and cons* of *comfort zones,* but generally *comfort zones* either support your life by giving you a safe haven to recuperate and heal, or it keeps you in a state of inertia, which is counter-productive. No one can make you leave your *comfort zone* unless you want to, and are willing to make the effort to change. Some do it willingly whilst others procrastinate. Which way forward is very much left to the individual and their current state of mind.

We will often make up excuses for *not* moving forward. We may even *dip our toe* into the future, but if it hurts, or if it reminds us of past wrongdoings then we will certainly be pulled back to our negative state.

But if we all learn through our experiences, can we change how we view our past? You cannot change your history of events. What's happened has happened and as they say "You can't turn back the clock". What you can do though is learn to look at the past differently. Doing so we can change your life story to be one where there is responsibility, accountability, new learning and determination to seek a brighter future.

I remember when I first began my life coaching training many years ago, and was taught that rapport building with my clients was essential to a successful coaching session. Many of my clients were able to talk about themselves, their strengths and weaknesses, and were able to set SMART goals (Specific, Measureable, Achievable, Realistic and Timely). However, I did come across a few clients who were so demoralised, so emotionally hurt that they were not able to even describe their problem. They were unable to focus their attention on their issues and spent many hours just switching from one topic to another. Was it me? I had doubts in my ability to get them to focus on the coaching process, but slowly I learnt that I had wrongly assumed that everyone has the ability to identify what their issues are. Now I recognise what a client may *think* is their issue, is not necessarily what their actual problem is. It was just the proverbial *tip of the iceberg*.

> **Case Study:** Take Clare (not her real name) for instance. When she visited me she stated that she wanted to overcome her low self-esteem. Three hours later, we still could not identify the main issues which were the cause of her self-sabotaging behaviour. Therefore, it was difficult to agree and set goals to move forward. I knew that she had the inner resources and strength to make the necessary changes that she identified, but there was something preventing her from doing so.
>
> My clue came when she said at the end of the session (unsuccessful I thought), that this was the first time she was able to talk freely to someone. Was this an indication that someone or something was preventing her from addressing

her problem? In later sessions I found out that by giving her the freedom and space to talk, something we all take for granted, she was able to talk about her three failed marriages, how she was a victim of domestic violence, why she was attracted to violent men and so forth.

Clare appeared to be a confident successful woman with her own hairdressing salon so her perceived negative self was not congruent with the image she presented to others. I decided that I needed to create a *safe zone* for her and slowly get her to make the changes that she chose for herself; moving her from a problem state (contaminative) to a solution state (redemptive).

I used my past experience working with learning disadvantaged adults, and improvised a method using pictures, to encourage narrative. Cutting pictures from a few magazines, I gave Clare a container filled with a mixture of happy, sad, angry and calm pictures and asked her to choose which pictures told her life story. It was interesting to see that she felt more comfortable speaking in the third person as she selected pictures that described her life, her current state of mind, and where she saw herself after each stage of our coaching sessions.

Slowly, she was able to change her picture selection from negative to positive and because she was narrating her life story in the third person, she felt *safe* enough to find the strength within to make the changes she chose for herself.

I am sharing Clare's story because I want people to understand:
× Don't always assume that everyone is comfortable talking about themselves.

- ✗ Don't assume that everyone can talk about their problems.
- ✗ Don't assume that conversation is the only way to build rapport and move forward.
- ✓ Do get to know your clients and their learning styles, life experiences and values.
- ✓ Do look at other methods of communication be it via pictures, painting, or music.
- ✓ Do be creative.

What's the way forward?

A lot has been written about the mind psychologies such as Neuro-linguistic Programming, Matrix Re-patterning, Cognitive behavioural Therapy (to include Mindfulness CBT), and hypnotherapy and so on. Then there are the *Energy psychologies* such as: Emotional Freedom Techniques, Acupuncture, Colour and Crystal Therapy, Chakra and Aura Therapy and many more. There is none that is better than the others and which you choose is up to you.

The key shared by all is to identify the problem and move from a destructive to a productive state of mind to achieve a state of balance in mind, body and spirit. When in this state of emotional, mental, spiritual and physical harmony, a person has the ability to be empowered, to find and use their inner resources to heal, to deal with and more easily change from one state of mind (negative/ contaminative / destructive) to another (positive / redemptive, self-growth and awareness).

When we reminisce over any period of our lives, we either smile at the thought of it, or frown. When you smile at the happy memories your brain and body produces *feel good* hormones such as serotonin which keeps you albeit temporarily in this state of bliss. However, when your memory makes you sad, equally your brain and body will produce hormones such as: adrenalin to *fight, flight or freeze* and cortisol the well-known stress hormone. There are numerous medical studies into each state of mind and the long term effect of adrenalin and cortisol. I won't go into these as I am not a medical professional. What I can say though is that by changing our mood, and our reaction to certain negative events we actually change the way we feel, and how we respond to a situation.

Stoics teach us that negative emotions often arise because we have become mentally attracted to something external, such as the good opinion of other people, being popular, rich, young and beautiful. Simplified, it means that we often chose to have the *grass-is-greener* syndrome meaning we are not satisfied with *our lot* and want what others have. When we are dissatisfied we indirectly undergo a metamorphosis for the worst. Unhappiness with our current situation, our job, friends or worse; we may develop secondary negative traits such as the *Failed Potential Syndrome* (FPS). It doesn't help that in our age of multimedia it is difficult to avoid being confronted with the success of our contemporaries. So how can you avoid this trap?

DO:
- ✓ Learn to recognise the emotions that are holding you back. Get honest feedback from friends and family, and be honest with yourself.
- ✓ Learn to let go of negative memories.
- ✓ Learn to compartmentalise your past life story into

Get Out of Your Own Way!

- ✓ childhood, adolescence and adulthood and look at these as life's lessons, not downfalls.
- ✓ Celebrate your achievements and accomplishments.
- ✓ Don't dwell on what you have not done, but look ahead at what you can achieve.
- ✓ Recognise that life is too short to hold grudges, or to be paralysed by your emotions and negativity.
- ✓ Set positive and happy goals for yourself and learn to take baby steps.
- ✓ Become aware of your *can't do, won't do* state of mind.
- ✓ Stop taking a look at what others are up to on social network sites. If others appear to have a better life, maybe they earned it and worked harder for it. Don't begrudge them their success.
- ✓ Learn to concentrate on your strengths and what you can offer others.
- ✓ Surround yourself with a good network of family and friends and learn to laugh more at life's foibles.
- ✓ Start to take control of your life story and make a personal promise to yourself, to make each memory a happy one.

If you can't forgive and forget, just forgive. Forgive yourself, forgive the offending party. Forgiveness does not mean what has happened is okay. It just means that your time and love is precious and could be spent with people who respect, love and support you unconditionally. "To err is human; to forgive is divine". Alexander Pope.

You can't change your past but you can certainly change the way you want to memorise the event. Don't let unpleasant memories prevent you from enjoying your present and

Get Out of Your Own Way!

future. Leave the past alone. Moving on may not be as easy as some people profess. Yes, it takes inner strength and resolve, but it is not impossible to do it just needs focus, determination, and resolve to *let go*. You can't move forward without letting go of the past.

Life is a story, the direction can change, but it has to be a choice we make. "We all have the ability to restore our physical and mental selves" says Dr Richard Millica of *Harvard Medical School*. "Many people mistakenly believe that while a knife will heal, an injury to the mind is impossible to repair".

Over the course of our lives about 75% of us will experience major life crisis that are traumatic enough to trigger stress related disorders. Dr Mollica also states that "only eight to twelve per cent of people develop stress related disorders while others go on to lead normal, positive lives proving that we are more resilient than we realise" which is good to know!

To help readers implement their own strategies for successful change I am offering a FREE half hour consultation until the end of the year. Contact me at my website www.lifemaxxinternational.com and quote *DAG – Yes to Change!*

Jennifer Rahman - Biography

Jennifer Rahman is an accredited life coach, emotional wellness coach and holistic therapist with more than 12 years' experience in each respective field.

Jennifer was born and raised in Singapore where she gained a Bachelor of Arts in two majors; Sociology and Social Work. She started her career in Singapore in public relations before moving with her family to England where she held senior positions in public relations and management.

In 2003, she decided to make a career change and embarked on a life coach training course that was to change the course of her life. As her three daughters completed their tertiary education and embarked on their own careers, Jennifer was left with the proverbial *empty nest syndrome*. Rather than spend her days staring at the four walls, she decided to find a niche for her many skills and life coaching offered many opportunities.

Encouraged by life coaching, Jennifer decided to extend her skills and embraced a parallel career in holistic therapy. She is an accredited Advanced Practitioner of Emotional

Get Out of Your Own Way!

Freedom Techniques (EFT), Colour therapy, Chakra and Aura Therapy, Feng Shui and Crystal Therapy.

Jennifer believes that being multi-disciplined has given her the expertise, experience and confidence to approach a problem from more than one perspective, or discipline. This she believes has given her an ever ready *toolkit* of skills that is of benefit to her clients.

Jennifer set up her own life coaching and holistic therapy business in 2006. Since then, her thriving practice includes offices in England and Spain.

Jennifer is also an accredited life coach (APC) with the International Institute of Coaching and Mentoring where she is presently their International Head of Far East.

Section Eight
7 Keys to Vitality
Success Strategies for your Personal and Business Life

by
Dawn Ann Campbell

"Self-care is never a selfish act - it is simply good stewardship of the only gift I have, the gift I was put on earth to offer others. Anytime we listen to true self and give the care it requires, we do it not only for ourselves, but for the many others whose lives we touch." - Parker J. Palmer

Get Out of Your Own Way!

Self-care is not selfish

7 Keys to Vitality and Longevity: Success strategies for your personal and business life because self-care is *not* selfish!

"So many people spend their health gaining wealth then have to spend their wealth to regain their health." A. J. Reb Materi

What do *you* think is the number one most important resource you'll ever need to succeed in your personal and professional life?

Take a moment to brainstorm this question by jotting down here, right now, the key resources that pop into your head:

Now prioritise them in order of importance from one to ten, with ten being the absolute must have key resource that will ensure you live a happier, healthier and wealthier life.

After a decade of coaching and mentoring individuals, and small business owners, I've observed interesting key resources being listed. Typically people respond by saying the key resources they think they need, or want are:
- ✓ Love
- ✓ Freedom

- ✓ More money
- ✓ To be slimmer
- ✓ Have more leisure time
- ✓ A more active social life and fun
- ✓ Better career path or working conditions
- ✓ Loving relationships and family environment.

Undoubtedly, these are great resources; achieving them will all add value to the quality of our lives. But where does *health* figure on the list? I'm amazed that sometimes it's not even there! Maybe we're so busy achieving goals, and acquiring *stuff*, that we forget that virtually nothing of value is achievable when we don't enjoy good health?

When we don't preserve vital health we may not be able to work as long, or in the field that fulfils our vocation. Consequently, there will be insufficient funds to raise a family, build a home, or even benefit from an active social life with hobbies. All of these factors ensure we enjoy a zest for life.

Good health is our birth right. We are born with health, it's always there. Maybe that's why we take health for granted - until it's gone - then all we want above anything else, even money, even love is to have our health back.

Luckily for the majority of us, health is probably the resource we have the most control over. It's also the resource that's central to the success of pretty much everything we do.

If we don't value health as our number one best resource, I'm not sure what else could possibly be more important? After all, when we don't look after our body, we won't have anywhere else to live! Additionally, if we don't take care of ourselves, we'll have nothing left to give others. Why is this important? Because "You can't live a perfect day without doing something for someone who will never be able to repay you". John Wooden

What is the definition of health anyway?

It used to be "the state of being free from illness or injury". That doesn't sound like a particularly positive benchmark to live life by does it! This definition was later expanded in1948 by the World Health Organisation (WHO) to "Health is a state of complete physical, mental and social well-being and not merely the absence of disease or infirmity". Getting better; still not a great definition though. Then in 1986 WHO said "health is a resource for everyday life, not the objective of living. Health is a positive concept emphasizing social and personal resources, as well as physical capacities". Much better, by changing the focus to the *environment* and *life-style habits*, we gain a sense of responsibility and control. We are also better able to understand *how* our choices influence our health status.

An absence, or decline in good health means it's difficult for anyone to achieve their maximum potential in any area of their life, personal or professional. You (as in your mind, body, spirit) will suffer; your relationships with suffer; even your home and business life will not function as efficiently, or effectively as they could *if* you were in good physical and mental health. That's why the concept of self-care is *not* selfish, or self-indulgent, it is absolutely essential not just so we survive, but so we *thrive*. "Life is not merely being alive, but being well". Edward Smith-Stanley

<u>If you doubt the wisdom of any of this, check your priorities</u>

Get Out of Your Own Way!

<u>by circling your answer in each of the following questions:</u>

Q. Which is more important your health or more money?

Q. Which is more important your health or your home?

Q. Which is more important your health or your relationships?

Q. Which is more important your health or success?

Q. Which is more important your health or time?

Q. Which is more important your health or freedom?

Q. Which is more important your health or love?

Q. Which is more important your health or career?

Q. Which is more important your health or family?

Q. Which is more important your health or ….?

Q. Which is more important your health or ….?

Q. Which is more important your health or ….?

Fill in the blanks with *your* priorities and repeat this exercise *until* you believe like Henri Frederic Amiel that "Health is the first of all liberties" and Richard Baker that "Health is the wealth of wealth" because "When you have your health, you have everything. When you do not have your health, nothing else matters at all". Marcus Valerius Martialis

Get Out of Your Own Way!

What does it mean to practice self-care?

Assuming we're now in agreement that health is our wealth, and a resource we need to prize over anything, or anyone else. We need to learn how to master extreme self-care by first attaining a good health status. Secondly, by maintaining our most valuable asset so we not only *add yours to our life, but life to our years* which is what we all want!

To begin with, let's explore what it is to even practice self-care. There is no definitive dictionary definition of *self-care* (except in medical terms). As we're exploring self-care from a perspective of taking responsibility and control of our lives, medical definitions don't apply. Remember the wise words of Desiderius Erasmus *"Prevention is better than cure" that's* what practicing self-care is about. It's also about practicing empowerment, being self-aware and honouring our boundaries as assertively as necessary to protect our rights.

So when we talk about self-care, we are talking about positively, purposely and actively taking time for ourselves in a way that rejuvenates and energises us. Ultimately, self-care makes us a better person to be around at home, and a more productive person in the workplace. To deny our need for self-care gradually leads to an air of negativity as we become increasingly resentful, repressed and energetically unbalanced.

Of course self-care may be misjudged by some people as selfishness. This is never truer than it is for women, especially mothers who are considered to be the *nurturers* in society. Regardless of sex, status, or culture, someone who practices self-care understands their limitations and know what their needs are.

They appreciate that unless they are taking responsibility for themselves on as many levels as possible; they are in no fit state to take care of anyone, or anything else. So it's about leading by example. A case in point which we've probably all experienced is when we're about to take off in an aircraft and the steward tells us in the event of an emergency to put on our own oxygen mask *before* helping anyone else. There's nothing selfish about that, it's just common sense. When we put our own mask on first, we are able to help many people. When we don't put our own mask on first, it's not long before we pass out, so can't help anyone.

Get Out of Your Own Way!

7 keys to vitality

What are the key self-care resources we need to enjoy vital health and longevity?

"No one else can breathe for you, drink for you, sleep for you, exercise for you, eat for you, or get sunshine for you. Health is your responsibility. No one else can do it for you. Health is self-built." Life Science

The above quote details a few of the *many* self-care resources we need to practice in order to enjoy a happy, healthy and wealthy personal and business life.

Here's a complete list of natural health principles:
1. Breathe clean pure air because pollution is destructive to health and well-being.
2. Maintain a temperate climate, excessive cold or heat drains our nerve energy.
3. Maintain internal cleanliness to minimise the risk of disease.
4. Drink plenty of pure water, ideally distilled to stay adequately hydrated.
5. Quality sleep allows the body to heal, repair and become rebalanced.
6. Eat a natural diet suited to our physiology; raw fruits, vegetables, nuts & seeds.
7. Fast regularly to improve assimilation, elimination and self-heal.
8. Expose skin and eyes to daily sunshine to top up essential natural vitamin D3.
9. Participate in daily activity to keep fit, supple, co-ordinated and independently mobile.
10. Rest and recuperation is essential for the mind body

and spirit to grow and develop.
11. Recreational, playful activities that are fun and rejuvenate our creative self.
12. Peace of mind to enhance emotional well-being and compassion for all.
13. Harmonious pleasant environment to live in.
14. Community of like-minded people to share, participate and interact with.
15. Self-mastery of oneself.
16. Secure outlet and work activities that provides a sense of purpose and income.
17. Inspiration, motivation and commitment to achieve goals with enthusiasm.
18. Instinct to reproduce.
19. Aesthetic pleasures from being in touch with nature to help us feel connected.
20. Expression of natural instincts; love, appreciation, gratitude and creativity.
21. Positive self-esteem builds self-confidence, self-reliance, and a sense of self-worth.

These self-care principles nurture vital health as well as promote longevity as originally taught by the likes: of T.C. Fry, Graham, Jennings, Shelton and Schulz et al. These and many other earlier proponents championed the virtues of a natural plant based-diet and holistic lifestyle as essential health giving practices.

What is the difference between being alive and truly living?

"Just by switching from a poor diet and bad lifestyle to a healthier one can add 14 years to your life" Dr. L Breslow

Get Out of Your Own Way!

Most modern day natural, holistic health practitioners are still in agreement that these 21 self-care practices are as valid today as they were centuries ago. In fact, some go so far as to say that considering the emotional, physical and environmental stresses we experience today, self-care is more important than ever.

Of the 21 health principles listed above, I consider the following seven key resources to be the most essential.

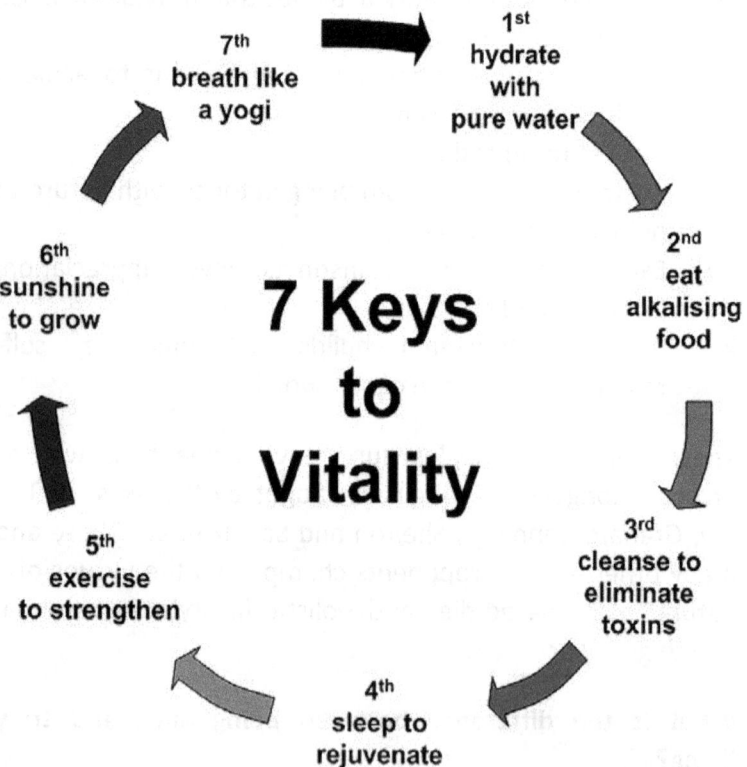

Consequently, I suggest they play a major role in any successful self-care plan because they make us feel truly alive, in love with life and full of zest each morning. Don't

Get Out of Your Own Way!

make the mistake of fixating on just one or two areas though like nutrition, or exercise as many people do. There is a direct correlation between our health and *all* the health principles, so be sure to apply at least these seven because good health is never merely the result of any one principle.

Practicing these essential self-care principles on a daily basis will not only ensure vital health is achieved and maintained, it will also create a positive work life balance too. You owe it to yourself and everyone around you to practice self-care first and foremost. Remember, self-care has nothing to do with being selfish, despite what you may have been brought up to believe. Instead it has everything to do with being honest about your needs and honouring your boundaries. "If you feel *burnout* setting in, if you feel demoralized or exhausted, it is best, for the sake of everyone, to withdraw and restore yourself. The point is to have a long-term perspective". His Holiness the Dalai Lama

Exercise: start by completing your *wheel of health*

Here is an example of one filled in.

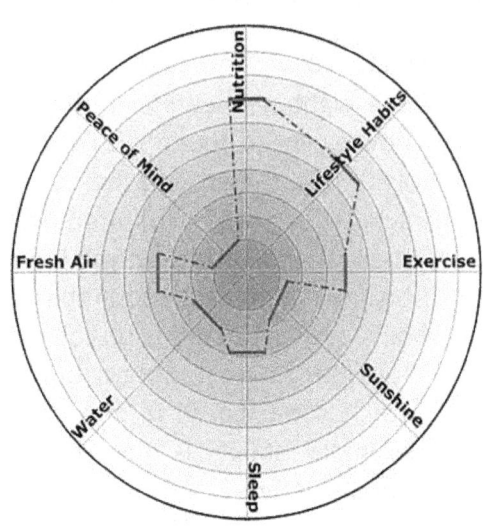

Get Out of Your Own Way!

Objective of this exercise:

To score each of the categories of your health, then join the dots up to see at a glance *if* what you think is going on, is actually representational of your *current* situation. Following which, it becomes easier to a) identify the weak links in your health protocol that need urgent attention b) decide the best course of action to achieve the greatest results.

Benefits of this exercise:

By utilising this visual life coaching tool you will be able to discover at a glance which areas of your life you need to improve to achieve a happier and healthier balance.

Other benefits include it helps with motivation because it shows us how near, or far, we are to achieving our goals. It helps us to focus on exploring choices, and it helps us make informed decisions due to increased understanding into difficulties we are experiencing.

Directions:
1. The eight segments in the *wheel of health* represent how balanced your life is right now. Regard the centre as 0 (unsatisfied) and the outer edge as 10 (perfectly satisfied). Using a coloured pen, you need to indicate the level of satisfaction you feel with each area of your health by putting a dot on the relevant line. When you have graded all areas of your health, join all the dots together to create a new outer edge that is right for you. Don't worry, it is rarely a circle. Typically the example above is representational of what most people draw.

2. With another coloured pen, you may like to re-plot your dots based on *where* you would *ideally* like your health categories to be. That way, you will immediately see what you are aiming for and how big the gap is.
3. Finally, date your wheel and set a date in your diary to revisit it a month, three months, or even a year from now to see how your health is improving.

"Our past may be blemished, but our future is spotless, so our past is a point of reference, *not* a place of residence". It's up to each and every one of us to decide what we want for our future; more of the same, or something different. To help us decide what those differences will be, here is your blank wheel of health to complete.

Get Out of Your Own Way!

Strategies for becoming a Centerian

Here are the 7 keys to vitality and longevity:

1st Why is breathing *fresh* air imperative?

"Forests are the lungs of our land, purifying the air and giving fresh strength to our people." Franklin D. Roosevelt

We simply cannot survive long without taking a breath (longest recorded is 22 minutes Guinness Book of Records) which we do 21,600 times a day. Our brain, and the trillion cells in our bodies, all need a fresh constant supply of fresh oxygen to be delivered by our red blood cells to live. Additionally, our white blood cells need oxygen to do the hard work of keeping us disease free. Athletes know this more than anyone because they understand the direct correlation between oxygen intake and muscle efficiency.

Without fresh air, our lungs become as stale and polluted as the air around us. A lack of fresh air leads to a lack of energy amongst other symptoms. Longer term, lungs eventually become overwhelmed and disease is the result.

Unless we exercise, we only use a third of our lungs capacity. Combine that with the fact many of us lead sedentary lives, are insulated indoors, and it's easy to understand the reasons for the increase in health related issues such as asthma and allergies.

Most people are surprised to learn that the air *indoors* is often more polluted than city air hence the real condition called *Sick Building Syndrome*. This is due to the vast array of chemicals in our homes and offices. Chemical fumes emanate from: dyes and glue in carpets, wallpaper, paint and furniture. Chemical fumes from smoking and air fresheners are killing our sense of smell and nasal hair that protect us from breathing in pollution. Chemicals in cleaning products (the garage, bathroom and kitchen being the worst offenders), and last but not least, beauty products; yes, I really do mean those expensive beauty products and perfumes you loving spray and apply to your skin, hair and nails are more dangerous than you realise!

Benefits of breathing fresh air include: keeping our lungs free from air borne pollutants, oxygenating our blood and muscles which increases energy, stamina, and feel good endorphins so lowers blood pressure and stress.

Solutions and top tips for improving lung capacity:
- ✓ Stop smoking.
- ✓ Keep windows open, especially at night because nature is constantly cleaning the air.
- ✓ If that is not possible, select a plant appropriate for the bedroom.
- ✓ Avoid the use of personal, household, garden and workplace chemicals to decrease the chances of your health being compromised. The EU bans almost 1,400 chemicals in personal care products every year. Yet 3,000 new, mostly untested chemicals are launched onto the market every year; always read the labels!
- ✓ Take up more vigorous exercise because it ventilates the entire body.
- ✓ Start each day by standing by an open window and emptying your lungs by puffing out all the stale toxic air you've accumulated overnight, puff until you cannot puff anymore. Only then breathe in fresh air which is full of negative ions and makes you feel alive.

Get Out of Your Own Way!

- ✓ In fact, whenever you're tired, or stressed, do this for an instant energy boost.
- ✓ Practice holding your breath to exercise you lungs.
- ✓ Explore natural friendly ways of keeping your environment clean and fresh.
- ✓ Learn to belly breathe: the aim is deeper, slower, quieter, regular breathing
  - breath out to release negative emotions > puff hard > hold
  - breath in to heal > hold
  - repeat several times
  - you may feel lighted headed to start with, but the lungs like any muscle need exercise to improve, so practice.

EXERCISE – Try it now, hand on belly and feel your breath lift your diaphragm up and down – lie down if it helps.

2nd Why is drinking pure water so critical?

"Water is the only drink for a wise man." Henry David Thoreau, or as others like to say "never drink the crap from the tap" because tap water is full of chemicals and inorganic minerals, fluoride, chlorine, carcinogens, agricultural fertilisers, industrial chemicals, pesticides and drugs.

We are able to survive a long time without food (duration depends on our fat reserves), typically, 3-4 months. However, no one will survive more than a week without water. Other than air, water is the body's single most essential nutrient.

The ancient healing properties of water have been practiced

by therapists for *ever*: water only fasting for religious, cultural, medical reasons and more recently, as a means of weight management.

Interestingly, in 1987 for the first time since records began, the amount of water consumed was superseded by all the other liquids we now drink: pasteurised juice, pasteurised milk, fizzy soda, sugary pop, dehydrating spirits, fattening wines and beers, chemically coloured sports drinks, and of course, the nation's favourite stimulants: tea, and coffee.

Maybe it's because humans are not naturally water drinking creatures. Our preferred water source is fresh juicy ripe fruit which contains the purest form of drinking water. Perhaps that's why sugary drinks are now the norm? Consequently, people are consuming way too much sugar and increasing their risk of diabetes to name but a few diseases.

Interesting consequences are that today we use 50% less embalming fluid than we did 50 years ago because what we drink is already embalming us! Also, despite all these liquids being consumed, 75% of the population are *still* chronically dehydrated. As a result, doctors say *many issues they deal with such as fatigue, headaches, migraine, weak muscles, brain fog, and constipation could be improved simply by drinking more water.*

Chronic dehydrated is due to a lack of understanding about:

1. Our bodily composition:
    o 90% water as a baby
    o 75% as adults
    o 60% in old age (hence wrinkling like a grape)!

- 70% of our brain is water
- 80% of blood is water

2. Our bodies need a *constant* supply of fresh water daily because we eliminate over a litre a day depending on age, size, activity, climate through our skin, lungs, kidneys and colon, yet most people don't replenished nearly enough.
3. The *type* of fluids the body needs to thrive:
    - Juicy fruit
    - Distilled water
    - Reverse osmosis water
    - Coconut (full of electrolytes)*
    - Young leafy greens and other tender vegetables.
        * Electrolytes are important to cells (especially nerve, heart, muscle) to carry and maintain electrical impulses (nerve impulses, muscle contractions) to other cells. Kidneys keep electrolyte concentrations in our blood constant despite changes in your body e.g. sickness; exercising etc. = electrolytes are lost; particularly sodium and potassium so need to be replenished daily.
4. Part of the problem is that we *eat on the go 24/7* so thirst signals are often misinterpreted for hunger. This false hunger is habitually dealt with by eating more dehydrating foods, so it becomes a vicious cycle because tissues and cells can't absorb nutrition as effectively when dehydrated, hence fatter people are more malnourished and need even more water.

Chronic dehydration is fixed by learning to interpret the body's cry for water; whenever you think you're hungry drink water and wait 30 minutes. If you're still hungry after that then go ahead and eat, if not, you know you were just thirsty.

The exact amount of water required depends on other variables such as size, climate and activity. The primary role of water is to transport toxins out of the body as quickly as possible. Drinking water does not as some people think cause *water retention*, the opposite is true, drinking water flushes away excess salt responsible for bloating.

People obsessed with their figures and skin knows that drinking water naturally suppresses the appetite and is necessary for a clear complexion; it also prevents sagging skin as we age, or lose weight. Adequate water is necessary for muscle tone, it balances our hormones and keeps our blood thin enough to flow freely, thus improving heart health to name but a few benefits of staying hydrated.

EXERCISE - Pinch the back of your hand and see how slowly it pings back into place, the slower it is, the more dehydrated you are. Other ways of testing is by your breath (smell) and urine (colour and smell) and the frequency.

Solutions and top tips for becoming better hydrated:
- ✓ Filter your tap water.
- ✓ Swap artificial sugary fizzy, caffeinated drinks for fresh ripe juicy fruit.
- ✓ If you buy bottled water, drink out of glass, not plastic, which leeches into the water, especially in sunlight, and has been proven to be carcinogenic.
- ✓ Understand that all liquids are not equal, if you don't believe me, try washing a wall with a cup of coffee, or a coke then you'll understand why drinking coffee, or

- coke does not flush our body of toxins (decaf has more chemicals than regular so compounds toxicity and dehydration).
- ✓ To avoid your heart getting dehydrated overnight (common reason for heart attacks in between 6-9am), drink a glass of water before bedtime and first thing on rising.
- ✓ If you have food allergies, or hay fever keep hydrated, histamine is used in the body as a water regulator, the more you drink, the more histamine is produced.
- ✓ Drinking water at room temperature is best.
- ✓ You know you're dehydrated when you realise you're thirsty, by which time it's too late.
- ✓ Sip water throughout the day rather than gulp a glass periodically which will just flush straight through you rather than hydrate you at a cellular level.
- ✓ As an added bonus to becoming rehydrated, you'll be managing your weight more effectively too.
- ✓ Drinking sufficient amounts of water means you'll also experience more energy because often feelings of fatigue are simply early warning signs of dehydration.

3rd Why does the best nutrition come from a natural diet?

"The golden rule of eating is; Thou shalt not poison thyself."
TC Fry

The western world has never seen so many malnourished people with 1 in 8 now suffering.

World Health Organisation (WHO) reported hunger and malnutrition are the greatest single threats to the world's public health. *The United Nations Food and Agriculture Organization* estimates 925 million people were undernourished in 2012. 16 million of which were living in developed countries, 3 million of them in Britain. That's an increase of 80 million since 1990 *despite* the fact that the planet produces enough food to feed 12 billion people! That's why I ran the London Marathon for Health Poverty Action in 2014.

"Food is the most widely abused anti-anxiety drug." People are often surprised to learn that fat people also suffer from malnutrition due to dehydration, constipation, and poor absorption of nutrients. Other factors include eating the wrong foods, at the wrong times, in the wrong combinations and exercising poor portion control.

Other problems arising from eating poor food choices include symptoms like: bloating, food intolerances / allergies, indigestion / heart burn / acid reflux, colon diseases like IBS, Candida / yeast overgrowth, depression (hence mood food and comfort eating), obesity and of course diseases like diabetes, Alzheimer's and cardiovascular issues. Of course there have always been diseases, even Cleopatra was known to have had cancer, so disease isn't new, what *is* new is the scale of the problem, particularly since the agricultural revolution.

Pre-agricultural revolution we relied on what Mother Nature provided. There is nothing faster or easier to eat than a piece of fruit! Natural foods are easy to recognise as foods coming from the ground. They include a wonderful abundance of fresh, natural, seasonal, local, ripe fruits, vegetables, nuts, seeds, seaweeds, herbs and flowers. These foods are what nourish us best because they are alive so they provide us with first class nutrients. Natural foods are perfectly packaged and balanced. They have exactly the right value of essential and non-essential micro and macro nutrients, vitamins, minerals, phytochemical, antioxidants, enzymes and amino acids that we need to thrive.

Nutrition doesn't need to be complicated. There is no one type of nutrition that has the capability to heal or cure. What we eat, or rather don't eat, is what helps the body create an environment for healing itself. For instance, when we abstain from solids and participate in a water only fast, our repair mechanisms are triggered and the body's energy, normally reserved for digestion, is focused on healing instead.

It doesn't have to be a full blow water fast, calorie restriction / intermittent fasting / 5:2 diet are all now popular adaptations of the traditional water fast.

Benefits come from swapping shopping at the supermarket for the local green grocer's market because supermarket trollies are typically filled with denatured, low nutritional, fortified for profit only foods. These are items that need an ingredients label to explain what it is as it's unrecognisable as food. This type of shopping is bad for your health *and* it's bad for the environment. The only people who benefit from you shopping at the supermarket are the supermarket shareholders.

Shopping at the green grocers or outdoor markets on the other hand means you will be making healthier choices about what to eat. Additionally you are supporting your local suppliers, all the while taking better care of the environment by minimising the need for excess (and expensive) packaging.

Get Out of Your Own Way!

Choose to consume a higher quantity and quality of foods that are rainbow coloured. They denote foods that are fresh, ripe, juicy, local (ideally organic), seasonal and above all, are completely natural. This is one of the most effective and quickest ways to instantly feel better and rid yourself of niggling health issues that make you feel sluggish and irritable. Only then will you be truly free to feel alive and revitalised!

Don't let your diet quietly and slowly kill you; too many people are literally digging their graves with their teeth!

<u>Solutions and top tips for eating a more natural plant based diet:</u>

- Eat mindfully for enjoyment and health.
- Eat when hungry, not when society says it's time to eat!
- Don't drink and eat at the same time.
- Observe food combining practices for better digestion and less fermentation.
- Eat sitting down in a calm relaxed space.
- Prepare food with love and appreciate for the journey it made to your plate.
- Support the local farmers and eat locally.
- Better still, grow your own.
- Start a kitchen garden.
- Eat foods that are in season.
- Eat a big raw salad every day.
- Eat as much fruit and veg. as you like every day.
- Think of fruit as fast food for snacks rather than saving them for desserts.
- Stop thinking about organic versus non-organic, instead think natural versus chemical to help you make the right choice.

Get Out of Your Own Way!

> In *Heal Your Life Holistically*, the next book in *the Dial A Guru* series, I will be writing in more detail about our relationship with food, especially disordered eating.

4th Why do we need to exercise?

"Those who think they have not time for bodily exercise will sooner or later have to find time for illness." Edward Stanley

You know what they say *use it or lose it*. That's because exercise develops our strength and endurance. It's cumulative and helps is maintain our independence as we age.

> We need CASS:
> - Coordination
> - Agility (flexibility)
> - Stability (balance)
> - Strength (endurance)
>
> All of which decrease with age.

Exercise is quite literally *body building* because our whole being is involved (cells, blood, lungs, heart, muscles, circulatory, cardiovascular and respiratory systems). So exercise helps us age well, it makes us feel better about ourselves because we look good (with or without our clothes), so it improves our self-esteem. Even our mind is improved with exercise because we're producing endorphins that make us feel happy. We're sleeping better because of the additional activity and our weight is managed so it's a win-win situation.

However, not many people like *exercise* per se. The key to

any successful exercise programme is making it fun, varied and just doing more of it.

Regardless of calling it exercise, keeping fit, working out, or training, we must move more vigorously if we are to ensure a comfortable, mobile independent old age. Doing *anything* that increases the heart rate for at least 30 minutes a day (be it sex, housework, gardening, rambling etc.) will all improve the tone of our body as well our emotions.

People who sit too long at a work station, computer desk, in front of the TV, in the car or have a specialisation at work which means an overuse of some body parts to the detriment of others, are in serious danger of health issues from poor posture. The only anti-dotes are regular brisk walks, swimming and cycling which are still some of the best supportive forms of exercise. So get up off the sofa or office chair and start moving, every hour on the hour.

> I will be writing more about the benefits of walking to distress in *Building a Profitable Business* another book in the Dial A Guru series later.

Solutions and top tips for can't exercise, won't exercise excuses:
- Change your negative beliefs around exercise by changing the word so something more positive like training, keeping fit, working out or whatever appeals.
- Then think of Plan A activities (outdoors in the fresh air and sunshine) and Plan B activities (indoors when it's cold and wet outside) so you don't need to over think it.
- Plan in advance where you will work out, who you work out with, how long and how often (start small

Get Out of Your Own Way!

- and gradually build up), until it's fun and something you don't want to miss.
- Set a SMARTER* goal and chunk it down into mini goals. *SMARTER: specific, measurable, achievable, realistic, time-orientated, evaluated, reviewed.
- Get educated about your activities, reading tips and inspirational stories about others who have succeeded will motivate you when the going gets tough.
- Treat yourself to the gear so you look and feel the part.
- Get the equipment that will support you, when we *act as if* you are on our way to success for instance, if walking is you exercise of choice, use a pedometer to record your daily steps (10,000 steps = about 4 ¾ miles or 8km).
- Build variety into your schedule like swimming, yoga, and cycling, dancing, they're all fun sociable activities.
- Take it gently, one day at a time, if you miss a day, so what, start again tomorrow.
- Use a journal to log progress.
- If you don't want to do it for yourself, do it for others, e.g. be a role model for your children, or raise money for a charity.
- Take up rebounding, do it in front of the TV if that's what it takes. Just start moving more.

Exercise: Excuses - *no time, too tired, hate exercise, no buddy, no place blah* **but...**

We have 168 hours a week. Less 56 hours sleeping. Less 40 hours working = 72 hours spare!

President Obama runs daily for an hour, if we can't find time to exercise, does that mean we're busier than the president of America?

Write down what your self-sabotaging reason(s) are for not nurturing yourself by moving more. Then write down what you have to do to fit it into your schedule.

There are plenty of self-sabotaging excuses answered and over-come at www.walkasyoutalk.com also, plenty of top tips for getting you started.

5th Who gets enough sleep *and* rest?

"One hour of sleep before midnight, is worth 2 after midnight."

This saying may or may not be true, but what *is* true is that adequate sleep is essential if we are to function properly during the day. And I've yet to meet anyone who says they get enough sleep!

Sleep has its own natural restorative cycle of repairing itself after an active day. Cells, tissue, muscles are all healed, toxins are eliminated and nerve energy is regenerated so sleep prepares us for another day. Consequently, health is dependent upon adequate rest and sleep. If we don't get a balance between rest and activity, our nervous system becomes wired, edgy and overly emotional. It's this over sensitivity to constant stimulation that wears us out physically and emotionally. Insufficient sleep and rest create longer term health issues hence the sayings 'running on autopilot' or 'going through the motions' where we're essentially running on adrenaline. Eventually, like a car, we

Get Out of Your Own Way!

burn our engine out.

If we're in the lucky minority who do *not* suffer with a sleep disorder, a third of our life will be spent healthfully experiencing the 4 stages of sleep (light sleep stage 1 & 2 theta activity followed by stage 3 & 4 deep or delta sleep which is a cycle that is repeated 4 or 5 times a night). However, a lack of this basic need for sleep is for a growing number of people, a vital clue to what lies behind their poor health and poor performance.

Adequate sleep is especially difficult to achieve for people who have changed the regulation of their internal biological clock due to shift work, or are living in areas with light and or excess noise pollution. Interestingly, when clients chill at our retreat, sometimes they'll initially say 'they can't sleep because it is too quiet and too dark" they are so used to traffic, white noise and light pollution lulling them to sleep at home.

Business leaders know the value of practicing daily power naps to prevent this happening to them. Just by switching off for 20 minutes a day allows their creative juices to become renewed. As the wise Thich Nhat Hanh says *'doing nothing is doing something'*. Switching off even if we don't nap is essential to our well-being, creativity, productive and decision making skills. Shame we're not all allowed or encouraged to take a power nap!

The brain is wired to respond differently depending on whether we're awake or asleep. When awake and aware we're in a catabolic state, when we are asleep our brain is cleaning and detoxing, anabolic state. So the function of sleep is to clear the mind of the day's chemical clutter. It's the only organ that doesn't rely on the body's lymphatic system to drain away toxins which explains our biological purpose of sleep.

Don't worry no-one can sleep too much. The body will sleep only for as long as it needs to repair, heal and eliminate. Healthy sleep essentially equates to a healthy mind and body enabling us to function safely and calmly. Adequate sleep is especially important while we're growing up, or engaged in physical or athletic activities.

People struggling to manage either mental issues such as depression, or physical issues such as obesity (we're 27% more likely to become overweight if we're sleep deprived), will benefit from improved sleep because of better balance hormones.

Chronic lack of sleep promotes pre-mature aging; it can result in dirty brain diseases like Alzheimer's and other neurological diseases. Sleep deprivation primarily arises for those that don't have the benefit of peace of mind. They are stressed, anxious, worrying, living in the past or the future. Business people especially are always planning ahead. Additionally, those that eat late in the evening have more trouble sleeping because energy is still being directed towards digestion, rather than shutting the body down. Or, people are so stimulated by alcohol, or an exciting movie, working on the laptop, reading a thriller etc. that they can't switch off.

The top reason for couples avoiding sex is being too tired. Apparently that's because 'it takes a man two minutes to get ready for bed, but it takes a women an hour because of all the jobs she has to do first: turn off the TV, and lights, close

Get Out of Your Own Way!

doors, let the dog out, lock up, set the washing machine, load the dishwasher, make packed lunches, take off makeup and so on. No wonder women have more trouble sleeping"!

Added to which, bedrooms are no longer the safe peaceful spaces they used to be. Today they are used for more than just sleeping; we watch TV, eat, read and use our laptops so bedrooms are no longer conducive to rest and relaxation.

In the short term, we tend to just feel tired, grumpy and maybe a bit overwhelmed when we don't get enough sleep. Longer term it actually becomes quite dangerous. Our risk of disease increases. We suffer with poor mental health; 90% of people suffering with depression are insomniacs; we suffer with poor memory function; our creativity and decision making process slows down; our general functionality and performance declines.

Billions are spent on medication and billions are lost in productivity and absenteeism. We increasingly make mistakes so more accidents happen which impact on health and safety at work, and on the roads. Annually statistics say 60% of people admit to driving while sleepy and 37% admit to having fallen asleep at the wheel resulting in 100,000+ collisions and 1,500 deaths.

Solution and top tips for achieving better quality sleep:
- Power nap like a CEO. There are common characteristic between successful leaders including the ability to take 10-20 minutes downtime every day (40 minutes max. between 2-4pm so night time sleeping isn't disrupted).
- Choose to feel full of zest in the morning, ready to jump out of bed and start the day with joy rather than

feeling sleep deprived and having to drag your sorry carcass out of bed. It's as simple as that; your attitude will help you decide to either stay up late to watch another hours TV, or enjoy feeling rested, alert and bright over breakfast the following morning.
- Keep a daily journal to reflect what you've achieved that day and visualise what you plan to do the next day, this frees up your mind to switch off and rest.
- During particularly busy times, keep pad and pen by your bed so if a thought or action wakes you, write it down and go back to sleep knowing it hasn't been forgotten in the morning.
- Make a regular bedtime a good habit. The body responds well to routine, it will become programmed to unwind ready for sleep. Then when you're in bed, focus on relaxing your body one limb at a time. At the same time, belly breathes.
- Make sure your bedroom is not wired with lots of electrical equipment like electric blankets, clock radios flashing, computers, mobiles being charged, TVs on standby all of which are running electrical charges that disturb your natural bio rhythms.
- Supplement with serotonin, magnesium, calcium, melatonin, and tryptophan.
- Eat a low GI food before bedtime like a banana or a few nuts that offer the magnesium, potassium and calcium needed.

> **Exercise - True or False – we get 20% less sleep than we did 100yrs ago?**
>
> False, the issue isn't the amount which is the same; it's the quality that's deteriorated. Today we have shift work, later

> eating patterns, light pollution, white noise pollution, traffic pollution and longer working days etc.
>
> We are naturally programed to sleep when it gets dark and wake up when it gets light but we no longer follow that pattern, we are no longer cooperating with our body's natural clock.

6th Why is sunshine vital to our health and well-being?

"Just living is not enough; one must have sunshine, freedom and a little flower." Hans Christian Anderson

Nothing on this plant is capable of surviving without sunshine; not us, not animals, no plants, nothing, literally everything would gradually wither and die. Nicknamed the *sunshine vitamin* because it offers everything subtle nourishment plus its energy generally makes us feel good. Actually, it's not really a vitamin at all; it's a steroid hormone that regulates growth. Perhaps that's why it's a nutrient not readily available through food, except in shitake mushrooms, oysters and eggs. Not to be confused with fortified vitamin D used to supplement breads and cereals which are synthetic so to be avoided.

The body converts sunshine into natural vitamin D3. Vitamin D3 strengthens and conditions our skin; regulates our glands and improves the quality of our haemoglobin in the blood. Natural vitamin D3 is absolutely essential and the darker the skin pigmentation, the more sun exposure is need.

Low blood levels of vitamin D3 are associated with a whole host of illnesses; especially bone related issues such as osteoporosis and generally increases the risk of mortality. So by taking every opportunity to expose your skin *and* eyes to direct sunlight, even on a cloudy day, you'll enhance your health and general well-being. It's the sunlight that is synthesised through the *eyes* that regulates the thyroid. Consequently, we need to expose our eyes to natural day light without reactor light, tinted or sunglasses daily.

Sunlight is directly related to the quality of haemoglobin and insufficient light causes a decrease resulting in anaemia. Sunlight prevents disease by killing pathogens and plays a vital role in preventing and mitigating many diseases. Vitamin D3 controls calcium absorption for healthy bones and triggers apoptosis (natural death of cells) so it's an important anti-cancer vitamin too.

Symptoms of deficiency are *Season Attention Disorder* (SAD), depression (major impact on the economy though loss of production and sick days, sever cases include rickets, heart attacks, loss of muscle strength and increased risk of breaking bones.

Sunshine also balances hormones and regulates our biological clock which is why we feel so good when the sun comes out. Yet we've become frightened of exposing our skin and eyes to the sun without protection when it's recently been proven that it's the over use of sunglasses and chemically based sun screens blocking our pores that are doing us more harm than good. Lines between fact and fiction have become increasingly blurred due to propaganda from the media and sunscreen producers who want to sell more of their products. We now know it's not that sun causes cancer per se; it's about it being the right amount of sun *at* the right time of day because cancer related deaths

Get Out of Your Own Way!

are actually *lower* in lower altitudes.

Sunshine is the best natural cosmetic helping scarred skin heal as well as strengthening pigmentation and tone making us less sensitive to the heat or cold. So skin, organs, muscles and blood all improve with sunshine all of which reduces the risk of disease.

A growing number of people, if the media are to be believed, are vitamin D3 deficient, yet traditionally, people under 50 aren't vulnerable. However, if you're concerned, you can calculate ultraviolet exposure levels in your area and assess your vitamin D3 status by Googling your latitude / geographical location for example see http://nadir.nilu.no/~olaeng/fastrt/VitD-ez_quartMED.html.

Solutions and top tips to be safe in the sunshine:
- Expose skin to the sun for at least 20 min. a day and build up gradually, even on a cloudy day, you're still getting the benefits.
- Ditto expose your eyes; it's only through the iris being exposed to ultraviolet light that your glands, especially the thyroid will be regulated.
- Avoid the mid-day sun which means 11am-3pm depending on the time of year and geographical location.
- Increasing your fresh food intake of rainbow coloured food high in antioxidants naturally increases our skins ability to protect itself.
- Give up wearing sunscreen, except for totally natural products, even then, check the labels for hidden nasties. Use coconut oil to protect skin naturally.

> **Exercise – go outside for 20 minutes today without sunglasses or sunscreen protection and top up your natural vitamin D3**

7th Why is peace of mind central to our well-being?

"Do not confuse peace of mind with spaced-out insensitivity. A truly peaceful mind is sensitive and aware." H.H. The Dalai Lama

Stress is the opposite of peace of mind. Both feelings are internal. Wherever you go, there they are. Hence the saying when people go off in search of peace that it was right there under their noses all the time!

Because the level and type of stress we're experiencing is constantly changing with the times, people are increasingly complaining about their lack of peace. This imbalance between peace and stress impacts our physical and emotional health and eventually, weakens our immune system thus increasing our chances of become diseased.

<u>Benefits</u> of practicing mindfulness helps us live in the present moment. Likewise, switching off from negative influences (including negative people who drain our energy) and learning to meditate both limit the constant stimulation that pervades our life 24/7.

Mastering *monkey mind* helps develop mental poise, maintains healthy blood pressure and protects our adrenal hormones. Unless we take time out to quieten and tame the mind we will always be a slave to it and know no peace.

There are many international surveys reporting on levels of

happiness, satisfaction and misery country by country e.g. http://www.earth.columbia.edu/articles/view/2960 United Nations 2011 where citizens of Denmark rated their life satisfaction at 7.8 out of 10. Citizens of Canada, Norway, Switzerland, Sweden, The Netherlands, Australia, Israel and Finland were next most satisfied, followed by people in Ireland, Austria, and the United States, where people rated their life satisfaction at 7.2. Chinese and Hungarian people reported the lowest overall life satisfaction, both at 4.7 with Brits in the middle at 5.2.

Sad to think that we've never had it so good with so much stuff, so many choices yet been so unhappy and dissatisfied! Proof that *stuff* only brings temporary happiness, and higher levels of stress (think road rage, computer rage, sleep deprivation induced rage...), plus owning *stuff* brings extra financial responsibilities such as insurance and stress over having to look after and protect our *stuff* so stuff usually ends up becoming a liability.

A lack of peace of mind kills our creativity. Negative self-talk stunts our growth, our inner critic is harsher on us than we'd allow others to be added to which, we have over 60,000 thoughts a day and over 80% of them are negative. Still, we try and control everything and everyone around us and perfectionism creates more stress by setting us up for failure. Stress does not exist outside of us; it is only our interpretation of external events, meaning, all misery is created by the mind.

To protect our immune system (apparently a minute of rage lowers our immune systems capacity to function for 6 hrs. but a minute's laughter can increase our immune system for the next 24 hrs), we need to understand the direct link between mental well-being and physical health.

Solution and top tips for regaining peace of mind:
- Breathe deeply for instant calming effect.
- Live in the now by being mindful and present.
- Practice gratitude for what you have, who you are and where you are.
- Decluttering your life will declutter your mind.
- Understand that other people/things can't destroy your peace of mind unless you let them.
- Learn to control 'monkey mind' chatter.
- Use affirmations, visualisations, anchors, gratitude journals etc. to reflect.
- Don't put off until tomorrow what needs doing today.
- Live each day as if it's your last.
- Meditate don't medicate, it gives you the ability to respond consciously and rewire old patterns of behaviours, attitude and beliefs.
- Let go of negative judgements.
- Learn to forgive 'holding onto hurt is like drinking poison but expecting the other person to suffer'.
- If you have a *stuck* perspective about something, get a life coach to help you become unstuck.
- Avoid self-talk that uses words like should and must, they normally belong to other people's goals.
- Remember everything is just energy, that includes things that are robbing you of your peace of mind like stress, you are not your brain, you simply have a brain and like any software it can be reprogrammed to respond differently to external stimulation
- Of course not all stress is bad, short term stress e.g. getting ready to present, or run a race helps us perform better.

Get Out of Your Own Way!

- Practice, practice, practice; you go to the gym; learn a new language, instrument etc. it all takes practice, same with training the mind.
- Your mind does not like discipline so will resist efforts to discipline it and procrastination will set in. However, the choice is yours, be mastered by your mind and its whims, or be the master. It is a muscle like any other, it needs to be trained to respond the way you want it to.

Ho'oponopono is an ancient Hawaiian teaching based for manifesting what we want for ourselves and others through continual cleansing. It's also a problem solving technique meaning 'to make right'. What does cleansing mean here? Well, quite simply it's a mental process. It's about letting go of negative and painful thoughts, deeds, words and actions.

The idea is to *clean and transform our mind of all our old stuck memories.* This is achieved through love, because we know love is the greatest healer. So ho'oponopono is a process of repentance, forgiveness and transmutation for which this mantra is repeated:

I am sorry

Please forgive me

I love you

Thank you

So the way regain peace of mind is to let the past go without apportioning blame then we are free to heal ourselves, before healing others. Just keep cleansing by repeating the manta *I love you, I'm sorry, please forgive me, thank you.*

Exercise – Practice walking mediation, even if you are only able to do around your bedroom.

Get Out of Your Own Way!

Summary

The *Blue Zones* are places where people healthily live to 100+. A concept used to identify a demographic and geographic area of the world where the highest population of centenarians live; healthy, without disease, drug free and who die of natural old age as described in Dan Buettner's book *The Blue Zones: Lessons for living longer from people who live the longest.*

Longevity Hotspots include:
1. Okinawa (Japan)
2. Sardinia (Italy)
3. Nicoya (Costa Rica)
4. Icaria (Greece)
5. Vilcabamba (Ecuador)
6. and Seventh-day Adventists in Loma Linda, California.

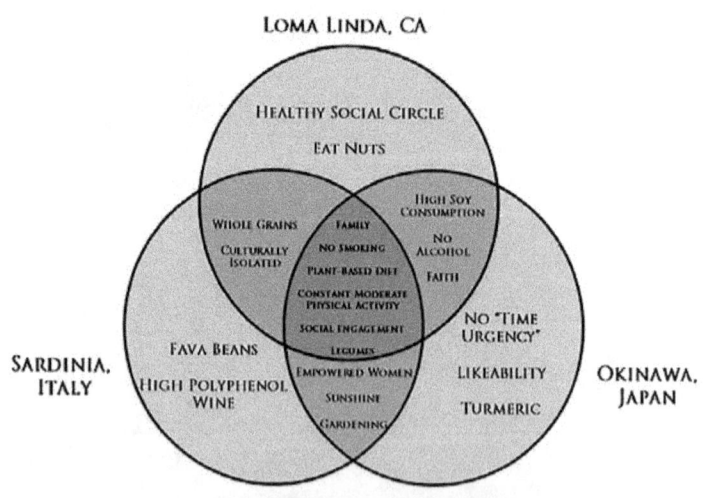

http://apps.bluezones.com

Blue Zones uses evidence-based practices of groups and

cultures from around the world to help people live longer, healthier and better lives.

The eight Common lifestyle characteristics that contribute to their longevity are:
1. Family are put ahead of other concerns.
2. Less smoking.
3. Semi-vegetarianism - except for the Sardinian diet - the majority of food consumed is derived from plants.
4. Constant moderate physical activity is an inseparable part of life.
5. Social engagement, people of all ages are socially active and integrated into their communities.
6. Legumes are commonly consumed.
7. Geographical area; all blue zones are located near volcanoes. The local water source is high in colloidal mineral content. There has been some speculation and claims that the drinking of water high in colloidal mineral content and consumption of fruits, vegetables and vegetation irrigated with water rich in colloidal minerals may play a part in increased health and life span.
8. They eat like a poor man.

By comparison with developed, but less healthy countries like US and the UK, 90+% of the population are at some point worried or unhappy about their weight or body image. And 1 in 3 have cancer, 1 in 3 suffer with degenerative heart diseases, 1 in 3 experience mental illnesses, and 1 in 2 relationships breakdown. We also have the some of the highest suicide rates in the world all of which indicate higher health care costs in the future.

Solutions and top tips include:

Get Out of Your Own Way!

- Adopt each of the 21 natural health principles and apply them to your own life.
- Treat your mind, body and spirit with the respect it deserves by not abusing it with over stimulation, wrong foods, poor lifestyle choices etc.
- Understanding that good health is a normal natural state of being.
- Appreciate why the only cause of disease is toxicity and continue learning about what to do to avoid it.
- Invest in ongoing education to better understand how your body works and reacts to its environment.
- Surround yourself with a positive support network that encourages and empowers you to achieve your goals.
- Implement our own health care protocol that promotes the philosophy 'prevention is better than cure'.
- Be committed not to gamble with your constitution.
- Learn to control your environment (practicing self-sufficiency), diet (gown own food) and lifestyle (observing the principles we discussed).
- Listen and cooperate with your body's needs (naturopathic principles).
- Respond to symptoms *by* eliminating the causes.
- Fast to allow the body to recover its health.
- Lead by example.

Final Word

"A man too busy to take care of his health is like a mechanic too busy to take care of his tools." Spanish Proverb

Only *you* can decide to take action and make the right

choices for both your personal and business health. You can either have more of what you've already had in your past, or else you can opt for something more empowering and nurturing for your future. One things for certain 'if nothing changes, nothing changes'. So don't just read this book, commit to taking action right now.

Learn to master each of these seven self-care strategies by focusing on them one at a time, in any order you like until each new habit is formed (circa. 21 days). Consequently, in less than six months you too will be on the road to healthy success both at home and in the workplace. Additionally, you'll become a great role model for your family and colleagues alike.

These words seem like good ones to end on "No matter how much we acquire, or fulfil our every desire, what good is wealth when we've lost our health and have to suffer till we expire"!

Share your thoughts with me and I will send you a complimentary copy of my Self-Assessment Health Questionnaire which will help you build on the insights gained here. Alternatively, contact me if you'd like to know more about a Natural Healing Protocol – Part 1 - Self-care & health maintenance and Part 2 - Annual maintenance habits.

Wishing you and your business vibrant health!

Get Out of Your Own Way!

Dawn Ann Campbell - Biography

Following a fast track 20 year corporate career in management consultancy, Dawn has vast practical and qualified expertise in establishing and developing small businesses. A combination of business and human resource skills enables Dawn to coach, mentor and train others to take responsibility for their own lives. Which is why she has two niche areas: personal health and business health, not least because what's going on in one, is often a reflection of what's going on with the other.

Dawn has been a solo entrepreneur for over a decade. She's a sought after Master Coach who mentors and assesses student coaches for Noble Manhattan, Europe's leading coach training provider. She is now Head of Assessment for the International Institute of Coaches & Mentors.

Dawn's also a *Heal Your Life* teacher (based on the Louise Hay philosophy); a Callahan trained *Thought Field Therapist*, a *Holistic Practitioner* and a *Nordic Walking & Fitness Instructor*.

Get Out of Your Own Way!

An almost lifelong vegetarian, Dawn's also a high raw vegan food chef who follows a natural hygiene lifestyle. At 50 + years young, she's fitter, healthier and happier both physically and mentally than ever before. She's currently studying Naturopathy and Buddhist philosophy as well as writing a recipe book and training for her next marathon.

"You know how people always want more health, happiness and success in their lives, well that's exactly what Dawn helps her clients achieve" so Dawn's mission is to inspire others to reclaim responsibility for their personal and professional life.

Consequently, she offers tailored mind, body spirit detox retreats at her idyllic home in North West France. She also takes public and business groups on walking and coaching trails to help them re-gain their fitness, health and happiness. See http://walkasyoutalk.com/ for more details.

"BBC radio interviews, writing for national and local press, presentations, in-house company training and workshops with 1 -1 follow up sessions mean that hundreds of clients have benefited from Dawns result orientated supportive style". Erica Connelly, Business Link, UK

Get Out of Your Own Way!

Dial A Guru Series

This dynamic and interactive series of personal and business self-development co-authored books is for anyone and everyone who has ever experienced self-sabotage.

Guru means *guide;* it's someone who shines *light* on a situation in an educational, encouraging and entertaining way that empowers us to reach our true potential at home *and* in the workplace.

Therefore, our collective aim as authors is to inspire and motivate you to become your own Guru. After all, there is *no greater authority on you than you!* Or to quote *Dr. Seuss* "Today you are you, that is truer than true. There is no-one alive who is YOUER than YOU"! So the *Dial A Guru* series is here to help you become the best *you,* you can be.

This is what Sam Thorpe, International Speaker, Trainer and Author of *METAMessages from Your Body* said about this series "There are many self-help books available; books about the struggles and plights of the individual, books about success and achievement. It is sometimes difficult to know where to start. This is where I consider Dawn Campbell to have ignited a spark of pure genius with her idea to facilitate the collaboration of inspirational experts in the field of personal growth.

I have read many books, and am a published author myself, but what has always been missing is a book that gives me a collaboration of like-minded souls. Each author – let's call them *Gurus* as they truly offer light in the darkness - has openly and lovingly revealed themselves, sharing their steps and stumbles along the path of discovery. You will find

Get Out of Your Own Way!

> yourself on a journey with friends, intimate and encouraging, supportive and uplifting.
>
> Extract from Sam's foreword in *Awaken Your True Potential**

We hope you receive as much enjoyment and benefit from reading our words and doing the exercises we've prepared for you, as we had creating them. All books come with an accompanying workbook to help you successfully move from A to B because our books are packed with opportunities for personal discovery; also available from Amazon.

Forthcoming books for 2016 in this series include:
- Heal Your Life Holistically to Thrive!
- How to Turn your Hobby into a Profitable Business

Existing books in this series include:
- *Awaken Your True Potential: How to awaken your true potential in your personal and business life

Get Out of Your Own Way!

Feedback

We hope you've enjoyed reading this book that we created for your benefit.

We also hope we've achieved our aim in entertaining, educating, encouraging and empowering you to press ahead, and achieve even greater things in your personal and professional life.

Naturally, we would appreciate hearing your feedback which will help us to further improve this series for the benefit of you, and new readers. Please take a few minutes to visit us at http://dialaguru.eu/contact-us/ and tell us what you thought, and more importantly, what you want more of next time.

As a **thank you** for taking the time to share your thoughts with us, you are free to choose a complimentary copy of one of Dawns' eBooks, just say which one you'd like.

You'll also find plenty of Free Resources available here http://dialaguru.eu/news-and-updates/

Get Out of Your Own Way!

Calling all authors-in-waiting

If you're an experienced professional who wants to add a published book to your product profile then consider joining us and writing for our readers.

You'll need to be passionate about sharing your specialist subject for the benefit of others. In return you'll be supported as you develop the discipline of writing with others to a deadline. I'm a hands on editor, so you'll be guided throughout the whole process of structuring your chapters to marketing your published book.

Having a published book to promote is the new business calling card so make sure you have one soon. Becoming a co-author has many benefits:

- It's a great opportunity to raise your profile as an expert in your field.
- It helps to build trust, credibility and perception of your expert status.
- It'll become easier to increase business through workshops and webinars.

- It will bring in some passive income.
- It opens doors to new networking opportunities.
- It's a quality gift to either reward clients or incentivise prospects with.
- Finally a book becomes a wonderful part of your legacy that you were here and details *how* your contribution, knowledge and experience made a difference!

If this is what you want too, then please contact me at http://dialaguru.eu/contact-us/

Please note there is no charge for this opportunity, co-authors are paid equal royalties for the life time value the book is in print and authors retain copyright of their own material.

Dawn Campbell, CECI, MNMC, AMC

Business and Personal Coach, Master Coach & Mentor, Holistic Practitioner, Author, Editor

About PenCraft Books, LLC

At PenCraft Books (PCB) we know what it's like to have a dream of being a published author. Individually, we have been through the publishing process. It isn't easy and the entire process from writing to having books sold requires a huge learning curve.

At PCB we're committed to taking the stress out of having to know everything from editing to publishing to marketing. This means our authors are free to do what they do best and write. Consequently, we mentor writers through the visioning and goal setting process. Essentially, we help them become authors and achieve a finished manuscript. We work hand-in-hand with our authors, guiding them through the entire process to help them succeed.

We also format finished manuscripts so they're available for readers both physically in bookstores, and on-line for our Kindle readers. Following which, we mentor our authors in the marketing of their published work to reach the widest possible audience.

We recognise that there are a lot of choices out there for publishing services. That's why PCB researched what authors really want and actually need. It's also the reason why we offer a tailored approach.

Our research consistently said that writers *wished they'd had a personal mentor when they first started writing.* Someone who cared and had the expertise to guide them along the path from original idea; to beating the dreaded procrastination, which is really about overcoming limiting self-beliefs and where our writing coaches come in handy;

right through to seeing their work in print.

However, the journey doesn't end there as most authors think it does. It's said that *writing a book is the easy part; it's the marketing of it when the real work starts.* That's why PCB also helps its authors stand out in a crowded market place with a marketing strategy to reach the widest possible audience and achieve maximum sales.

Our expertise enables us to provide support to new writers going through every tough spot imaginable, to just being there for the more experienced authors.

www.PenCraftBooks.com

Get Out of Your Own Way!

Editor and co-author of the Dial A Guru initiative.

Dawn's corporate life provided a variety of professional writing opportunities. Following which she became a writer and editor for the International Institute of Coaching & Mentoring when she produced their award winning e-zine.

Dawn has also co-authored 4 published books; *Breaking Free of Self-Sabotage, Getting Well, Breaking the Barriers* and *The Young Professional Women*. All books are available here http://www.nyasa.biz/books/.

Since then, Dawn has written and published four eBooks: *14 Day Raw Weight Loss, Water Fasting, The Virtual Home Detox* and *Walking for Health*.

Having enjoyed the process of writing with other people Dawn created her own co-authored book series called *Dial A Guru*.

This initiative was extended to co-authors because she kept coming across potential authors who *talked* about writing a book, but needed the encouragement and discipline to write.

A co-authored book provides the perfect compromise; new authors don't have to worry about having enough material to fill a whole book which may be a bit daunting. The entire process is taken care of for them, not least there's a schedule to honour so accountability increases. Also we know collaboration makes the process more fun not least because writing is a lonely business!

A major benefit is sharing the workload of PR & Marketing when the book is published and ready to be launched which is a real bonus.

Joining forces with a community of like-minded writers helps us develop our strengths and build confidence. Now nearly half of our new co-authors are penning their own books thanks to going through this learning curve.

As a result of networking and promoting this exciting book series *Dial A Guru* boasts an impressive group of professional, qualified, experienced and passionate writers. Backgrounds range from existing authors, magazine owners, therapists, teachers and coaches to name but a few.

Our growing writing community is represented across the globe to include: India, Poland, Ireland, Wales, Poland, France, England, Spain, Hungary, Philippines, Romania and Scotland,

As Commissioning editor, Dawn provides co-authors a huge amount of support and valuable information for each step of the process from writer's top tips, to PR & Marketing, to Press Release Templates and much more. Everything they

Get Out of Your Own Way!

need to add a book to their signature platform and raise your profile as an expert in your chosen field.

> "Dawn makes for an excellent editor. With many years' experience as a Coach, Holistic Practitioner, Author and Editor Dawn understands my work and the message I wish to convey fully. She is able to turn my writing around at the drop of a hat into something that is more fluid, eloquent and to the point. I recommend her not only as an editor but as a business coach too." ~ <u>Wendy Fry</u>, Emotional Health & Relationship Consultant, Author of Find YOU, Find LOVE

> "Dawn is such a fabulous Editor! She is very efficient, lays everything out really clearly and supports you by sending through useful bits of information to help you with writing your book. I would not have known where to start but with Dawn's expertise I've not only crafted my chapters for my book but also learnt lots of new things about writing along the way too". <u>Ruby McGuire</u>

> What can I say? I am totally impressed. I think that running a group effort like this takes a very special mix of talent and you are doing a stellar job! Thanks for this amazingly clear document, considering the numbers and the complexity, it is quite an accomplishment. I just want to say bravo!! I firmly believe that my text, for whatever it's worth, is much better for having had you there. I am now convinced I need an editor! Now I know why writers love their editors so much! <u>Elaine Rudnicki</u>

Get Out of Your Own Way!

> Dawn thanks for this. I am so impressed with your comments – thank you so much for taking so much time and care in giving them. Really helpful. <u>Bettina Pickering</u>

> Dawn is a great editor and extremely helpful with any little bumps I have had on my way to becoming a co-author. She has been very helpful with advice on how to promote myself and also giving me ideas on what else I can add to help educate people about the benefits of Reflexology and Homeopathy. She has been a great listener and hope that we will work together again on many books in the future. To my amazing Guru, Thank You <u>Danni Lindsay</u> x

In addition to other books in the *Dial A Guru* series, Editor & Author Dawn Campbell has produced the following eBooks published by PenCraft Books.

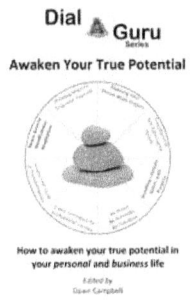

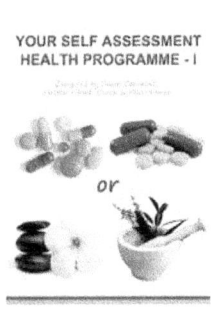

A comprehensive self-assessment health questionnaire.

Everything you need to know about enjoying a detox in the safety of your own home.

Get Out of Your Own Way!

The diet to end all diets; simply eat what Mother nature provided to achieve your ideal body weight.

An ancient practice of promoting healing through rest and water fasting.

Walk out of the office and destress; learn about the physical and mental health benefits of walking.

www.ingramcontent.com/pod-product-compliance
Lightning Source LLC
Chambersburg PA
CBHW071651160426
43195CB00012B/1423